EXCAVATIONS AT MEI
CRIPPLEGATE, LON

Archaeology after the Blitz, 1946–68

EXCAVATIONS AT MEDIEVAL CRIPPLEGATE, LONDON

Archaeology after the Blitz, 1946–68

*Based on the work of Professor WF Grimes for the Roman and Mediaeval London Excavation Council,
and related research by the Museum of London and by University College London*

Gustav Milne
with Nathalie Cohen
and with contributions by Tony Dyson, Jacqueline Pearce and Mike Webber
illustrations by Susan Banks

ENGLISH HERITAGE

2001

ARCHAEOLOGICAL REPORTS

Published by English Heritage at the National Monuments Record Centre, Great Western Village, Kemble Drive, Swindon SW2 2GZ

Copyright © English Heritage 2002

ISBN 1 85074 771 7

Product Code 50094

British Library Cataloguing in Publication Data
A CIP catalogue record for this book is available from the British Library

Edited by Christine McGee
Indexed by Veronica Stebbing
Designed by Tracey Garrett at Multiplex Techniques Ltd
Edited brought to press by David M Jones and Andrew McLaren, Publications, English Heritage

Printed by Snoeck-Ducaju & Zoon

Contents

Illustrations

Frontispiece London after the Blitz: an archaeological opportunity.

Acknowledgements

A report such as this, incorporating fieldwork and research conducted during a 50 year period, builds on the expertise, knowledge and support of far more people than can be mentioned individually: the list of authors in the bibliography gives an all too brief indication of the debt owed by any modern scholar to the labours of others, for example. The following acknowledgements cannot claim to be comprehensive, and do not intend to demean the contributions of the many who are not named. My first debt must be to John Shepherd, a learned colleague and cheerful friend (formerly the Curator of the Grimes London Archive) who established the project using his unrivalled knowledge of the RMLEC's work, and to Jenny Hall who managed the programme for the Museum of London, showing tolerance when it was most needed. Thanks are due to many others on the museum staff, such as Roz Sherris, John Clark, the library team, the photographic department and those in the Archaeological Archive.

Of my co-authors, Nathalie Cohen worked long and hard on the project producing thought provoking reinterpretations of the original field records, while Jacqueline Pearce significantly reassessed the post-Roman pottery with new insight. Mike Webber was responsible for the revised interpretation of the City ditch sequence and also helped supervise parts of the 1996 fieldwork programme on the Cripplegate sites, together with Nathalie Cohen, Stuart Brookes, Ken Walton, and the rest of the recording team from University College London.

The artwork was prepared for publication by Susan Banks (MoLAS) from material drawn up by many hands including N Cohen (Figs 46, 55, 63, 69, 72, 73, 99 and 100); N Constantine (Fig 89); C Harrison (Figs 123, 124, 128, 129 and 130) and M Webber (Figs 18 and 19).

The photographs are from several sources: Frontispiece and Figs 1, 2, 26, 44, 70, 71 and 146 are from *The Sphere* magazine.

Figs 74, 75, 76, 77, 94, 95, 110, 111, 119, 120, 121, 122 and 148, are all from the incomparable collections in the *Guildhall Library*.

Figs 125, 126, 127, 131, 132, 133, 134, 135, 136, 137, 138, 139 and 149 are by Ken Walton for the *London Archaeological Research Facility*.

With the exception of Fig 21, which is by the Museum of London, the rest of the photographs are from the Grimes London Archive now held by the Museum of London.

The discussion of St Mary Elsing benefited greatly from the input of Jane Camps-Linney and from Simon Roffey (UCL), and also from Ellen Barnes (EH) and Philip Gale (CoL); while my knowledge of the tradition of a Saxon palace in Cripplegate was transformed by the research of Tony Dyson (formerly of MoLAS). Other points of detail have been clarified through information provided by Niall Hammond on Saxon buildings, Professor James Graham-Campbell (UCL) on the finds from Bastion 14 and from Dave Lakin and Liz Howe on the most recent programme of MoLAS excavations in the study area. An earlier version of this report was read by Dr Grenville Astill (University of Reading) and his most useful suggestions have been incorporated in the revised text wherever possible: we were most grateful for all his comments. The errors, omissions and obscurities that remain are, however, still my responsibility.

In conclusion, the results of this volume are dedicated to the memory of all who worked for and with the RMLEC, especially Professor Grimes, Audrey Williams and their hired hands. Their investigations were undertaken in circumstances and conditions far removed from those experienced by later generations of City archaeologists, but the first systematic study of medieval London's archaeology unquestionably began in those RMLEC trenches dug in the basements of bomb sites.

Abbreviations

BM *British Museum*

CBA *Council for British Archaeology*

CoL *Corporation of London*

DoE *Department of Environment*: government department responsible for archaeology, which succeeded MPBW, but was replaced by English Heritage in 1983

DUA *Department of Urban Archaeology*: the Museum of London's professional team working in the City 1973–91

EH *English Heritage*

GLA *Grimes London Archive*: the collection of RMLEC field records and associated data held by the MoL

LARF *London Archaeological Research Facility*: independent organisation based at UCL founded in 1992: it organised the recording of the surviving monuments in the City for this report

MoL *Museum of London*: opened in 1976, amalgamating collections from the Guildhall Museum and the London Museum, of which Professor Grimes was the Keeper (later Director) from 1945 to 1956

MoLAS *Museum of London Archaeology Service*: established in 1991, replacing the DUA and the other museum based archaeological units

MoW *Ministry of Works*: government department with responsibility for archaeology when RMLEC began its excavation programme in 1947: subsequently replaced by MPBW

MPBW *Ministry of Public Buildings and Works*: government department responsible for archaeology when RMLEC completed its excavation programme in 1968: subsequently replaced by DoE

RCHM *Royal Commission on the Historical Monuments of England*

RMLEC *Roman and Mediaeval Excavation Council*: the organisation set up to investigate archaeological sites exposed by bombing during the London Blitz; Professor Grimes was the honorary Director of Excavations

UCL *University College London*: this university in Bloomsbury incorporates the Institute of Archaeology: Professor Grimes was the IoA's director from 1956 to 1973: now also the home of the *London Archaeological Research Facility*

WFG1, WFG2 etc Site codes that are now used by MoL to identify archaeological investigations conducted by the RMLEC from 1946–68

Summary

This report is an illustrated appraisal of the excavations conducted by the Roman and Mediaeval London Excavation Council (RMLEC) between 1946 and 1968 on 25 bomb damaged sites in the north-west corner of the City of London. This area was occupied by the Cripplegate fort in the Roman period, but the excavations of these sites also uncovered medieval artefacts and features, and it is with these later materials that this volume is concerned.

Although the excavation director, Professor WF Grimes, published a major interim report of the Council's work in 1968, circumstances prevented the full publication of the sites in his lifetime. A major post-excavation programme funded by English Heritage from 1992 to 1997, however, has resulted in the production of five major reports covering his work. The first volume is a report on St Bride's church (Milne 1997), the second, on the Temple of Mithras (Shepherd 1998a), and the third is a gazetteer and summary of the entire RMLEC's excavation programme (Shepherd 1998b). The final reports are concerned with the excavations around Cripplegate, one evaluating the Roman fort (Shepherd forthcoming) and the other – this volume – the medieval developments in that area.

The post-Roman report is divided into six sections, beginning with an introduction providing the background to the RMLEC's programme and to the development of medieval archaeology in the post-war period. The results of the excavations are then reappraised in a series of thematic chapters – according to new dates, assigned by specialists from the Museum of London, for the surviving finds – a fresh analysis of the excavation archives, and where possible, the rerecording of the surviving masonry structures by a team from University College London.

In Chapter 2, London's medieval defences are described and discussed. The chronology now established begins with the identification of an extramural Saxon ditch cut beyond a wide berm. It had silted up by the twelfth century, and a new ditch was cut much closer to the wall in *c* 1200. Later in the thirteenth century bastions were added to both the northern and western walls, a statement that is supported by ceramic evidence not only from Bastion 11a, but also from Bastion 14, from which evidence of thirteenth-century ceramics had previously been overlooked. There were modifications to the wall and to the bastions during the later medieval period, and the ditch was recut in the sixteenth and seventeenth centuries. A summary of the pottery from the best preserved sequence is presented by Jacqueline Pearce, and a report on the post-medieval ceramics and crucibles from the upper fills of the ditch is being published separately (Bayley, forthcoming).

Chapter 3 discusses the evidence for medieval secular buildings, including two Saxon sunken-featured buildings on the Addle Street site, the major masonry built town house known as Neville's Inn excavated at Windsor Court, and the remains of two company halls, one belonging to the Brewers and the other to the Barber Surgeons.

The next chapter considers the archaeological evidence for three parish churches and a medieval hospital. The excavations of St Alban's church, which were published in interim form in 1968, are substantially reinterpreted, redated and a more complex sequence presented showing that it was founded no earlier than the eleventh century. The work at St Mary the Virgin, Aldermanbury was the last major excavation conducted by the RMLEC. The development of this church, which was established in the twelfth century, is published in detail for the first time. The north wall of St Alphage survives as part of the City's defensive wall, the north face of which was only exposed after bombing had destroyed the later buildings, which had encroached upon it. A fourth ecclesiastical structure, the tower of St Mary Elsing, is the last surviving remnant of a fourteenth-century hospital for the blind, which later served as a parish church after the Dissolution of the Monasteries in the sixteenth century. This structure is also published in detail for the first time, following a new survey.

A wider view is taken in Chapter 5, in which an attempt is made to date the development of the street pattern around Cripplegate. It is suggested that the area was open fields in *c* 900, but that settlement encroached from south to north from the mid to late tenth century onwards. The evidence of this expansion is used to discuss and evaluate implications for the layout and dating of the City's ward structure, and the much vexed question of a Saxon palace in the Cripplegate area reviewed.

In conclusion, Chapter 6 summarises the role provided by Professor Grimes, not just as the RMLEC's excavation director, but also as the Corporation of London's consultant on matters relating to the preservation and display of ancient monuments. To paraphrase the words of Professor Grimes himself, this report might be described as a discussion of the RMLEC's medieval excavations in the Cripplegate area – which incorporates some detailed archaeological information that has not been published before as well as desultory comments on one or two other matters – (Grimes 1968, xi).

Résumé

Ce compte-rendu consiste en une évaluation illustrée des fouilles menées par le Conseil pour les Excavations Romaines et Médiévales de Londres (Roman and Medieval London Excavation Council, RMLEC) entre 1946 et 1968 sur 25 sites endommagés par des bombes dans le coin nord-ouest de la Cité de Londres. Ce quartier était occupé par la forteresse de Cripplegate à l'époque romaine, mais les excavations de ces sites ont également révélé des objets artisanaux et des témoignages datant de la période médiévale, et c'est de ces derniers matériaux que traite ce volume.

Bien que le directeur des fouilles, le professeur WF Grimes, ait publié un important compte-rendu intérimaire sur les travaux du Conseil en 1968, les circonstances ont empêché que la totalité des sites soient publiés de son vivant. Cependant, un important programme de suivi de fouilles financé par English Heritage entre 1992 et 1997, a eu pour résultat la production de cinq comptes rendus majeurs couvrant ces travaux. Le premier volume est un rapport sur l'église de St Bride (Milne 1997), le deuxième porte sur le temple de Mithras (Shepherd 1998a), et le troisième est un répertoire géographique et un résumé de l'ensemble du programme de fouilles de RMLEC (Shepherd 1998b). Les derniers comptes rendus s'intéressent aux fouilles autour de Cripplegate, l'un évaluant le fort romain (Shepherd à paraître) et l'autre – le volume dont il est question ici – les développements médiévaux dans cette région.

Le rapport consacré à la période post-romaine se divise en six parties, il commence par une introduction qui présente l'arrière-plan du programme de RMLEC et le développement de l'archéologie médiévale dans la période de l'après-guerre. Les résultats des fouilles sont ensuite réévalués dans une suite de chapitres thématiques – autour de nouvelles dates, attribuées par des spécialistes du musée de Londres aux trouvailles subsistantes – une analyse récente des archives de fouilles, et, quand cela était possible, la reclassification des structures de maçonnerie subsistantes par une équipe d'une université londonienne, University College London.

Dans le chapitre 2, on décrit et discute les défenses de Londres au Moyen-Age. La chronologie maintenant établie commence avec l'identification à l'extérieur des murs d'un fossé saxon creusé de l'autre côté d'une large berme. Il s'était ensablé avant le douzième siècle, et un nouveau fossé avait été creusé bien plus près du mur vers 1200. Plus tard, au treizième siècle, des bastions avaient été ajoutés aux deux murs nord et ouest, assertion que confirment des témoignages sous forme de céramiques provenant à la fois du Bastion 11a et du Bastion 14, dont on n'avait pas précédemment tenu compte. Des modifications furent apportées au mur et aux bastions au cours de la dernière partie de la période médiévale, et le fossé fut recreusé aux seizième et dix-septième siècles. J.Pearce présente un résumé de la poterie provenant de la séquence la mieux préservée, et un rapport sur les céramiques et les creusets post-médiévaux des couches supérieures du remblai est publié séparément (Bailey à paraître).

Au chapitre 3 on examine les témoignages relatifs à l'existence de bâtiments séculaires médiévaux, parmi ceux-ci on trouve deux bâtiments à structure enfoncée sur le site d'Addle Street, une importante villa construite en maçonnerie, connue sous le nom de Neville's Inn et mise au jour à Windsor Court, et les vestiges de deux salles appartenant à des guildes, l'une propriété de la compagnie des brasseurs et l'autre de celle des barbiers-chirurgiens.

Le chapitre suivant traite des témoignages archéologiques relatifs à trois églises paroissiales et un hôpital médiéval. On offre une nouvelle interprétation et datation des fouilles de l'église de St Alban's, qui avaient été publiées sous la forme d'un bulletin intérimaire en 1968, et on présente une séquence plus complexe qui montre que sa fondation n'est pas antérieure au onzième siècle. Les travaux à l'église de la Vierge Marie, St Mary the Virgin, à Aldermanbury constituèrent la dernière grande campagne de fouilles organisée par RMLEC. C'est la première fois qu'on publie en détail l'histoire du développement de cette église, qui fut établie au douzième siècle.

Le mur nord de St Alphage subsiste et a été intégré dans le rempart défensif de la Cité dont la face nord ne fut exposée que lorsque les bâtiments plus tardifs qui avaient empiété sur elle furent détruits par les bombardements. Un quatrième bâtiment à vocation écclésiastique, la tour de St Mary Elsing, est le seul vestige qui nous reste d'un hôpital pour aveugles datant du quatorzième siècle, qui plus tard servit d'église paroissiale après la dissolution des monastères au seizième siècle. On publie également pour la première fois un relevé détaillé de cette structure à la suite d'une nouvelle étude.

On adopte un point de vue plus large au chapitre 5, dans lequel on tente de dater le développement d'un quadrillage de rues autour de Cripplegate. On suggère que le quartier consistait en champs ouverts vers 900, mais qu'à partir du milieu ou de la fin du dixième siècle l'occupation humaine gagna du terrain du sud vers le nord. On utilise les témoignages relatifs à cette expansion afin d'en examiner et évaluer les implications pour l'organisation et la datation de la structure de ce quartier de la cité ; on revient également sur la question maintes fois débattue de l'existence d'un palais saxon dans le quartier de Cripplegate.

En conclusion, le chapitre 6 résume le rôle joué par le professeur Grimes, non seulement en tant que directeur des fouilles à RMLEC, mais encore comme conseiller auprès de la corporation de Londres pour tout ce qui touche à la conservation et la mise en valeur des monuments anciens. Pour paraphraser les paroles du professeur Grimes lui-même, on pourrait décrire ce rapport comme étant une discussion des fouilles médiévales de RMLEC dans le quartier de Cripplegate "qui inclut des renseignements archéologiques détaillés qui n'ont pas encore été publiés ainsi que des commentaires à bâtons rompus sur un ou deux autres sujets." (Grimes,1968,xi)

Traduction: Annie Pritchard

Zusammenfassung

Diese Studie ist eine illustrierte Beurteilung der Ausgrabungen durch den Römischen und Mittelalterlichen Ausgrabungsrat (RMLEC) zwischen 1946 und 1968 auf 25 bombgeschädigten Standorten im Nordwesten Londons. Dieses Gebiet war Standort des Krüppeltor Forts zu römischen Zeiten, doch wurden bei den Ausgrabungen auch mittelalterliche Artefakte und Merkmale freigelegt, und es sind diese späteren Materialien mit denen sich dieses Volumen befaßt.

Trotz einer umfangreichen Zwischenstudie bei dem Direktor der Ausgrabungen Professor WF Grimes in 1968, Umstände verhinderten die gesamte Veröffentlichung der Standorte während seiner Lebenszeit. Ein umfangreiches Post – Ausgrabungsprogramm finanziert bei English Heritage von 1992 bis 1997, hat jedoch zur Produktion von fünf Studien über seine Arbeit geführt. Das erste Volumen ist eine Studie über die St Brides Kirche (Milne 1997), die zweite über den Tempel von Mithras (Shepherd 1998a) und die dritte Studie ist eine Übersicht und Zusammenfassung der gesamten Ausgrabungsarbeiten des RMLEC (Shepherd 1998b). Die letzen beiden Studien befassen sich mit den Ausgrabungsarbeiten um das Krüppeltorgebiet, eine mit dem römischen Fort (Shepperd bevorstehend) und diese Sudie über die mittelalterlichen Ereignisse in diesem Gebiet.

Die post – römische Studie ist geteilt in sechs Abschnitte, eine Einleitung über den Hintergrund des RMLEC Programmes und die Entwicklungen von mittelalterlicher Archäologie in der Nachkriegszeit. Die Resultate der Ausgrabungen sind dann neubewertet in einer Serie von thematischen Kapiteln – und in Übereinstimmung mit den neuen Datierungen, zugeteilt bei Spezialisten des Museums von London für die bestehenden Funde – eine frische Analyse der Ausgrabungsarchive, und wenn möglich, die Wiederaufnahme von überlebenden Mauerstrukturen bei einem Team des Universitätsinstitutes London.

Im zweiten Kapitel werden die mittleralterlichen Verteidigungsanlagen erklärt und diskutiert. Die jetzt erstellte Kronologie beginnt mit Identifizierungen eines anglosächsischen Burggrabens geschnitten jenseits einer weiten flachen Ebene. Es wurde aufgeschwämmt bei dem 12. Jahrhunderts und musste neu näher zu Mauer um 1200 gegraben werden. Später im 13. Jahrhundert wurden Bastionen an den Nord – und Westmauern angebaut, eine Aussage bestätigt durch Keramikstücke nicht nur von Bastion 11a sondern auch von Bastion 14, Beweise von 13. Jahrhundert – Keramik, welche vorher übersehen wurde. Modifikationen wurden ausgeführt an den Mauern und Bastionen im späteren Mittelalter, und der Schnitt des Grabens wurde im 16. und 17. Jahrhundert geändert. Eine Zusammenfassung der Töpferarbeiten der best erhaltenen Stücke ist präsentiert bei J Pearce, und eine Studie über die Keramik- und Metalarbeiten wird separat veröffentlicht werden (Bailey bevorstehend).

Das dritte Kapitel diskutiert die Beweise für mittelalterliche sekuläre Gebäude, zwei tiefgelegte sächsische Gebäude an der Addle Street Seite, das bedeutene steingemauerte Stadthaus bekannt unter dem Namen Neville's Inn und ausgegraben bei Windsor Court, und die Übereste von zwei Handelshallen, eine zu einer Brauerei gehörend und die andere zu Barber – Chirurgen.

Das nächste Kapitel erwägt die archäologischen Beweise für drei Pfarrkirchen und ein mittelalterliches Hospital. Die Ausgrabungen der St Alban Kirche, publiziert in der Zwischenstudie von 1968, sind substantiel neu interprätiert, neu datiert, und präsentiert eine mehr komplexe Sequenz, welche zeigt, daß sie nicht früher als im 11. Jahrhundert gegründet worden war. Die Arbeit an St Mary the Virgin, Aldermanbury war die letzte bedeutene Ausgrabung ausgeführt bei der RMLEC. Die Entwicklung dieser Kirche, geschaffen im 12. Jahrhndert, ist jetzt erstmals im Detail veröffentlicht. Die Nordmauer von St Alphage überlebt als Teil der Stadtverteidigungsmauern, das Nordgesicht nur durch sichtbar durch die Bombenzerstörung der späteren Gebäude, von welchen es überbaut wurde. Das vierte kirchliche Gebäude, der Turm von St Mary Elsing, ist der letzte überlebene Rest eines Krankenhauses für die Blinden, welches später als Pfarrkirche eingesetzt wurde nach der Auflösung der Klöster im 16.Jahrhundert. Einer neuen Untersuchung folgend ist diese Struktur nun erstmals im Detail veröffentlicht.

Ein weiter Blickwinkel wird im fünften Kapitel genommen, in welchem versucht wird die Entwicklung des Straßenmusters ums Krüppletor zu datieren.

Es wird angenommen, daß es Gebiet von offenen Feldern war um ca 900, das es aber dann vom Süden und vom Norden Mitte bis Ende des 10. Jahrhundert immer begrenzter wurde. Der Beweis für diese Expansion wird benutzt um die Implikationen für den Aufbau der Stadtamtsstruktur zu diskutieren und einzuschätzen, und um die schwierige Frage nach einem anglo-sächsichen Palast in dem Krüppeltorgebiet zu überprüfen.

Als Abschluß wird im sechsten Kapitel die Rolle von Professor Grimes, nicht nur als der RMLEC Direktor für Ausgrabungen, sondern auch als der Corporation of London Berater in Sachen der Erhaltung und Austellung von altertümlichen Monumenten zusammgefaßt. Um es in den Worten von Professor Grimes zu beschreiben, diese Studie kann als eine Diskussion der RMLEC mittelalterlichen Ausgrabungen in dem Krüppeltorgebiet gesehen werden, – welche einige nie zuvor veröffentlichte detailierte archäologische Informationen entält sowie flüchtige Kommentare in ein oder zwei anderen Angelegenheiten – (Grimes 1968, XI).

Übersetzung: Norman Behrend

1 War and peace

Medieval archaeology after the Blitz

Terrible bomb damage was inflicted upon British towns during the Second World War (1939–45): the civilian loss of life was heavy. Much property was destroyed, including many historic buildings in Bristol, Canterbury, Coventry, Hull, Liverpool, Portsmouth and Southampton, to name but a few of the towns that were targeted. As for London, it endured 57 consecutive nights of aerial bombardment between the 7 September and 2 November in 1940 alone: the docks, the City and the suburbs all suffered. At 6pm on Sunday evening 29 December 1940, the sirens sounded again, heralding the imminent arrival of 136 enemy bombers. In three hours they dropped more than 130 tons of high explosives and 600 incendiary bombs, the latter proving to be the more destructive. Some 1500 fires were started, including one vast conflagration that took hold over an area extending from Aldersgate underground station to Moorgate station in the north to Cheapside in the south: street after narrow street was burnt out. London also lost its medieval Guildhall, company halls such as the Barber Surgeons, as well as eight churches, including St Bride's, St Lawrence Jewry, St Alban's, St Mary Aldermanbury: remarkably St Paul's Cathedral survived, although incendiary bombs were seen bouncing off the dome. In that one night, the City suffered its worst fire since 1666 (HMSO 1942; Johnson 1980).

By 1945, once hostilities were over, large areas of the City had been flattened, with many streets represented only by lines of debris-filled cellars (see frontispiece). Such extensive bomb damage would clearly take time to make good, since the economy of the war weary country was as battered as its buildings. With so many historic sites and buildings lost in such a brutal way, this was a time for reflection as well as replanning, with bodies such as the new Council for British Archaeology (CBA), the Survey of London and the Society of Antiquaries, the Ministry of Works and the Corporation of London contributing to the general debate that actually began during the Blitz. Kathleen Kenyon, secretary of the CBA, went as far as to suggest that a programme of City excavations should start with the large site between Blackfriars and Ludgate. That particular request went unheeded, for that site was not investigated for a further 40 years. Nevertheless there was a strongly held view that the archaeological opportunity presented by the summary clearance of such large areas of the ancient City was one that should not be missed: here was 'potential knowledge that can now be acquired for relatively modest cost but can never again be bought' (Wheeler 1944, 152).

Accordingly, a committee was formed in 1945 and the Society of Antiquaries sponsored trial excavations in 1946, supervised by WF Grimes, a distinguished archaeologist and the newly appointed Keeper of the London Museum. This led directly to the formation of what was initially known as the Roman London Committee, but the name was changed to the Roman and Mediaeval London Excavation Council on the insistence of Grimes, who had been invited to become its Honorary Director of Excavations. The inclusion of the term 'Mediaeval' in the title was one that caused comment at the time, and not just because of the idiosyncratic spelling. The contemporary consensus supported by the CBA was that archaeological research spanned the period from the Palaeolithic up to the Saxons, ending in AD 700: later medieval studies were the province of historians rather than archaeologists. It should be remembered, however, that the 'excavation' of major medieval sites such as the monastic remains at St Mary's Abbey in York, date back to the early nineteenth century.

Church archaeology can therefore claim some antiquity, certainly more so than medieval urban archaeology, which was a rather later development. Although there is a distinguished history of urban archaeology in Britain, the archaeological investigation of Roman towns adopted different approaches from those of medievalists. That distinction can be shown by comparing the large scale excavations of the deserted Roman town of Silchester in Hampshire, which began in the 1890s, with the aim of examining the whole settlement, whereas the work at the deserted medieval town of Old Sarum, Wiltshire (1909–15) concentrated on the cathedral, castle and Bishop's palace, with minimal attention to the lay settlement (H de Shortt 1965). The archaeological study of the medieval burgage plot is largely a post-war development.

The use of 'modern' scientific archaeological techniques on a multiperiod urban site like London in an investigation that gave equal weight to the Roman as well as the later medieval periods was therefore still a novel concept in the 1940s. Certainly Professor Grimes thought it so, since he felt obliged to provide an explanation for the title of the RMLEC in the *Archaeological Newsletter* for July 1948, to enlighten the (presumably) baffled readership: '...the Council has the word mediaeval in its title to avow its interest in the later as well as the earlier periods of London's history, of which in fact, just as little is known from the archaeological point of view. It is in any case clear already that the complicated interlocking of work of varying periods in the deep deposits that cover a large part of the City is such that their separation without detailed study would be impossible. The Council's policy of dealing with every phase of London's history is therefore dictated by practical necessity as well as principle'.

The Society for Medieval Archaeology itself was not founded until 1956, a decade after the RMLEC, the work on the London Blitz sites being one of the catalysts for the development. Indeed, London's role in the genesis of this 'new' subject area goes back well before the war. The British Museum's Department of British and Medieval Antiquities was established in Bloomsbury in 1866 (BM 1907, vi), for example. Medieval pottery and other artefacts had appeared in quantity during nineteenth and early twentieth-century redevelopments in London: these had created interest, with some being published by the Guildhall Museum (1908), others in Sir Mortimer Wheeler's *London Museum catalogues* (1927; 1935) dealing with the Vikings and then the Saxons, and by GC Dunning and J Ward-Perkins (Dunning 1932; 1933; 1937; London Museum 1940). When Grimes took charge of the London Museum in December 1945, he established a new departmental structure, which included a separate Medieval Department. From 1952 this was under the control of Brian Spencer, 'one of the best appointments ever made by the museum' (Sheppard 1991, 121). The director who succeeded Professor Grimes in 1956 was Donald Harden, a founder member of the Society for Medieval Archaeology, and the first editor of its annual journal. In addition to three distinguished officers from the British Museum, there were no less than four past and present London

archaeologists serving as officers on the first council of the newly formed Society for Medieval Archaeology: Gerald Dunning, Donald Harden, Professor Grimes and Sir Mortimer Wheeler.

The London Museum was by no means alone, however, in its advocacy of medieval archaeology: John Hurst from the Ministry of Works has suggested that medieval village studies were developing nicely in the 1930s, but 'the Second World War intervened and set the study of medieval archaeology back ten years' (Beresford and Hurst 1971, 77). In 1948 the British Museum's Rupert Bruce-Mitford called for a concerted study of medieval archaeology as a subject in its own right, taking into account the pre-war work on finds, on rural sites such as Great Beere in Devon, and on urban sites such as the Bodleian extension in Oxford. Neither was London the only town to mount an excavation programme of bomb damaged sites: important work was subsequently undertaken in Southampton, a town with no Roman precursor (Platt and Coleman-Smith 1975) and on the Bristol church of St Mary le Port in Bristol (Watts and Rahtz 1985) for example. Thus it could be argued that the

Fig 1 Modus Operandi: *workmen open up a new trench for the RMLEC on a City bombsite at Windsor Court.* (The Sphere)

Blitz served as a stimulus to the development of the concept of medieval urban archaeology as well as to multiperiod urban archaeology: the Roman and Mediaeval London Excavation Council was a principal agent in the van of both those advances.

Sadly, once the main RMLEC programme came to close in 1962, the priorities for salvage excavations in the City often focussed rather more on the Roman than on the medieval levels. This was a period of retreat, in which London's archaeology was not well provided for. The situation changed dramatically after 1972 following the work on Baynard's Castle, from which site well preserved medieval masonry buildings and waterlogged artefacts were recovered in quantity. Pressure from the Guildhall Museum and from bodies such as *Rescue* led to the formation of a professional rescue archaeological unit in the City (Hebditch 1978), with a determination to record the medieval levels with the same degree of detail as the Roman (Biddle 1973), the principle first avowed by the RMLEC nearly 30 years before.

RMLEC excavations in Cripplegate

To return to the City in 1946: the inaugural meeting of the RMLEC was held at the Mansion House on 23 September, with the Lord Mayor, Sir Charles Davis, in the chair. The task facing the Excavation Council was vast: there were 103 acres 'available' for excavation, of which 50 acres could be cleared to basement level for a cost of £800,000 (at 1940s prices). Clearly, such sums were well beyond what the RMLEC could ever hope to raise, and thus no case could be sustained for a programme incorporating the total excavation of large areas. Instead, the Director advocated a system of trial trenching all available sites within the walled City, at an estimated cost of £30,000, followed by a programme of extended clearances in selected areas, which could come to a total of up to £100,000. By the end of 1962, the Council had only managed to raise £40,000 (itself not an inconsiderable sum,

DELVING INTO LONDON'S PAST : Mr. W. F. Grimes, Keeper of the London Museum, assisted by Miss Adrienne Farrell

Fig 2 City archaeology in 1947: Professor Grimes publicises the work of the RMLEC at Bastion 12. (The Sphere)

but quite inadequate for the task), and thus had to trim its excavation objectives accordingly. The methodology subsequently adopted involved the employment of a small team of labourers to dig trenches under the guidance of a foreman or supervisor, while the Director of Excavations would make regular visits to record the exposed sections and collect such finds as had been recovered, which would then be placed in numbered bags. On some sites, the trenches would be extended or joined up to form a larger open area depending upon the interest of the features and the available time (see Figs 1 and 2).

On the face of it then, it would seem that the RMLEC's vision of subjecting the City to an intensive research programme of scientific archaeological investigation for the first time was not realised. Indeed, looking at the distribution of their sites across London as a whole, this pessimistic view is confirmed. There are but 53 numbered sites shown on his map covering the whole of the intramural area of the City (Grimes 1968, fig 2), many of them modest in size. There are, however, three significant concentrations of sites, one in the Walbrook valley, one at Cheapside, but by far the largest grouping is in the north-west corner of the City. This was part of the

largest single zone of destruction, which spread between St Paul's, the Barbican and Moorgate, much of it destroyed in the fire bomb attack of the 29 December 1940. In all, some 24 sites were investigated (WFG1; 2–14; 14a; 15; 15a; 16–22) in that Cripplegate area during the RMLEC's main excavation programme that ended in 1962, while two more sites, Bastion 11a (WFG1a) and the church of St Mary Aldermanbury (WFG22a), were added in 1965 and 1967–8 respectively. In other words half of the RMLEC's City wide excavation programme was concentrated in Cripplegate (Figs 3, 4 and 5).

The principal thrust of that research programme was the elucidation of the plan and occupation sequence associated with a Roman fort, the presence of which had not previously been suspected. It had been built in the second century to house a complement of some 1000 soldiers. It was c 200m east–west × 240m north–south, and evidence for the masonry wall and ditch, interval towers, corner towers, the west gateway, internal buildings and streets was recovered. By the third century the City wall had been built to enclose the fort within the intramural area of the town, and the north and west walls were thickened to the same width as the new town wall itself.

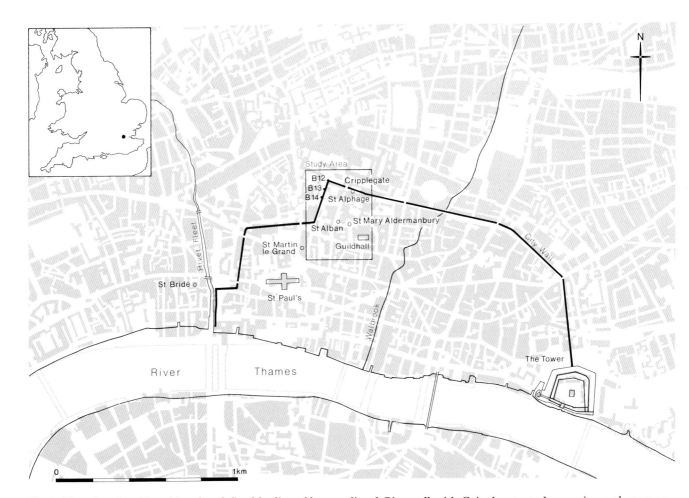

Fig 3 Plan showing City of London defined by line of late medieval City wall with Cripplegate study area in north-west corner extending from Bastions 12 to 14 in west to Guildhall in east, and from Cripplegate in north to St Alban's church in south: see also Figs 4 and 5.

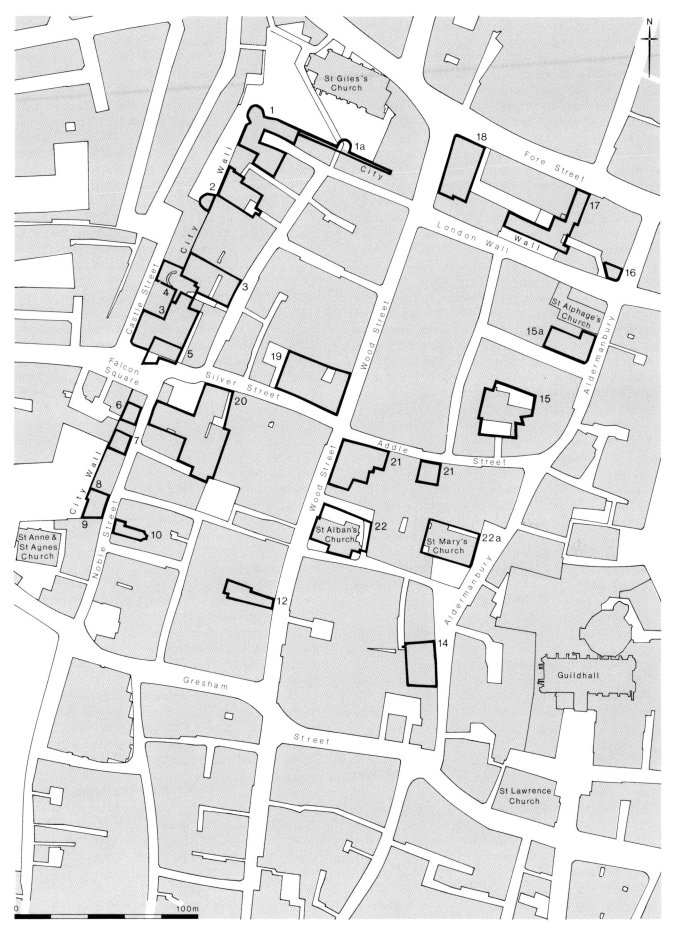

Fig 4 Plan of Cripplegate study area showing location of RMLEC excavations in relation to 1940 street pattern.

The fort's eastern and southern walls, however, seem to have been demolished in or by the end of the third century, showing that the fort fell out of use within the Roman period. The RMLEC therefore mounted a remarkable programme of archaeological research in the ruins of Cripplegate, in which some sites were deliberately selected to answer particular questions relating to the layout and use of the fort. This was a luxury no other agency had ever been afforded. However, a number of the excavations were conducted with the more familiar catalyst of imminent redevelopment hanging over them, as the works associated with Route 11, the broad highway now known as London Wall, gathered momentum. This involved a large swath of land running diagonally across the Cripplegate area, directly covering sites WFG3, 5, 15a and 19, and obliged Professor Grimes to mix research with rescue archaeology.

The fort's discovery was hailed as the single most important achievement of the RMLEC, and a detailed reappraisal of it has recently been compiled (Shepherd forthcoming; Howe and Lakin forthcoming). Since the post-war excavations were therefore principally focussed on the Roman levels, the overlying medieval material examined on all those sites was not initially studied with the same degree of intensity. Nevertheless, summaries of elements of that work have been published (Grimes 1968), although not as an area study. It is the prime objective of this new volume to present just such an area study of the post-Roman levels from the sites excavated by the RMLEC between 1946–68, following the Museum of London's redating of the pottery recovered from those sites.

Some idea of the value and scope of this new approach can be gained by reviewing the range of medieval sites that were investigated. These included a comprehensive study of the City defences, examining the ditch sequence, the town wall and Bastions 11a, 12, 13, 14 and 15; domestic occupation from the late tenth century onwards, which was studied through the excavation of pits, wells, sunken-featured buildings and the masonry foundations of substantial town houses, including Neville's Inn; the halls of two famous City companies, the Brewers and the Barber Surgeons; no less than three parish churches with the upstanding remains of St Alphage and the sites of St Alban's and St Mary Aldermanbury; as well as the tower of St Mary Elsing, part of a fourteenth-century hospital that somehow survived the Dissolution, the Great Fire, the Blitz and post-war redevelopments.

Taken together, it can therefore be argued that the RMLEC investigations in Cripplegate provide a database from which a concerted attempt at an intensive archaeological study of a sample of the medieval City could be mounted. The study area lies in the northwest corner of the City sheltered by the wall on two sides with Guildhall, London's civic centre from at least the thirteenth century, immediately to the east. Its southern boundary lies just north of Cheapside,

the largest and busiest intramural market street in the late medieval City, which ran up to the east end of the massive minster church of St Paul's, the spire of which rose some 160m above the medieval townscape. Such a location unsurprisingly attracted 'divers fair houses', as described in John Stow's celebrated survey of the City published in 1603 (Wheatley 1956, 260–71). The half dozen parish churches here once contained numerous memorials, which also demonstrate the standing of the neighbourhood, for several mayors are represented among the parishioners from Lord Northampton (d 1381) to William Brown (d 1507). Those memorials also list the range of professions followed by the richer parishioners and include haberdashers, mercers, drapers, grocers and goldsmiths. Three more goldsmiths are mentioned in a property dispute in 1321 (Chew and Kellaway 1973, no 255) while another one, Thomas Spora, complained about his neighbour, William de Lyon who lived in the Cripplegate Hermitage in 1336 (Chew and Kellaway 1973, no 333). To that mix can be added the companies and company halls that were established in and around the area: the Brewers (c 1292), Curriers (c 1300), Barbers (c 1308), Bowyers and Haberdashers (c 1371). The presence of heavier industry in 1357 is implied by the building of a forge in Wood Street, 'gravely impeding the inhabitants and common people passing by' (Chew and Kellaway 1973, no 483). The City's judicial records for 1244 also mentions the presence of a strong Jewish community in the ward, when Leo the Jew, Joce the Jew and Elias the Bishop, also a Jew, were all separately reprimanded for conducting building works that encroached upon the street (Chew and Weinbaum 1970, nos 411, 413, 414). Such an economically diverse and prosperous picture reflects a partial view of the later medieval situation. Two cases considered by the judicial sessions in 1276 provide a rather different image, recording that John Le Surr was dragged to his death by two pigs he was leading, while the body of another man, never identified, was discovered drowned, having lain unobserved for some five weeks (Weinbaum 1976, 155, 211).

The general development before that period, particularly from the tenth century onwards, would rely more heavily on archaeological evidence. The purpose of the present volume is to begin that work, looking first at the individual elements, be they bastions, buildings or churches, in the light of the new dating provided by a fresh analysis of the field records and a major reappraisal of the surviving finds. Then attention will turn to the development of the area as a whole, looking at the dating of the street system and what effect the earlier Roman fort had on the layout of the medieval roads and defences. The burning question of the location of a possible Saxon royal palace of Offa, the late eighth-century Mercian King (757–96) in the area is also discussed in the light of documentary research and the recent revelation that

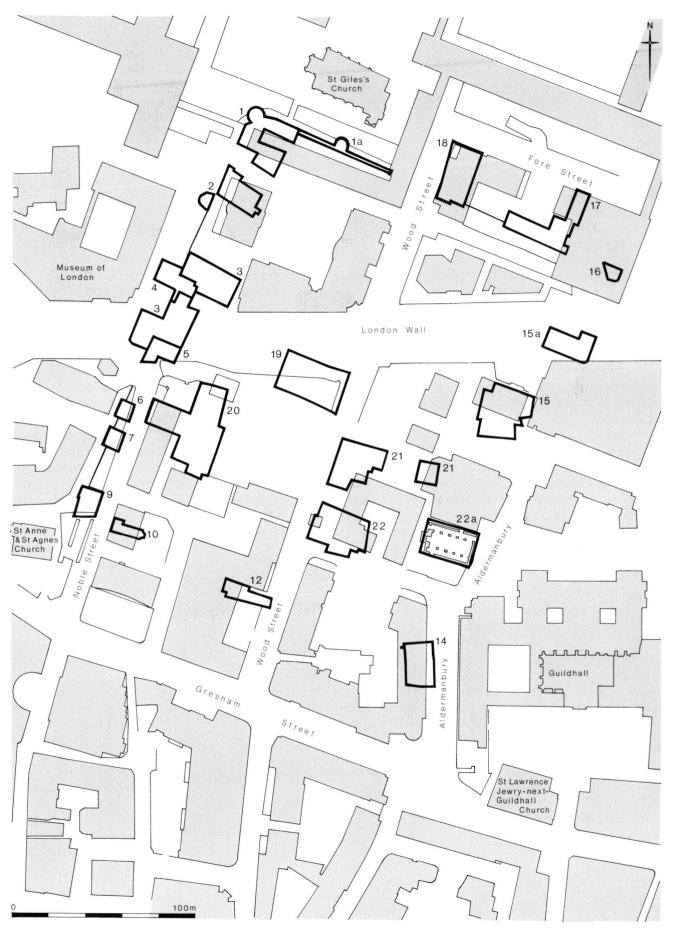

Fig 5 Plan of Cripplegate study area showing location of RMLEC excavations in relation to modern street pattern.

the mid Saxon settlement of Lundenwic lay not within the walled City, but well to the west (Vince 1990), a discovery made long after the RMLEC had completed their investigations. As a consequence it is argued that our understanding of medieval Cripplegate as a whole is considerably greater than the sum of the superficially meagre parts recovered from the City's bomb sites. Old data have current value and can still provide a chronological and topographical framework upon which more detailed archaeological records from current excavations (Howe and Lakin forthcoming) can build.

2 London Wall

Revealing the City's medieval defences

At 12.15am in the early morning of the 28 August 1940, the first bomb of the London Blitz exploded, destroying buildings between Fore Street and the City wall in St Alphage's churchyard (Hill 1955, 21). The northern (external) face of part of the City wall was thus revealed for the first time for more than 300 years, once the remains of the buildings that had been erected right up against it had been stripped away. During the course of the Blitz, other sections of London's wall were revealed, notably in the Cripplegate area (Figs 6 and 7). The RMLEC therefore decided that its first excavations would be conducted here 'with the particular aim of learning more about the City wall, its date and structural features' (Grimes 1968, 15). This research objective was one that was pursued with some vigour for a high proportion of the RMLEC sites were located on and adjacent to the City wall, its bastions or it ditches (Fig 8). As a consequence, more than a fifth of the main published report produced by Grimes is concerned with the Roman fort at Cripplegate or with London's defences. Those chapters describe and discuss the fort that he had discovered and dated to *c* AD 120, the strengthened town wall of *c* AD 200 and the associated ditches, the later medieval ditches and the new evidence of the thirteenth-century dating for the hollow bastions on the City's western side (Grimes 1968, 15–91). Thus the work of the RMLEC made major contributions to our understanding of London's defences. In this chapter, the work relating to the medieval period will be reassessed and reviewed in the light of more recent research, and a Late Saxon date suggested for the earliest medieval modification to the City ditch.

City ditch
with Mike Webber

A series of trenches were cut outside the City wall to examine the sequence of defensive ditches, which subsequently proved to date from the Roman period to

Fig 6 Section of external face of City wall immediately south of Bastion 14 (WFG4 visible on extreme left). The lower section had been incorporated within a later building and has been extensively refaced in brick, whereas the upper levels still retain the original medieval masonry facing. (GLA GR114)

9

Fig 7 East (internal) face of City wall, with modern brick facing on basement and ground floor levels, but with medieval masonry still visible at first floor level. This whole section, having survived the Blitz, was demolished in 1957 to make way for a sliproad into what is now the Museum of London's car park. (GLA GR111)

the seventeenth century (Fig 9). Of these only two cuttings (WFG17 and 18) were long enough to establish the relationship between all the major phases (see Figs 8 and 10), while some confined themselves to examining ditch deposits beneath the floor of the Bastions 11a (WFG1a), 12 (WG1), and 14 (WFG4) and others only looked at the ditch profiles closest to the wall face. Nevertheless enough was recorded from seven sections on five sites to establish a sequence and to recover sufficient pottery from the fills or from later features cutting into them to provide a working chronology. The interim report work on this important work was published in 1968, but since then the ceramics from the sites have been studied in more detail by Jacqueline Pearce for the Museum of London. As a consequence, more precise dating is offered in the following report, which was compiled largely by Mike Webber.

Saxon ditch

The earliest medieval ditch is of Late Saxon date and although it was seen and recorded by Grimes (Fig 11), it was neither unequivocally identified nor closely dated by him. It had been dug to a depth of at least 1.5m beyond a *c* 15m berm away from whatever survived of the Roman city wall, and could have been up to *c* 15m wide. A complete profile was not recovered from any one single site, and the sections shown in Fig 12 have therefore been combined to provide the composite profile illustrated in Fig 13. The northern (outside) edge was recorded on two sites (WFG17, WFG 18) and what was taken to be the southern (inside) edge on WFG1, although no pottery was recovered from that part of the feature. The deposits that filled the ditch were broadly horizontally bedded, suggesting a long period of silting up. The recent study of the pottery from the silts has

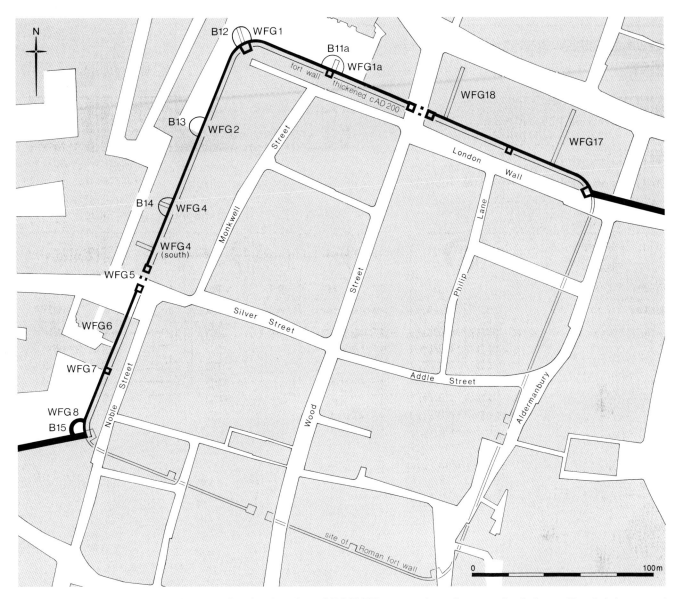

Fig 8 Plan of Cripplegate study area showing location of RMLEC excavations that examined the medieval defences and Bastions 11a, 12, 13, 14 and 15 shown in relation to 1940 street pattern (see Fig 4).

identified a sequence in which pottery dated from 950–1150 came from the lower fills, 1000–1200 from the middle fills and 1150–1200 from the upper fills. This seems to imply that the ditch was cut perhaps in the tenth century, certainly by the early eleventh century, and had subsequently silted up by the late twelfth or early thirteenth century.

Medieval ditch

A new ditch from which late medieval pottery was recovered was then cut through the infilled Saxon ditch much closer to the City wall (Fig 14). The parts of the ditch were identified in most of the cuttings made beyond the wall, and a full profile can therefore be reconstructed with some confidence working from sections recorded on WFG1 and WFG4 in particular. The inside edge was cut beyond a very narrow berm some 1.2m from the wall face. The initial fills were cut by the

footings of Bastions 11a and 14, and pottery from the ditch, which has been dated 1200–1225, was recovered from a sealed context below the floor of Bastion 14 (WFG4: Figs 15 and 16). This demonstrates that the bastions were built after the wider medieval ditch was dug. This later phase of the medieval ditch presumably represented that described in Stow's survey; 'the ditch which partly now remaineth, and compassed the wall of the City, was begun to be made by the Londoners in 1211 and was finished in the year 1213... this ditch being then made of 200 foot (*c* 60m) broad' (Wheatley 1956, 11). The width revealed on the RMLEC sites, however, can only have been *c* 20m. A documentary reference in 1348 to the berm between the City wall and the ditch south of Newgate describes it as 10 ells wide (Dyson 1984, 5), some 30ft or 10m, whereas the evidence from the Cripplegate sites suggests that the berm was less than 1.2m wide there in the early thirteenth century.

Fig 9 General view of RMLEC excavations at the Cripplegate Buildings site in Fore Street (WFG18) with the gutted shell of St Giles church to the north. (GLA GR420)

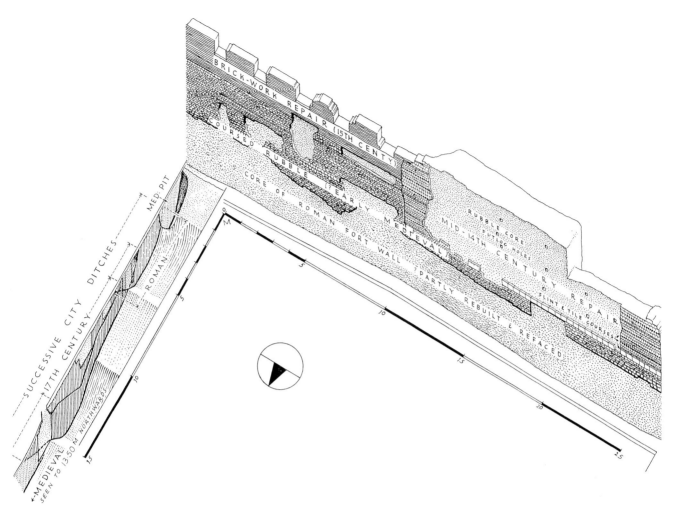

Fig 10 Isometric projection of external face of City wall (with crenellations) adjoining north wall of St Alphage church, shown in relation to series of defensive ditches of Roman, Saxon, Medieval and later date beyond berm to the north of the wall. Drawing by Professor Grimes, based on surveys conducted by the RMLEC and the Corporation of London. For more detailed ditch sections, see Figs 12, 13; for wall elevation, see Fig 116.

Fig 11 North end of silted up Late Saxon City ditch exposed by RMLEC at Fore Street in 1954 (WFG17). (GLA GR403)

Pottery from the fills of a medieval recut identified in sections recorded at WFG17 and WFG18, beyond the bastions, contained pottery broadly dated 1350–1500 from the lower fills and to 1480–1550 from the upper fills (WFG18; bag nos 35, 114, 115, 141, 156, 233).

Sixteenth-century recut

A substantial recut was evident on three sections (WFG1 WFG17 WFG18: Fig 17 and see Figs 18 and 19), and pottery groups from the infill has been dated from 1580–1620 (WFG18), although other less closely datable assemblages have been given a wider range of 1500–1700. The ditch fills were cut by a well associated with pottery dated 1500–1600. The ditch itself was up to 4m deep and 24m wide at the top with gently sloping sides. This phase presumably represents a ditch cutting event associated with the uncertainties posed by the Spanish Armada invasion threats of late sixteenth century.

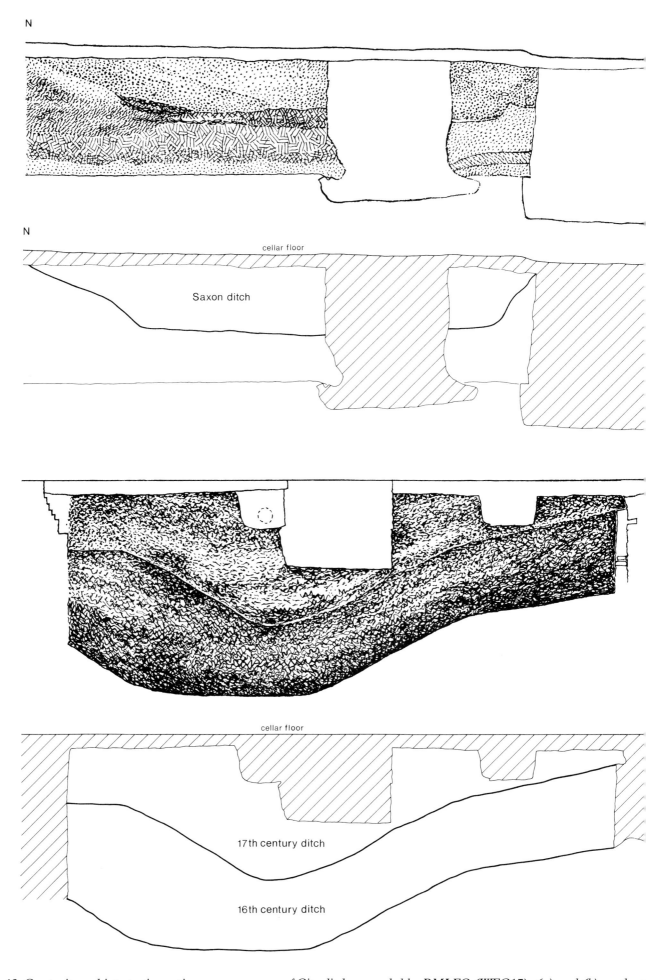

N

N

cellar floor

Saxon ditch

cellar floor

17th century ditch

16th century ditch

Fig 12 Composite and interpretive sections across sequence of City ditches recorded by RMLEC (WFG17): (a) and (b) north se

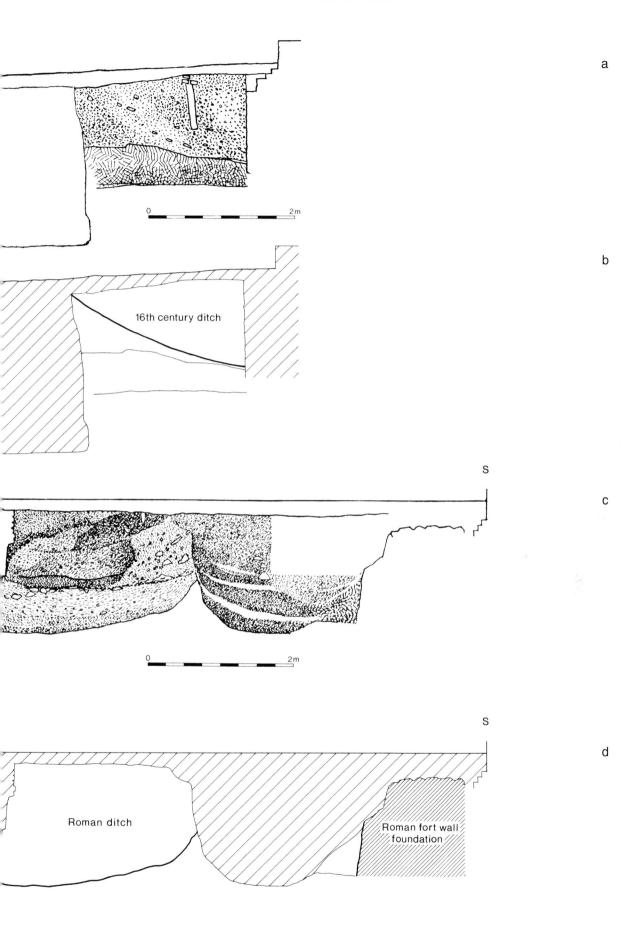

a

b

16th century ditch

0   2m

S

c

0   2m

S

d

Roman ditch

Roman fort wall foundation

g Saxon and sixteenth-century ditches; (c) and (d) south section, showing Roman, sixteenth- and seventeenth-century ditches.

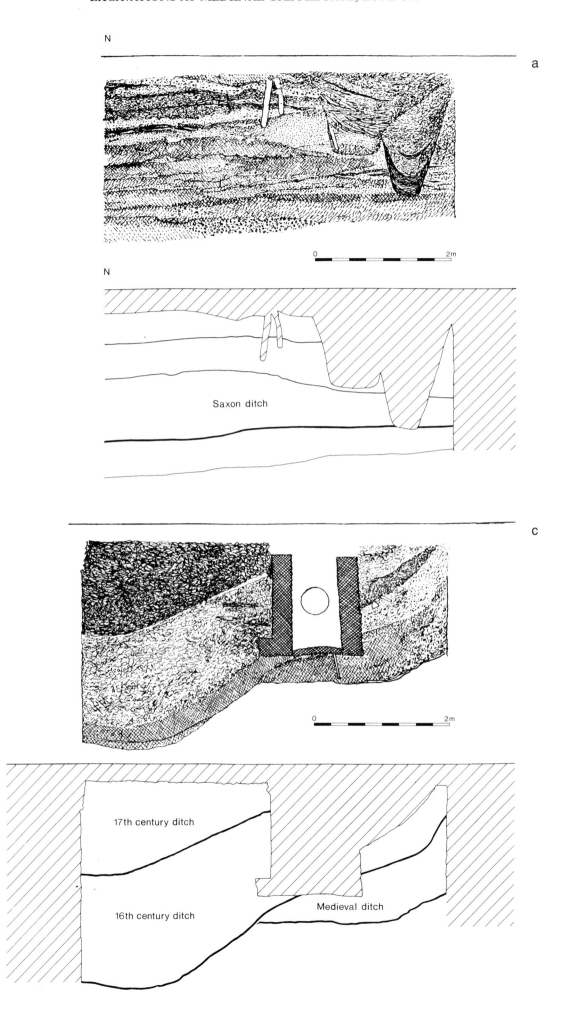

N

a

0   2m

N

Saxon ditch

c

0   2m

17th century ditch

16th century ditch   Medieval ditch

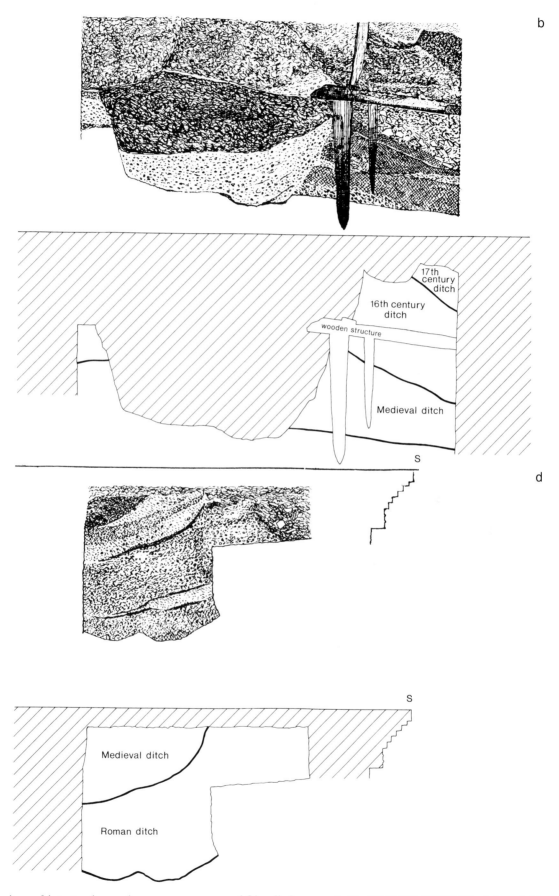

Fig 13 Composite and interpretive sections across sequence of City ditches recorded by RMLEC (WFG18): (a) and (b) north section, showing Saxon and later ditches; (c) and (d) south section, showing Roman and later ditches.

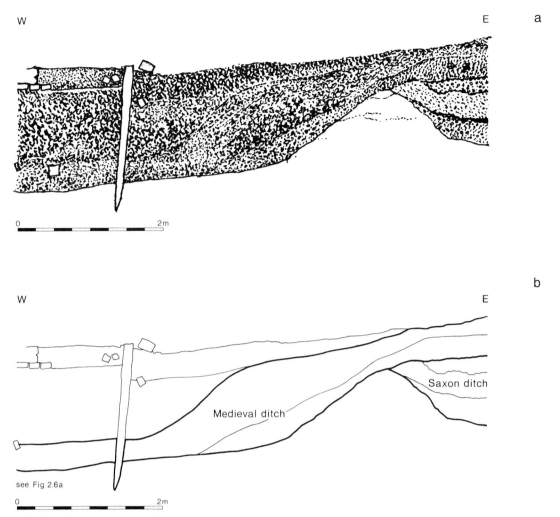

Fig 14 (a) Section through City ditch sequence recorded by RMLEC on WFG1; (b) interpretation showing later medieval ditch cutting eastern edge of Saxon ditch.

Fig 15 City ditch profile exposed by RMLEC below floor of Bastion 14 (WFG4 to left) and base of Roman wall (to right), looking north-west. (GLA GR118)

A group of distillation vessels and crucibles probably used in the assaying of metals was recovered from the fills of this recut, and is reported on elsewhere (Bayley forthcoming).

Seventeenth-century recut

Another major recut was identified in WFG1, WFG17 and WFG18, clearly cutting through the late sixteenth-century infill material (Fig 20 and see Figs 18 and 19). It was similar in profile to the sixteenth-century recut but was some 1m shallower than it and had a more rounded bottom. It was itself cut by features containing pottery dated to 1630–80, as well as a brick culvert, which Grimes identified as the main sewer built in 1648. The last phase of the City ditch must therefore have been infilled before the mid seventeenth century. The fills of that ditch contained ceramics dated from 1580–1650, 1620–50, 1580–1700 and 1610–40. Taken together, it seems that the ditch represented a short-lived feature the cutting of which was presumably occasioned by the mid seventeenth-century Civil Wars, in which London played a leading role as the headquarters of the Parliamentary cause.

Fig 16 City ditch sequence sealed beneath floor of Bastion 14 (WFG4) looking east towards footings of City wall exposed in RMLEC excavations. (GLA GR133)

Fig 17 Profile of infilled late sixteenth-century City ditch exposed by RMLEC in section on the Fore Street site (WFG17). Scale: 4 × 6in (c 0.6m). (GLA GR400)

Pottery sequence from the City ditch at Cripplegate Buildings (WFG18)

by Jacqueline Pearce

A considerable quantity of pottery was recovered from the section of the City ditch excavated at Cripplegate Buildings: 5248 sherds from a minimum of 3485 vessels (Estimated Number of Vessels or ENV). Most of these are post-medieval: 3984 sherds, or 2621 ENV (75%). Finds were selectively sampled during excavation and stored in individually numbered bags, several of which might come from the same context. This accounts in part for the high number of sherd links recorded between bags, some of which are the equivalent of medium or large contexts (ie 30–100 sherds and more than 100 sherds, respectively), filling several bags or boxes given the same number. A total of 29 bags contain medium sized groups (18 of which are post-medieval); eight are large and two are very large (multiple boxes), all post-medieval. Within samples, all pottery appears to have been collected, including small and uninteresting sherds, as well as numerous large sherds, many of which join to give complete vessel profiles.

The pottery was recorded using minimum quantification by sherd count (SC) and ENV. All figures given here are based on these data. Although their value is limited by the collection policy and the inadequacy of the stratigraphic records, they still demonstrate clearly discernible patterns. The ceramic evidence is now discussed chronologically, corresponding closely with the proposed ditch sequence as derived from other sources.

Tenth- to twelfth-century pottery

A total of 812 sherds (540 ENV) are dated between *c* 900 and *c* 1200, the period during which the first medieval ditch is thought to have been open. Very little appears to be residual (37 sherds), a marked contrast with later medieval pottery from the site. Sherds from cooking pots in early medieval sandy ware and early medieval sand and shell-tempered ware (Vince and Jenner 1991, 56–63) are the earliest pottery recovered, together spanning the period *c* 970–1150. A single sherd of Rhenish red-painted ware in bag 198 is broadly dated in London from *c* 900 to *c* 1250 (ibid, 100–102), but the main pottery used in the capital throughout the tenth century, Late Saxon shelly ware (ibid, 49–54), is noticeably absent, except as five abraded, residual sherds.

Most of the pottery from this period dates to *c* 1050–1200, and includes the usual range of domestic wares widely used throughout the City. The main fabrics, in addition to the above, are early Surrey ware, early medieval shelly ware and local grey ware (ibid, 73–5; 63–8; 76–9). After their introduction *c* 1080, London-type wares became a major element in the City's pottery supply (Vince 1991b, 268; Pearce et al 1985). Cooking pots, jugs and pitchers are the main forms,

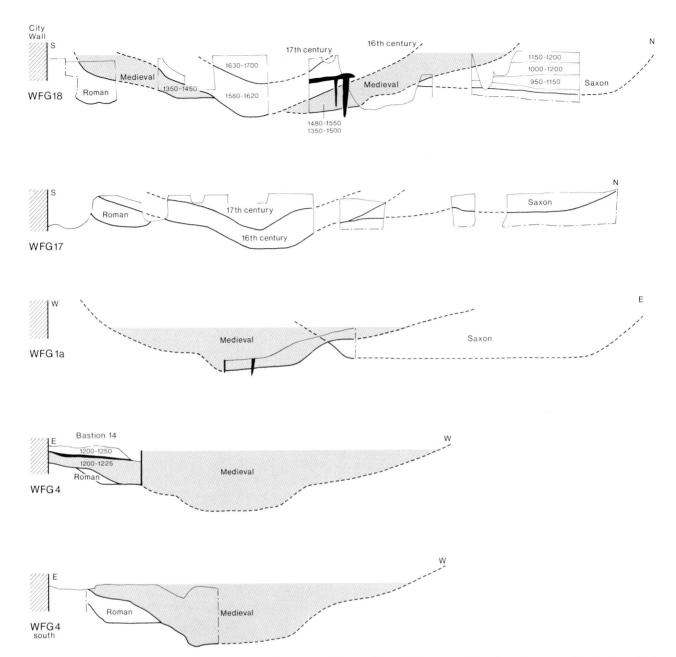

Fig 18 Interpretative drawings showing suggested comparative profiles of Saxon, medieval and post-medieval City ditches recorded by RMLEC on sites WFG1a, 4, 17 and 18, with locations of dated finds groups.

as elsewhere in London. There are also sherds from ten small hemispherical metalworking crucibles, mostly in early medieval sandy ware and early Surrey ware (cf Bayley 1992, fig 4). A very unusual find is part of a modelled bird in Stamford-type ware (residual in bag 2). It was originally applied to the body of a late twelfth-century highly decorated spouted pitcher; the only other example excavated in London comes from the site of the Guildhall Yard Extension (Nenk and Pearce 1994).

Late thirteenth- to fifteenth-century pottery

In all, 446 sherds (320 ENV) are dated between *c* 1270 and *c* 1500, associated with the use of the second wider medieval ditch. A large proportion are residual in later

contexts (254 sherds or 56%). Very little pottery can be dated to the early thirteenth century when the second ditch was first cut and the bastions constructed. The majority is broadly dated to *c* 1350–1500, consisting largely of cooking pots and jugs in Coarse Border ware and Cheam whiteware (Pearce and Vince 1988). There are no metalworking ceramics at this date.

A number of bags are dated to *c* 1400 or later by the presence of jugs and pipkins in late London-type ware and late London slipped ware (Vince 1985, 58), and Cheam whiteware barrel shaped jugs, dated after *c* 1430 (Pearce and Vince 1988, 86), showing the ditch was in continuous use throughout the fifteenth century. Part of a bowl in Paterna blue ware from the Valencia region of Spain (bag 43), is similar to a bowl from Mary-at-Hill, London, and is typical of the

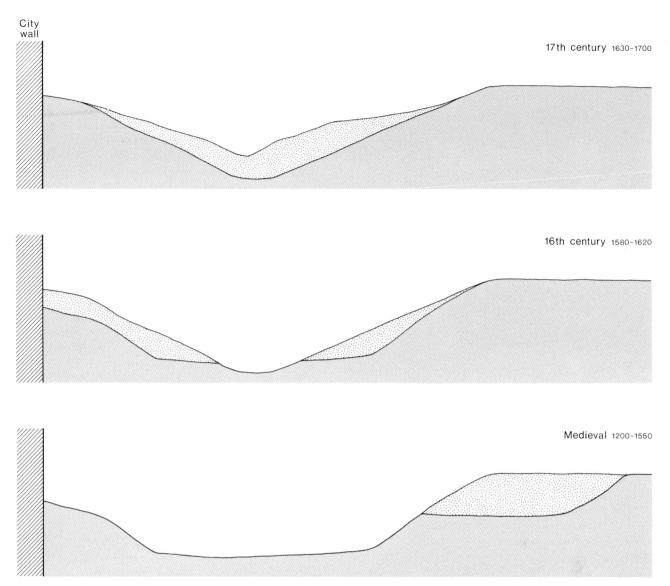

Fig 19 Suggested profiles of medieval and post-medieval City ditches shown schematically.

fourteenth/early fifteenth century (Hurst et al 1986, fig16, no36). This is the only imported pottery found at this date.

Post-medieval pottery

Most of the pottery is post-medieval, the main sequence dating to *c* 1480–1650 (3769 sherds/2496 ENV). Several medium or large groups are dated either before or after *c* 1550, and between *c* 1580 and 1630, presenting a representative sequence of the fabrics and forms in use in the City during this period (Pearce forthcoming b).

Groups dated to *c* 1480–1550 (684 sherds/506 ENV) are characterised by the absence of Frechen stonewares and Surrey-Hampshire Border ware, one of the most common kinds of pottery used in London *c* 1550–1700 (Pearce 1992). They consist largely of local (London area) redwares, but also include sherds from several drinking jugs and other forms in early Border ware (41 sherds/33 ENV),

which is intermediate between 'Tudor Green' (Pearce and Vince 1988, 79–81) and the later Border ware (Pearce forthcoming a).

A remarkable quantity of fine, well glazed, redware cups in a previously uncharacterised fabric were recovered (282 sherds/214 ENV), with a large concentration in groups predating *c* 1550 (15.2% ENV – the second most common fabric at this date). Following petrological analysis, and comparison with late fifteenth-century whiteware forms from Farnborough Hill (Holling 1977) and pottery recently excavated in Guildford (Guildford Museum RB3932), the fabric has been named early Red Border ware (Pearce forthcoming a), and dated to *c* 1480–1550. Although not yet identified in production waste, it is suggested that these cups predate the introduction of Red Border ware proper into London (*c* 1580+), and its first known production at Farnborough Hill *c* 1550–80 (Pearce 1992, 95). The cups come in three forms: a flared, corrugated vessel, a rounded form with straight-sided neck and a narrow-based cup with vertical fluting. They are,

Fig 20 Profile of infilled late seventeenth-century City ditch, in which base of 4 × 6in scale rests (c 0.6m), exposed by RMLEC on the Fore Street site (WFG17). (GLA GR394)

however, rare elsewhere in the City, making the concentration of finds at WFG18 all the more intriguing and significant (see below).

In late sixteenth-century groups (739 sherds/504 ENV), Border wares are the second most common type of pottery after local redwares (12.9% by ENV). There is a higher proportion of imports, principally Low Countries earthenwares and Rhenish stonewares, including part of a fine polychrome albarello in North Netherlands maiolica (bag 240), dated c 1550–80 (Hurst et al 1986, fig 56, no 172).

Most of the forms were used for cooking and serving: pipkins, cauldrons, bowls and dishes, dripping dishes and jugs, and an unusually high proportion of drinking vessels (22% ENV of all late sixteenth-century pottery). There is also a figurine salt in Cistercian ware (bags 240/242). Made in the form of a woman in early sixteenth-century dress holding a shallow dish, the form is extremely rare, with only three known parallels in London (two in the Museum of London reserve collection and one from the Tower Postern – TOL79). There is a more complete example in the National Museum of Wales (NMW Acc. No. 27.98), and scattered finds elsewhere.

A large number of industrial vessels were also recovered (Fig 21), mostly in unglazed early post-medieval redware (Pearce forthcoming a). These consist principally of long-necked distillation flasks or cucurbits (54 sherds/34 ENV), frequently with the powdery red haematite deposits associated with the production of nitric acid, used in parting precious metals (Bayley 1992, 6–7). A smaller number are

found in the early sixteenth-century pottery, but the quantity increases in groups dated to c 1580–1630 (148 sherds/83 ENV). Apparently associated with these in the same groups are numerous shallow, thick-walled, unglazed dishes in the same fabric (4 sherds/ENV c 1550–1600; 51 sherds/34 ENV c 1580–1630). These have a rounded base, and several show signs of heating. Their function remains unclear, although it appears they might have had an industrial use. There are also several crucibles, especially in groups post-dating c 1580 (16 sherds/15 ENV), including small and medium sized Border ware and triangular Hessian crucibles in various sizes, most probably used for working precious metals (Cotter 1992; Pearce 1992, 45, fig 46, nos.455–6). Finally there is a single bone ash cupel, with a lump of partially purified silver remaining. Used in separating precious metals for assaying, these are extremely rare finds in London (examples are known from Legge's Mount, Tower of London; Bayley 1992, 6, fig 7a).

There are several large, good groups of pottery dating to c 1580–1630 (2342 sherds/1475 ENV). None includes Metropolitan slipware, introduced in the second quarter of the seventeenth century (the earliest known example, in the Museum of London, is dated 1630); there is very little tin-glazed ware or other distinctive pottery of mid seventeenth-century date, such as brown-glazed Border ware (Pearce 1992, 101). This argues strongly that the ditch was infilled and no longer used for dumping by the 1640s. London area redwares still predominate, together with Border wares, Essex fine redwares (Orton 1988, 298) and Low Countries and Rhenish imports. Tin-glazed ware in Orton's group A, dated to c 1612–40/50 (ibid, 321; 27 sherds/20 ENV), includes several sherds from a tankard decorated in blue and white with leaf scrolls and part of an inscription reading '..O*RO..'. Other vessels of interest include an unusual green-glazed standing candlestick with handle in Red Border ware (bag 244); part of a dish in Beauvais double sgraffito decorated with a Tudor rose (bag 217; Hurst et al 1986, 109–14); and a dish in North Netherlands maiolica with an eight-pointed polychrome star design, together with a dish in North Holland slipware with cruciform decoration (both bag 217).

A total of 151 sherds (89 ENV) come from bags dated after c 1670, representing small scale domestic rubbish disposal, rather than extensive dumping. This includes the usual range of fabrics current during the late seventeenth and eighteenth centuries, but nothing of particular note.

Discussion

The City ditch was used for centuries as a communal dumping ground for all manner of household and other refuse, giving a series of invaluable snapshots of the range and variety of domestic and industrial apparatus used by the successive generations of Londoners.

Fig 21 Group of sixteenth to seventeenth-century metalworking ceramics recovered by RMLEC from City ditch at Cripplegate Buildings (WFG18). Back row: early post-medieval redware distillation flask necks; Front row (l to r): triangular hessian crucible; Surrey-Hampshire Borderware crucibles.

Considerable quantities of sixteenth- and seventeenth-century pottery were recovered from sections through the ditch excavated at Boston House, 90–94 Old Broad Street (BRO90; Pearce 1994) and Capel House, 54–62 New Broad Street (CAP86; Pearce 1992, 105), bearing close comparison with the material from Cripplegate Buildings, and revealing a similar pattern of successive dumping and recutting until the ditch was finally infilled in the seventeenth century. The concentration of pottery from WFG18 dating to the tenth to twelfth centuries corresponds with the use of the earliest ditch, after which there is a hiatus until *c* 1270. Then follows a lengthy period of dumping, during which the late medieval material was much disturbed by later activity, with the main and most significant period of use dating between *c* 1480 and *c* 1630. By the 1640s, as at BRO90, if not slightly earlier, the ditch at Cripplegate was no longer used as a communal dump.

The pottery recovered from WFG18 brings into focus certain activities centred on Cripplegate Ward or nearby. Among the most significant features are the concentrations of both fine redware cups and industrial vessels. The area appears to have been a focus of metalworking from the early medieval period. There are several small crucibles dated to *c* 1050–1150, of a

kind generally used in working precious metals. This compares closely with the large numbers of similar crucibles found on the nearby site of Shelley House, at the north end of Noble Street (NST94; Pearce 1996). There are no metalworking ceramics at either site from the late twelfth until the sixteenth century, when ample evidence for the industrial processes associated with working metals is provided by the large numbers of cucurbits or distillation flasks, as well as crucibles, and the enigmatic industrial dishes. Although these forms occur in groups predating *c* 1550, they are most common between *c* 1580 and 1630, suggesting that this was the main period of industrial activity.

Intriguing questions are raised by the large numbers of early Red Border ware cups recovered. They appear to have been made at a single workshop over a relatively short period, in the early to mid sixteenth century. Their occurrence in such a restricted area suggests that they were bought in bulk for use in large scale entertainments and dining, rather than by individual households. One of the more likely sources at this date might be one or more of the numerous Livery Company Halls situated in this part of the City, or a hall or tavern regularly used by some of the companies for their feasts and messes. Several Company Halls were established in the immediate vicinity by the early sixteenth century, including those of the Brewers, Curriers, Barber Surgeons, Bowyers and Pinmakers (Lobel 1989, map 3, c 1520). It might be that one of these contracted to purchase earthenware cups from one of the potteries of the Farnham region, for use at their feasts, in much the same way as the Inns of Court regularly bought whiteware drinking vessels in bulk from the same area from the late fifteenth century onwards (Matthews and Green 1969). These questions and the early history of the Border ware industry are treated in greater depth elsewhere (Pearce forthcoming b).

Other pottery from the sixteenth- to early seventeenth-century sequence is largely domestic in character, with few fine quality or unusual vessels that might be associated with better off households. One exception is the Cistercian figurine salt. It was probably used in a merchant or other middle class household, since the wealthy would no doubt own pewter or silver salts, serving for display as much as for practical purposes. Otherwise, there is a relatively low proportion of imported pottery at all periods on the site, and even fewer highly decorative, exotic or expensive items. With few exceptions, most of the pottery recovered was of a kind used by people across the social spectrum for the time honoured activities associated with the preparation and consumption of food.

Bastions

Bastion 11a

Although the term 'bastion' is not the correct technical description for the projecting extramural towers on the City wall, it is the term employed by Grimes in all his work and appears in much of the literature concerning London's defences; hallowed by such general familiarity, the term is retained here.

Bastion 11a was recorded by Grimes in 1965 (Figs 22, 23, 24 and 25), while acting as the consultant appointed by the Corporation to advise it on archaeological issues. The remains of two curving stumps of foundation walling up to 1.25m wide were exposed during the extensive landscaping programme associated with the Barbican redevelopment in St Giles churchyard (Grimes 1968, 71–8). The stumps projected up to 4m northwards from the line of the Roman City wall, built out over the southern edge of the Roman City ditch. These walls are seen as representing a semicircular bastion some 6.25m in diameter, which had clearly been butted against the northern face of the Roman wall. A number of intrusions and truncations had disturbed the feature: for example, the most northerly part of the wall had been cut away by a modern drain pipe connected to a seventeenth-century sewer, which, Grimes noted, 'was evidently still in use' (WFG1a, field notes). Nevertheless, a section of archaeological deposits

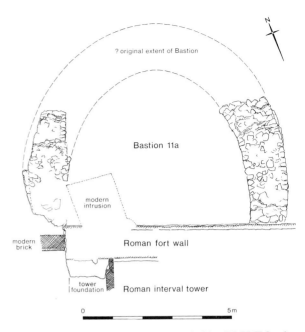

Fig 22 Plan of Bastion 11a as recorded by RMLEC, showing relationship to the remains of the Roman interval tower and wall (WFG1a).

between the two arms of the bastion survived for a depth of 2m from the modern surface of the churchyard to the Roman berm. On excavation, Grimes was able to show that the brick earth berm between the wall and the Roman City ditch was overlain by a surface of rammed gravel and stone, over which were

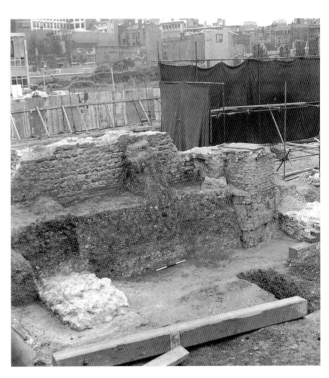

Fig 23 Eastern and western arms of Bastion 11a in 1965 (WFG1a) projecting northwards from the face of the City wall, still partially obscured by later deposits. Looking south towards the City. (GLA GR21)

deposits of mortar and silt that contained a sherd of medieval pottery. That horizon was sealed by a deposit of grey silts that contained a range of occupation material including cooking pot rims dated to the thirteenth century. It was also clearly cut by the masonry foundations, demonstrating unequivocally for the first time that at least one of the bastions was a medieval rather than a Roman addition to the City's defences.

This was a major discovery, which came just too late for inclusion in Ralph Merrifield's published discussion of the London bastions (Merrifield 1965, 320–25). Indeed, it was only added at the last moment to Professor Grimes' own book, which was at that time in page proof. Such was the importance of this find that hurried amendments were made, delaying the publication of the book, and for which the publisher charged the RMLEC £85 16s (GLA: RMLEC AGM 1969).

The position occupied by this clearly medieval bastion in relation to the Roman wall circuit is of interest. The medieval feature lies directly south of the fragmentary remains of a Roman interval tower associated with the second-century fort, which could suggest that the projecting bastion was built as a conscious replacement for a decaying internal tower.

A rammed gravel surface 0.25m thick was identified within the bastion, representing its only internal working surface, and this sealed the layer with the thirteenth-century pottery described above. Grimes notes that the gravel surface 'was exactly like that in Bastion 14' which he had recorded some 18 years previously. The new bastion was named 11a, since it lay between the previously numbered Bastions 11 and 12. Although when first revealed, the outer part of it had been cut away by the seventeenth-century sewer following the line of the infilled City ditch (Grimes 1968, plates 18 and 19), subsequent restoration work replaced the missing portion so that it now appears as a complete semicircular plan, projecting into the Barbican moat, with the core infilled with gravel.

Bastion 12 (WFG1)

This semicircular hollow bastion (Fig 26) marks the north-west corner of the Roman fort and the later City wall, which extends eastwards and southwards from this point. Today the tower stands exposed for a height of some 9m above the contemporary ground surface, which has been substantially lowered since the 1950s during landscaping (Fig 28). The Barbican lake now laps up against its external face, recreating in general terms the feel but not the form of the medieval moat. The bastion was excavated at the turn of the century by J Terry who recorded that the lowest 1m of the superstructure and the underlying footings were of a different character to the upper works. He also noted that 'the wall had, at various periods, undergone a great amount of repairing but unfortunately of a very injudicious character, large pieces of brickwork interspersed with flint, tiles and broken bits of slate having been introduced; and as the wall was originally built of ragstone, the bad taste of these earlier repairs was only too manifest'.

Fig 24 The eastern and western arms of Bastion 11a (WFG1a) fully exposed, projecting northwards from the northern face of the City wall, to the south of which the residential buildings in the Barbican Wallside development are under construction. (GLA GR24)

Fig 25 Detail to show the western arm of Bastion 11a (WFG1a) butting up against the Roman masonry exposed at the foot of the north face of the City wall. (GLA GR25)

Fig 26 Bastion 12: RMLEC excavations in the interior in 1947. (The Sphere)

The injudicious repairs were subsequently replaced with 'ragstone very carefully built in to match the old work' (Terry 1905).

Grimes published a comment that although much of the bastion clearly had a modern finish, where the original masonry was visible, it appeared to be the random rubble characteristic of the medieval bastions on the western side of the City. Unfortunately there are few surviving records or drawings made by the RMLEC during their investigations in 1946 to support this statement. Three trenches were recorded, one of which sampled the deposits within the bastion itself, one was set just to the east, while a third involved working with a north–south trench dug by contractors perpendicular to the line of the City wall. The first cutting, the only one from which results relevant to this particular discussion were obtained, showed that the bastion had a substantial gravel floor surface within it. No pottery or other datable artefacts were recovered from the associated sequence, and consequently Grimes was unable to provide an unequivocal independent date for it.

Photographs taken some twenty years later in the late 1960s (Fig 27), show that the ground surface was subsequently lowered very substantially during the Barbican landscaping programme, revealing more of the base of the bastion. Plans for its restoration were being drawn in 1968 while the RMLEC were excavating the nearby church of St Mary Aldermanbury. Grimes was also clearly involved with this stage of the work, the conservation and laying out of the monuments exposed by the bombing. In 1972, for example, he was sent more plans from CG Chandler, the Corporation's chief architect, to comment upon. That letter referred to the many discussions that had taken place between Grimes and the Corporation concerning the treatment of 'the Roman London wall', a term that included the medieval bastions (WFG 1 Corr 11/4/72). In this particular instance, Grimes was less forthcoming, and a follow up letter had to be sent five months later to solicit a reply (WFG1 Corr 24/9/72). Clearly the Corporation was loath to act on such matters without the benefit of advice from their distinguished, if reticent, consultant. That he did finally respond is shown by a note appended to another Corporation of London plan (C3/16/28a) showing the proposed new layout around Bastion 12: it is dated 11/10/73 and states that the 'dimensions shown are as agreed by Phrof (sic) Grimes'.

The bastion as it survives today is clearly of more than one build, but the meaningful phasing of the structure has been complicated by the substantial restoration works that have taken place during the twentieth century (Fig 29), usually without the accompaniment of detailed drawn records (see Terry 1905).

Bastion 13

Only the lower 2m of this hollow semicircular bastion survives, now substantially rendered. In the seventeenth century, it had been incorporated into the Barber Surgeons' courthouse, but that was replaced by a warehouse in 1864, which preserved the much mutilated lower portion of the bastion in the cellar. The nineteenth-century building was in turn

Fig 27 Bastion 12 (WFG1), north-west face with base exposed after ground level lowered during Barbican Wallside redevelopment in 1968. (GLA GR583)

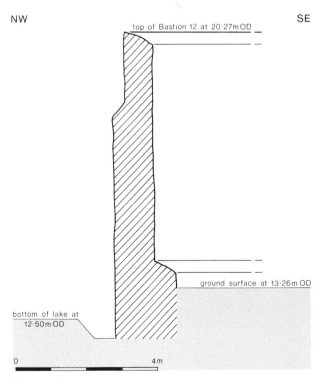

Fig 28 Bastion 12 in relation to bottom of present-day Barbican lake and ground surface: profile to show changing thickness of wall (WFG1).

Fig 29 Bastion 12 (WFG1): knapped flint course at base of uppermost surviving stage of the tower exposed during consolidation of the monument in the late 1960s. (GLA GR13)

destroyed during the Blitz, exposing the remains of the tower once again. Subsequent work by the RMLEC excavated the entire interior of the bastion (Fig 30). This showed that the foundations had been taken down to the base of the Roman City ditch through the silts that partially infilled it up to the level of the foundation offset. On the north side of the bastion where the junction survived, it had been butted against the City wall, which here comprised courses related to the Roman fort and also to a later medieval rebuilding (Grimes 1968, 67, plate 20). Once again, the evidence for this rests heavily on the contemporary photographic evidence (Fig 31), since few drawings or detailed field notes have survived. No datable pottery from any stratified context related to the construction or initial use of the bastion seems to have survived.

The internal area of the bastion has now been infilled to a height of *c* 1m above the excavated level, and laid out as a formal garden. The internal face of the bastion as exposed bears traces of its use as a warehouse, most obviously in the surviving top of the monument, which retains the bases of three windows dressed with yellow stock bricks. These mark the positions of the splayed apertures that allowed daylight into the basement of the warehouse, and thus indicate the level of the external ground surface to the west in the late nineteenth century, which was substantially higher than it is today. That was the general level from which the RMLEC began their labours, in marked contrast to the much lower landscaped surface seen today.

Bastion 14

This hollow D-shaped bastion had been so successfully incorporated within later warehousing that its survival had escaped the notice of the compilers of the Royal Commission's survey of the medieval monuments of London (RCHM 1929). It survived the Blitz undamaged and unseen, although the bombing destroyed many of the later accretions in the neighbouring properties. The Pioneer Corps was then sent in to clear up the bomb damage in this part of the ravaged City in 1942. The remains of Bastion 14 had been classified as an unsafe structure and was actually in the process of demolition, before the destruction was halted by timely intervention of an architect who finally recognised it for what it was: the incident was reported in a letter to the *Times* on 12 October 1942, some four years before the RMLEC began their work (Hill 1955, 55).

The excavations that Grimes subsequently conducted in 1947 below the floor of the shallow cellar within this bastion marked the inauguration of the RMLEC's main archaeological programme (Figs 32 and 33). The methodology adopted was explicitly recorded, and is of some significance. The area was not opened up in plan and taken down in a series of horizontal levels, separating out each phase in reverse order of deposition, as might be anticipated today. Instead, an east–west trench was cut along the main axis of the bastion, and the two long sections thus exposed were examined. These sections were then progressively cut back by some 0.3m at a time, cleaned and examined, but not every new exposure was drawn. In this way the entire fill of the bastion was removed, not layer by layer, but by the cutting back of sections comprising several different superimposed or intercutting features. The adoption of this technique on other RMLEC sites helps to explain why so many of the pottery groups retrieved from them contain 'intrusive' or 'residual' material.

A viable quantity of pottery was recovered from the basal levels of this bastion, but unfortunately the study of medieval ceramics was not sufficiently advanced to utilise that resource in the 1950s. Consequently, the published discussion of the dating evidence for this feature concentrates solely on a coin of Constans (AD 346–50) and a bronze pendant recovered from the gravel floor of the bastion (Grimes 1968, fig 16, 68–70). The pendant (now lost) was thought to be of Saxon date, and therefore showed that this western bastion need not be of late Roman date, as were those on the eastern side of the City. A fresh study of the drawings of the pendant (initially by Professor James Graham-Campbell, and subsequently by Nina Crummy) suggests that it is not a Saxon, but a late Roman artefact (J Graham-Campbell, personal communication). On the face of it, this would seem to prove that Bastion 14 was broadly contemporary, but the reappraisal by the Museum of London specialists of the pottery from the levels immediately above and below the gravel surface has provided convincing

Fig 30 Internal view of Bastion 13 (WFG2) exposed during RMLEC excavations, showing medieval masonry foundations incorporated within basement of a nineteenth-century warehouse illuminated by splayed brick windows. (GLA GR44)

evidence for a much later date (Fig 34). Pottery from underneath the gravel floor has now been dated to 1200–1225 (WFG4, bag no 4) while pottery overlying the floor is slightly later, at 1200–1250 (WFG4, bag no 3). This suggests that both the coin and the pendant must be seen as residual items incorporated within the gravel floor, and that an early thirteenth-century date for the construction of Bastion 14 has now been proposed. Ironically, the RMLEC had therefore recovered enough artefacts to date the construction of the western bastions in 1949, but this crucial material was not identified or published for almost 50 years.

Virtually all the medieval work on the internal face is masked by brickwork associated with the bastion's use as part of a modern warehouse prior to the Blitz. In marked contrast, the exposed external face of the bastion is built from rough rubble, irregularly coursed, and today stands to a height of 6.5m above the modern turf line (Fig 35). The base appears to be battered, but this effect might have been enhanced by the robbing of facing stones. At a height of *c* 3.5m above the present ground surface there is a pronounced string course comprising greensand blocks up to 0.15m thick. A number of regularly spaced putlog holes can be identified both above and below this level, forming at least

Fig 31 Base of Bastion 13 to right, exposed during RMLEC excavations (WFG2) that show its junction with the earlier masonry of the City wall on which the 3 × 1ft scale (c 1m) rests. (GLA GR41)

three horizontal sets 1m apart. Above the string course the facing is much mutilated, patched and repaired, but there is clear evidence of a band of knapped flints forming a decorative feature between 0.4 and 0.6m wide, set against the ragstone rubble matrix.

Cutting through that band are the remains of four apertures spaced between 3 and 3.5m apart, but all had been damaged or blocked to various degrees (see Figs 35, 36 and 37). The best preserved example was on the northern end of the bastion, and clearly comprised an arrow loop built with green-sand blocks, the upper section of which had been cut by the insertion of a narrow window. It seems likely that all four apertures enjoyed the same fate, and that the medieval windows had themselves been blocked by modern brickwork. Thus the overtly defensive function of the bastion can be seen to have been altered to one of later medieval domesticity, while these in turn succumbed to the needs of modern secure storage.

In spite of much alteration, it is clear that the general build of this bastion differs markedly from Bastion 12, the only other example in London in which substantial sections of the superstructure has survived. The lack of arrow loops or a string course in Bastion 12 for example, implies that 12 and 14 were built at different times or by different hands or suffered markedly different developments.

Bastion 15

This bastion sat across the external face of the Aldersgate re-entrant of the City wall, but was largely demolished in 1922. The surviving stubs were examined by the RMLEC during the cramped excavations in the basement of No 31 Noble Street in 1949–50, a site that is better known for the uncovering of the south-west corner of the Roman fort. Although so little survived, there was sufficient to show how Bastion 15 had been joined to the medieval wall. Unlike all the other bastions seen by Grimes, it had not been butt jointed, but had been toothed into a slot cut into the face of the wall just above foundation level. The shallow foundation rose over a wedge of occupation material at this point, from which some sherds of pottery were recovered. These were not considered datable in the 1950s, (ie before unequivocal evidence of a medieval date for some of the bastions had been established) although 'in general appearance they look to be of late Roman date' (Grimes 1968, 67–8). The pottery has since been lost, and so that statement can neither be challenged nor contradicted.

Discussion

In 1965 Ralph Merrifield published his authoritative book and gazetteer on the Roman City of London: this included a description of all the then known bastions on the City wall. These seemed to form two groups, an eastern one, which comprised in the main solidly based towers, numbered from B1 (now within the precinct of the Tower of London) to B11, next to All Hallows on the Wall, and a western group of 'hollow' bastions, numbered from B12 at Cripplegate to B21 near St Martin's at Ludgate (see Fig 3). The majority of the eastern group were clearly late Roman in origin, while the dating of the western series was less certain. 1965 was, however, also the year in which Professor Grimes discovered the remains of a hitherto unknown bastion just east of Bastion 12. He was able to show that the new bastion was an addition to the wall and that it could not have been constructed earlier than the thirteenth century, a date range that he subsequently applied to at least Bastions 14 and 15 in the western group. In a footnote, he went on to suggest that an appropriate context for their construction might be the documented defensive refurbishment dated 1257, in the reign of Henry III (Grimes 1968, 78). With typical caution, he did not apply that date directly to the western group as a whole, since he was, at that time, awaiting the opportunity to undertake further work on Bastions 12 and 13. In the event, his unpublished field records do not record any subsequent discoveries of relevance to this issue.

Rather than renumbering the whole series, Grimes called his new feature Bastion 11a in his report, published three years later (Grimes 1968, 71). Since then, more of the eastern group have been found from which

Fig 32 Internal view of Bastion 14 (WFG4), looking west, during the RMLEC excavations. The line of the Roman foundations of the City wall can be seen in the foreground, against which the bastion is butted. Below the contemporary ground surface the medieval masonry footings are visible: above that level, the face of the bastion is masked in the brickwork representing the period when it was incorporated into a warehouse. (GLA GR119)

it proved possible to suggest that there were not 11 but at least 22 evenly spaced bastions just on the eastern side of the City by the end of the Roman period (Merrifield 1983, 220–21).

It is not known how many of these were visible or were utilised in the defence of late Saxon London but by 1066, when William's Norman army laid siege to the City, it was clearly well defended. A document that describes the event records that London viewed by the Conqueror approaching from the west was 'protected on the left side by walls and on the right side by the river'. Siege engines, moles and battering rams were

therefore constructed, and threats made to destroy the walls and also, significantly, the 'bastions and a proud tower' (Brooke 1975, 27–8: Morton and Muntz 1972). If this description can be accepted, then it seems that, at the very least, some of the Roman bastions on the eastern side of the City might have been brought back into use in this period, although the 'proud tower' might have been one of the main gateways: Ludgate has been suggested, for example (Mills 1996, 61). Other contemporary defensive measures might have incorporated a stave wall protecting part of the waterfront excavated on the Thames Exchange site.

Fig 33 The junction of Bastion 14 (WFG4) to right, with the remains of the Roman City wall (left) revealed by the RMLEC. The shovel rests against the medieval foundation, above which the bastion has been refaced in brick. (GLA GR127)

Dendrochronological analysis produced a felling date in the winter of 1066/7 for the TX2 structure, which might have been protecting a river gate at the foot of what is now College Hill (Milne 1992a, 47–9). In the event the City was finally taken, surrendering to the Norman army in exchange for an agreement that the new King would respect London's laws and customs. He then set off to subdue the rebellion in the northern counties with appalling severity.

Before that turbulent century was out the Conqueror had seen work begun on his own proud tower in London, set in the south-eastern corner of the town to give him protection from the 'vast and fickle' populace. The White Tower seems to have been further defended on its eastern flank by at least three of the towers projecting from the line of the City wall itself, while the Bell Tower was constructed on the western side in the twelfth century: these elements seem to have utilised Roman foundations (Parnell 1993, 17–23; fig 18). The outer defensive works of the Tower were therefore arguably little different from the City's own defensive arrangements. Indeed, William Fitzstephen's oft-quoted description of late twelfth-century London records that it was already 'well towered on the north side with due distances between the towers' (Wheatley 1956, 502). That last phrase is important, since such projecting towers would only make strategic sense if they were built and operated as a group, in such a way that no part of the base of the main wall was beyond the range of whatever firepower was accommodated within one or other of the towers.

Gatehouse towers and perhaps even church towers that were built onto the wall could also provide firing platforms, and would also have been incorporated into the system. Indeed, it is not impossible that

Montfichet's Tower, a Norman work built to afford protection to the south-western side of the City, was just another mural tower or even part of Ludgate itself, rather than a moated castle with bailey, as some have suggested (Watson 1992). There is therefore a case to be made that there was a system of mural towers in operation certainly by the twelfth century. Certainly by 1235, Bastion 21, near Ludgate, is mentioned in a document that also goes on to refer to 'the other turrets in the said wall' (Dyson 1993, 22: Cal Patent Rolls 1232–47: 106–7). This is earlier than the AD 1257 date mentioned by Grimes, quoting Stow's sixteenth-century survey of London, in which the City wall was described as 'sore decayed and destitute of towers' (Wheatley 1956, 11). That date has unfortunately been reiterated without qualification by many subsequent commentators and appears in the standard guide to the City wall (Chapman *et al* 1985, no 17), for example.

In sum, it is suggested here that the bastions in the Cripplegate area are all of medieval date, but the surviving or excavated fabric shows that no two are identical in construction or in the history of their development. Some, such as Bastion 11a and Bastion 14, are clearly of thirteenth-century date. It is possible that others might have been built before then, in line with the admittedly incidental documentary references discussed above. The date of 1257 quoted in Stows' survey might therefore mark a major phase of rebuilding or the addition of further bastions to a more widely spaced system. The full extent of the medieval mural towers has yet to be clarified. Although there is space for several more between 11a and 11, the Moorgate marsh might have provided sufficient protection. Alternatively, it is possible that towers might have been utilised at Cripplegate itself, the pre-Conquest church of St Alphage on the wall and a tower in the vicinity of what became the Aldermanbury postern, all these features being set at the same distance one from another as Bastions 12 to 14.

It is also worth observing the relationship of the Roman fort's interval towers to some of the later projecting bastions: the thirteenth-century Bastion 11a, for example, was built directly in front of the second-century internal interval tower. This raises the possibility that some of these Roman towers might have been adapted and enlarged to function as watch towers with the early medieval defences, and that it was these structures that were referred to in Fitzstephen's twelfth-century description of London as 'having on the north side towers placed at proper intervals' (Wheatley 1956, 502). The sites of some of these towers might subsequently have been redeveloped as projecting more readily defensive bastions from the thirteenth century onwards.

What is clear is that during the thirteenth century, a series of projecting towers of cylindrical or semi-cylindrical form had been built at regular intervals onto all sides of the enlarged circuit centred on the White Tower (Parnell 1993, 32–4, fig 17). The function of

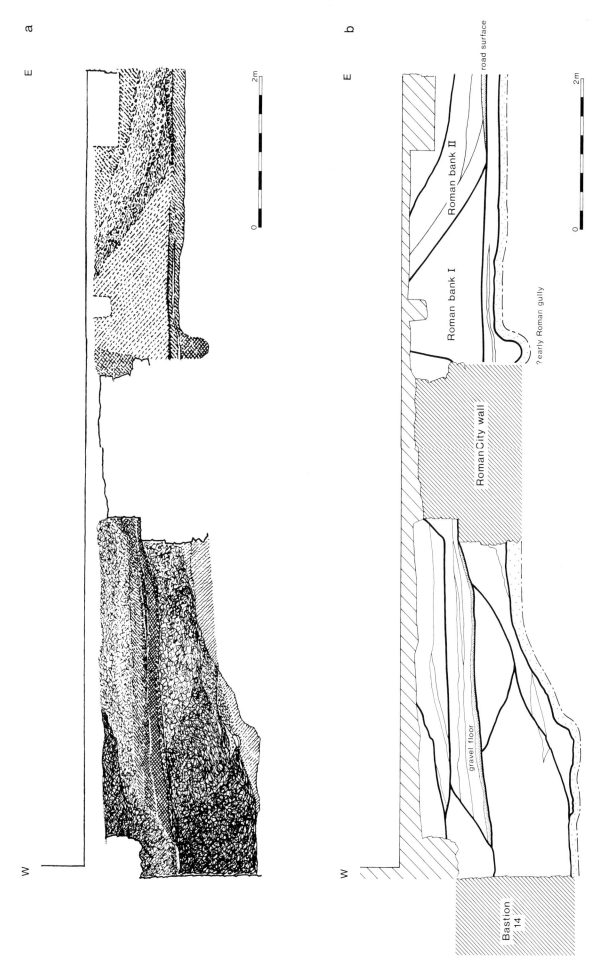

a

E

W

2m

0

b

E

Roman bank I

Roman bank II

road surface

?early Roman gully

Roman City wall

gravel floor

W

Bastion 14

2m

0

Fig 34 (a) West–east section recorded by RMLEC below Bastion 14 and (b) interpretation showing ditch fill cut and sealed by gravel floor within Bastion associated with thirteenth-century pottery (WFG4).

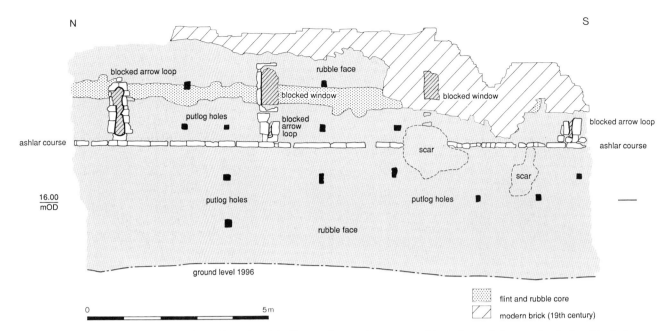

N

S

blocked arrow loop

rubble face

blocked window

blocked window

blocked arrow loop

putlog holes

blocked arrow loop

ashlar course

ashlar course

scar

16.00
mOD

scar

putlog holes

putlog holes

rubble face

ground level 1996

0   5 m

flint and rubble core

modern brick (19th century)

Fig 35 Schematic external elevation of Bastion 14, flattened out, showing position of surviving putlog holes, blocked arrow loops and blocked windows (WFG4): LARF/MoLAS. Compare with Figs 36 and 37.

these mural towers was not just to provide a platform for the provision of covering fire along the face of the wall itself: they were also consciously designed to provide secure storage and well equipped domestic apartments from the outset, as the late twelfth-century Bell Tower shows (Parnell, 1993, 26). As in the Tower, so in the City: the Mayor and Aldermen had also adopted that dual function for its bastions, and by renting out the towers they thereby defrayed some of the costs of the associated maintenance. For example, there is a record for the grant of the use of Bastion 21 to Alexander de Swereford in 1235 on condition 'that if a time of warfare shall arise in the realm...the turret shall

be exposed to receive the munitions of the City like the other turrets in the said wall' (Dyson 1993, 22: Cal Patent Rolls 1232–47: 106–7). Although detailed records of the uses of all the towers in the Cripplegate area have not survived, Cripplegate itself accommodated

Fig 36 External view of Bastion 14 (WFG4) looking east in 1950, before contemporary ground surface was lowered. Note blocked arrow loops. (GLA GR110)

Fig 37 External (west-facing) face of Bastion 14 (WFG4) showing blocked arrow loop above 3 × 1ft (c 1m) scale recorded by RMLEC. (GLA GR109)

a prison that is referred to in 1299 (Dyson 1993, 4). The tower in the north-west corner of the City, Bastion 12, is thought to have served as a Cistercian hermitage, a cell of Garendon Abbey, Leicestershire (Wheatley 1956, 268, 282), and was associated with the adjacent chapel of St James, the mid twelfth-century undercroft from which was removed and rebuilt in 1872 in Mark Lane on the site of All Hallows Staining (Schofield 1995, 205; Wickham 1999, 28). Hermits also inhabited towers at Aldgate and Bishopsgate, and were accommodated in gatehouses or towers in other towns as at Norwich, for example (Gilchrist 1995, 173).

City Defences viewed from Cripplegate

A chronological summary

The work of the RMLEC in the Cripplegate area has therefore provided a model for the development of the City's defences, the details and dating of which has now been refined by more recent research (Fig 18 and 19). The initial cutting of the Saxon City ditch has not been dated directly, but the earliest pottery from the fills could have been discarded no earlier than AD950. Given that the Lundenwic settlement is now known to have been protected by a substantial ditch on its north side, as revealed on the Royal Opera House site (MoLAS 1998), it would not be unreasonable to suppose that the City would have been defended in like fashion from 900 onwards, since the threat of Viking incursions continued until 1016. There seems to have been a substantial berm between the line of the Roman wall and the inside edge of that ditch, which could imply that the upcast from the digging of the ditch was thrown up to form a wide earthen embankment against the face of the wall, perhaps to strengthen areas where the masonry had collapsed. The height to which the Roman wall survived in the early medieval period remains unclear, although a marked change of alignment visible on both the western section and the northern St Alphage section suggests major rebuilding from a very low level in some areas.

Evidence of similar ditches set at some distance from the wall have subsequently been identified on several sites in the City. These include the Houndsditch site to the east of Cripplegate, from which a twelfth-century shoe was recovered (Maloney and Harding 1979, 350–53), as well as sites to the west, as at Aldersgate, which contained eleventh-century finds (Vince 1990, 90; Butler 2000), and at the Old Bailey, where mid eleventh-century pottery was found in the later fills (Rowsome 1984; MoL 1987, 138–9). Although Grimes was aware of this early medieval feature to the north of the City wall, he did not suggest a date for it in his published report (Grimes 1968, 86) even though the quantity of pottery recovered from the RMLEC excavations was larger than the groups recovered from the investigations of the feature

elsewhere by the Museum of London's archaeological team in the 1970s. In sum, all this work shows that there was a defensive ditch around the medieval City at least two centuries before the first surviving documentary record of the ditch in 1211.

The next phase saw a new ditch dug closer to the City wall, in the early thirteenth century, according to the pottery recovered from the earliest fills. The new position of this ditch suggests that its predecessor was completely infilled and no longer visible or operable, and that the concept of an earthen bank against the outer face of the wall was also not retained. Its alignment so close to the wall itself suggests that there were no projecting towers in the vicinity and that none had been planned at that precise time. Bastions 11a and 14 (and presumably the others in this area) were built shortly after this event, profoundly altering the defensive capability of this sector of the City. The bastions encroached into the moat, and therefore the water would have lapped around the bases.

The ditch itself continued to silt up and be periodically emptied, while the arrow loops in Bastion 14 were blocked as the tower was converted into a store or residence. The late fifteenth century saw a flurry of activity as the City wall was heightened with brick crenellations, as shown on the section of surviving wall adjacent to St Alphage church, for example. This was in part a response to the uncertainties of the conflict between the Yorkist and Lancastrian parties. The ditch was also presumably recut at this period then left to silt up again as the crisis passed, since groups of late fifteenth century pottery were recovered from the upper fills.

Other recuts of the ditch presumably reflect the fears of Spanish invasions in the late sixteenth century and Civil War in the early seventeenth century. By that date, London had expanded well beyond the City's boundaries and a defensive circuit extending for some 18kms was raised to protect the suburbs in the 1640s (Sturdy 1975; Flintham 1998, 233). Once the military threat had receded, the outer ring of defences was slighted and the City ditch backfilled: at Cripplegate it was replaced with a brick-built sewer in 1648. This feature was observed by John Terry in 1901 during the restoration of Bastion 12, as well as by the RMLEC in their investigations half a century later. By the mid seventeenth century encroachment over the area immediately behind the wall was commonplace: for example, in 1605 the hall of the Barber Surgeons was built well to the west of the original medieval building, utilising the City defences as its west wall, through which a series of large windows were cut. Such actions would not have been tolerated in an earlier century.

Changing responsibilities

One of the most marked features of this study of the City's medieval defences is the noticeable lack of uniformity in the treatment of the wall and ditch, as well as in the plan, construction and use of the bastions. This stands in marked contrast to the more regular Roman pattern, and is a distinction reflecting the fact that the responsibility for London's defences changed over the medieval period. The early tenth-century Laws of Athelstan records that every borough was to be repaired by a fortnight after Rogation Day (section 13) by the people themselves. A century later, Ethelred's V Law shows that every able bodied man was still expected to contribute time and muscle to the communal needs of military service and to repairing of fortresses and bridges: London was no exception to that general rule (Ethelred's V Law: section 26 (RL p 87). As for the manning of the defences, the late Saxon document known as the Burghal Hidage (Hill 1969) suggests that four men were needed to defend every pole (c 5m), then more than 2500 men would have been required to cover the line of London's land defences, which were calculated at 643 perches (Wheatley 1956, 12).

Following the imposition of the feudal Norman regime in the late eleventh century, military service was related to a series of obligations based on land ownership and tenure. The communal obligation to build or repair town walls was subsequently commuted into taxes or tolls, or shifted onto the shoulders of organisations such as the wards, the City's administrative districts represented by aldermen. In 1337, for example, Alderman Richard de Berking and Thomas Chamberlain were appointed 'to have a new wall made adjoining the Cripplegate & to repair & cover the said gate & the gate of Aldersgate & to make 2 small houses under the said gate for lodging the gatekeepers therein' (Dyson 1993, 6–7; Letter Book: Oct 1337). The Crown was certainly reluctant to make provision for London's defences from its own revenue, although the City was not afraid to ask. For example, in c 1215 it presented a list of demands to King John, including a call for assistance in walling the town, showing that it was the City (presumably through its ward structure) that shouldered the initial responsibility for its defence (see M Bateson A London Municipal Collection, section 27: Dyson 1993, 6). Indeed, although Stow records that 'in the year 1257 Henry III caused the walls of this City, which was sore decayed and destitute of towers, to be repaired in more seemly wise than before', he added that it was 'at the common charge of the City'. From the mid thirteenth century onwards there are records of Murage Grants that authorised the charging of tolls on goods brought into the City to raise the necessary money for the maintenance of the wall.

By the fifteenth century, during the unsettled period of the Yorkist – Lancastrian conflicts, the City companies also undertook some of the responsibility for maintaining the wall. Stow records that during the 1470s, 'Ralph Joseline, Mayor, caused part of the wall about the City of London to be repaired...he also caused the Moorfield to be searched for clay and brick therefore to be made and burnt'. Various companies such as the Skinners and the Drapers were named as being responsible for particular sections: the Goldsmiths repaired the 75 pole length (c 370m) from Cripplegate to Aldersgate, beyond which the wall seems to have been in better repair (Wheatley 1956, 11–12).

Conclusion

More recently, excavations by the Museum of London teams from the 1970s onwards have added to our knowledge of the medieval City defences, with the recording of the posterns at Tower Hill and Dukes Place, while the extensive work in the Fleet Valley revealed substantial sections of the late thirteenth-century extension to the defences on the western edge of the town (McCann 1993). Nevertheless, it can still be argued that the RMLEC excavations at Cripplegate have provided the fullest sequence through the medieval defences of the City yet recovered from any London excavation, uniquely showing the relationship between the ditches and upstanding bastions, for example. It was on these 50-year-old sites that the late Saxon ditch was first recorded (although apparently not identified as such) and sufficient stratified pottery recovered to date the 'hollow bastions' to the thirteenth century. The true value of those early excavations have now been realised, when set alongside the refined dating of medieval pottery sequences achieved by Jacqueline Pearce.

3 Houses and halls

by Nathalie Cohen and Gustav Milne

Secular medieval buildings in Cripplegate

This section brings together such evidence as was recorded on the RMLEC Cripplegate excavations for medieval buildings, and includes a Saxo-Norman sunken-featured building, a later medieval masonry town house and two company halls. The examples will be described and dated, and then briefly discussed in the context of other analogous finds that have been recorded in the City to set the RMLEC work in perspective. The sunken-featured building adds to the corpus of some forty such vernacular structures now known from the City: as is so often the case in the history of London's medieval archaeology, the first examples were identified by the RMLEC in the 1940s and 1950s.

At the other end of the social spectrum, the excavations of the grander masonry town house at Neville's Inn suggests that the area was not impoverished in the later medieval period. Such aristocratic houses, or 'centres of conspicuous consumption' as Caroline Barron terms them, played an important role in the City's economy, since 'the frequent and lengthy sojourns of the aristocracy in their London houses' ensured that a substantial proportion of the wealth recouped from their rural estates was spent in the City (Barron 1995a, 14). As for company halls, the sites of these buildings have been excavated on only a handful of occasions since the RMLEC ceased their field operations, and then often only in discrete trenches. There were some 100 livery companies based in the City in the late seventeenth century: of these 52 lost their halls in the Great Fire of 1666. Most were subsequently rebuilt in red brick or Portland stone. The City boasted thirty six company halls on the eve of the Blitz in 1939, but by 1945, 20 had been destroyed or rendered unusable, ten were badly damaged, three were but slightly damaged, with only a further three surviving more or less unscathed (Hill 1955, 132). There were four halls actually within the Cripplegate study area, the Barbers, the Brewers and the Parish Clerks, all seventeenth-century buildings, and the Coach Makers. All perished in 1940. The sites of two halls, the Brewers and the Barbers, attracted the attentions of the RMLEC, and this work still stands as rare examples of the excavation of this particular type of medieval urban site. The concluding summary considers some broader trends of medieval settlement development, which a new review of the RMLEC work in the Cripplegate area seems to show.

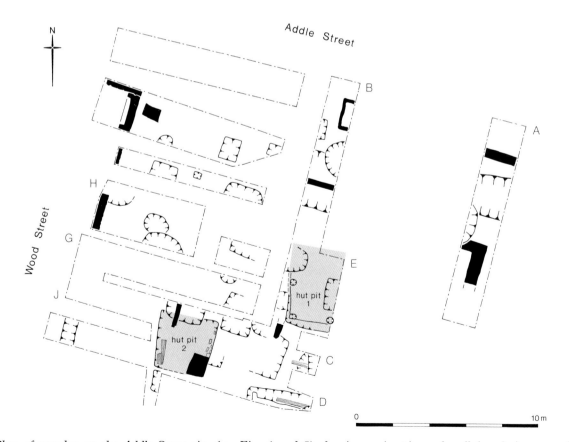

Fig 38 Plan of trenches on the Addle Street site (see Figs 4 and 5) showing major pits and wall foundations recorded by RMLEC (WFG21).

Sunken-featured buildings at Addle Street (WFG 21)

The Addle Street excavations were conducted on a large site bounded by Wood Street to the west and Addle Street to the north (Fig 38). Permission to excavate here was initially granted by the Corporation of London in June 1959, with the proviso that it must be handed back in September at the latest. This was because redevelopment was imminent, and thus the site was in effect, a 'rescue' rather than a purely 'research' project. Some thirteen trenches were opened up, starting on the eastern side of the site (Trenches A–E) in July 1959 and then moving over to the Wood Street frontage (Trenches F–L). In the event, work stopped on the site in January 1960, without unduly delaying the proposed redevelopment. More than 20 medieval pits or wells were identified, together with fragments of masonry wall foundations. In addition, two sunken-featured buildings were identified, according to the interim summary (Grimes 1968, 159), but no illustrated report on them was ever published.

WFG21: SFB 1 The southern and western sides of the larger of the two features were examined in the contiguous trenches B and E, and lay some 7 to 8m south of the Addle Street frontage (Figs 39 and 40).

The south-eastern edge of the hut pit had been cut into an earlier pit, but was itself cut by three other medieval pits (Pit B3, Pit B2 and Pit E1). This demonstrates that it lay within a backyard area, presumably to the south of whatever building occupied the contemporary frontage onto Addle Street. The southern edge of the hut pit survived for a length of 2.4m, the western for 3.6m, but the feature had clearly once extended further in both directions. The level from which it had been cut was not determined, but it was at least 1.5m deep. Three postholes were recorded, one in the south-west corner and one on each of the two surviving sides, set some 2m apart (Fig 41).

WFG21: SFB 2 The second of the two features was only 3m square but was at least 1.7m deep. While this seems rather large for a latrine pit, it is an unusual shape and depth for a building: certainly the majority of the London sunken-featured buildings recorded so far were rectangular rather than square in plan. Its identification as a sunken-feature building is open to question, but whatever its function, it lay at the rear of a property either fronting Addle Street, some 15m to the north, or more likely, Wood Street, some 6m to the west.

This feature has a particular claim to fame, in that it seems to be the first medieval pit feature in the City to have been subjected to environmental sampling procedures. Samples from it were washed through a 30 mesh sieve, and the following report was written in December 1959 by Dr IW Cornwall, Reader in Human Environment at the Institute of Archaeology:

'The lower part of the deposit contained masses of charcoal, mostly in rather small crumbs, shell, bone fragments including an entire caudal vertebra of a ?dog,

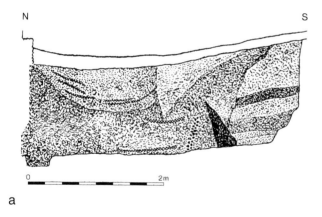

a

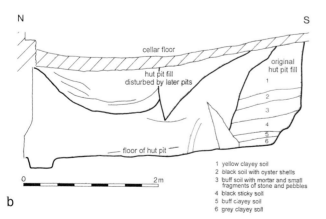

b

Fig 39 Section across hut pit 1 on the Addle Street site (WFG21)(a) as recorded by RMLEC; (b) interpretation showing disturbance caused by later pit digging.

Fig 40 RMLEC excavations at Addle Street, Trench B (WFG21). Hut pit 1, with wattlework from later pit visible, against which scale rests. (GLA GR495)

Fig 41 Beyond the 3 × 1ft scale (c 1m) resting on the floor of hut pit 1 is the posthole in north-east corner of the building. RMLEC excavations at Addle Street, Trench B (WFG21). (GLA GR491)

but not many recognisable uncarbonized plant-remains in comparison with the quantity of charcoal. Fish bones were present but not very plentiful.

The upper part contained much less charcoal and plant material (some seeds) but more animal remains, insect remains (?fly larvae), a rodent femur, masses of fish-bones etc. This looks like occupation debris- a midden to judge by the numerous insects apparently in situ.

The lower part of the deposit is more like ash, possibly the burning of the roof. There is little preserved that would suggest a fallen roof allowed to rot where it lay: in particular masses of reed, straw or similar thatch might be expected. Most of the uncarbonized organic matter, of which there was a great deal, was completely humified and amorphous' (WFG21, field records).

Sunken-featured buildings in the City

The recording of Grubenhauser is commonplace during the excavation of Saxon settlements in rural areas: they have been noted at Mucking in Essex (Hammerow 1993) and West Stow in Suffolk (West 1985) for example. When Professor Grimes published his report on the half a dozen sunken-featured buildings he had recorded on the Bucklersbury (WFG43), Financial Times (WFG35) and Addle Street sites (Grimes 1968, 155–60) in the heart of London, there was little else from an urban context with which to compare them, beyond Professor Jope's excavations on the Clarendon Hotel site in Oxford (Jope and Pantin 1958). Twenty years later, a report on controlled

excavations in the Cheapside and Billingsgate areas could list a further 15 examples from the City (Horsman et al 1988). These were classified into three types:

(a) the shallow sunken-floored outhouses
(b) deeper set sunken-floored buildings, which might have been used for domestic occupation
(c) the very deeply set cellared buildings in which the pit element lies beneath a surface laid structure.

A more recent study of sunken-featured buildings lists 37 from the City as a whole (Hammond 1995). This figure includes those recorded by the RMLEC, the one excavated on the St Nicholas Acon site by the Guildhall Museum, together with a further 30 examined between 1979 and 1990 on sites excavated by the Department of Urban Archaeology (site codes: CID90, DMT88, FMO85, HOP83, IRO80, KNG85, MLK76, PDN81, PEN79, St Mildred's MIL73, WAT78, WEL79). Subsequent work has identified fragments of further examples on an RMLEC site at Mark Lane (WFG52), where two sunken-featured buildings were examined in 1949–50. They were initially thought to represent Roman features (Grimes 1968, 124), but have subsequently been reinterpreted as being of Saxo-Norman date (Watson 1996, 94). The most recent discoveries have been on the Museum of London Archaeology Service excavations, at No 1 Poultry for example (MoLAS 1998, 7) and even in the Cripplegate study area itself, where three examples were excavated on the Shelley House site in Noble Street, as well as two more at 100 Wood Street (MoLAS 1998, 28).

Working with this wider database, it can be seen that the first Addle Street example was more deeply dug than many of the other London ones, there being only ten sunken-featured buildings that had been dug to a depth of *c* 1m or more in the City. Within this group, the Addle Street building is of similar size to the smaller of the two examples found on the Ironmonger Lane site (Horsman *et al* 1988, 64: IRO 1) or to the largest of those found on the Milk Street site (Horsman *et al* 1988, 52–3: MLK1), both of which are dated to the tenth–early eleventh century. It seems to have been significantly shorter than the 9m long hut pit excavated by Grimes on the Financial Times site in 1955 (Grimes 1968, 155–60) and significantly shallower than the deepest hut pit yet excavated in the City, at the Watling Court site in 1978 (Horsman *et al* 1988, 57–61: WAT 3), which was a little more than 2m deep (Fig 42). From this it can be suggested that the Addle Street sunken-featured building falls into the second category described above, a sunken-featured building that might have been utilised for domestic occupation rather than just as an outhouse or for storage. A sequence of relaid floor surfaces or a central hearth might have been anticipated, had more of the structure been available for excavation. It seems likely that such structures were not themselves built gable end onto the

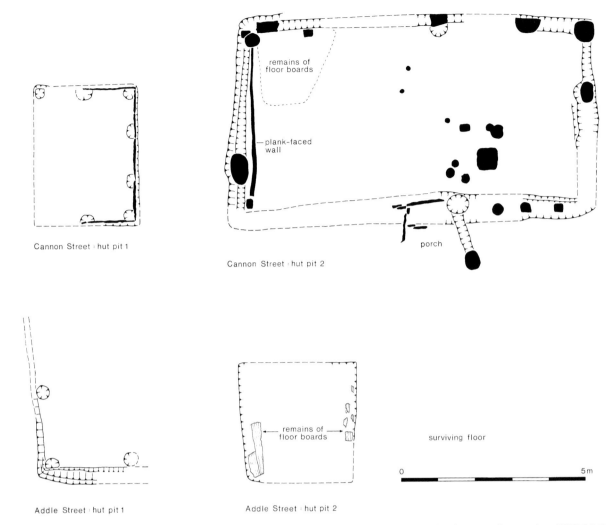

Cannon Street · hut pit 1

Cannon Street · hut pit 2

Addle Street · hut pit 1

Addle Street · hut pit 2

Fig 42 Comparative plans of sunken-featured buildings recorded by the RMLEC on the Cannon Street site (WFG35) and the Addle Street site (WFG21).

contemporary street frontage, but were set behind a surface laid building that was. As such they are seen as additional, ancillary buildings set behind the main 'hall' within a particular burgage plot.

Town House: Neville's Inn

Summary history

The site abuts the City wall on the western edge of the study area, and overlies the remains of the west gate of the Roman fort (Figs 4, 5 and 43). There are few surviving written records associated with Neville's Inn, but such documentary sources as there are complement the discoveries made by the RMLEC during the excavations of the site in the 1950s and into the 1960s. The earliest mention of the town house is in 1367 when, following the death of Ralph Neville, it was recorded that he had owned a tenement on the west side of Monkwell Street that served as an inn for himself and his retinue. His son John acquired further property to the north and east of that tenement in 1368 and 1374 (Kingsford 1917, 49–50). Stow describes the

property in the late sixteenth century as having a 'stone wall which encloseth a garden plot before the wall of the city, on the west side of Noble Street, and this is of Farringdon Ward. This garden plot, containing 95 ells in length, 9 ells and a half in breadth, was by Adam de Bury, mayor, the aldermen and citizens of London, letten to John de Nevil, Lord of Raby, Radulph and Thomas his sons for sixty years, paying 6s 8d the year... At the north end of this garden plot is one great house built of stone and timber, now called Lord Windsor's house, of old time belonging to the Nevils, as in 1396 it was found by inquisition of a jury, that Elizabeth Nevil died, seised of a great messuage in the parish of St Olave Monkswell Street in London, holding of the King free burgage, which she held of the gift of John Nevil of Raby, her husband' (Wheatley 1956, 282).

The house was known during the sixteenth century as Westmoreland Place or Windsor Place, reflecting the changing ownership of the property. There might have been some remodelling of the house and grounds during the early seventeenth century, after the death in 1600 of Katherine, the widow of the last recorded owner, Edward Windsor. The Great Fire of 1666

Fig 43 Neville's Inn (WFG3) in 1947: general view across the RMLEC excavations looking south towards Falcon Square (with traffic island and bollards) and Falcon Street: the two cars are parked just beyond the junction with Castle Street. The upstanding but ruined wall marking the western edge of the excavated area sits directly over the line of the Roman and medieval City wall: some of the exposed chalk foundations are thought to be associated with Neville's Inn, more of which were uncovered when the southern half of the site (below the spoil heap) was excavated in 1956. (GLA GR55)

destroyed the property, after which the site was given over to a variety of uses, including a nonconformist hall, light industry including a haberdashery and a blacksmith's shop according to Grimes' notes.

RMLEC excavations

The site of Neville's Inn was heavily bombed in 1940 and was subsequently cleared to facilitate construction of the new Route 11 (London Wall). Before work began on the road, the RMLEC carried out a series of excavations in the area over several years, starting in 1947. The main investigations began in 1956 with the principal aim of elucidating the chronology of the underlying Roman fort and its western gate. There are, however, problems associated with interpreting the records, especially those relating to the medieval material. The long chronology of the excavations remains somewhat confused and the information that has survived is incomplete. At least four different hands,

Fig 44 Falcon Square (WFG5): view across the RMLEC site in 1956 looking northwards on the approximate line of the City wall towards the church of St Giles Cripplegate before the Barbican redevelopment began. In the foreground is the north turret of the west gate of the Roman fort (now under the street called London Wall) that lay just to the east of part of the medieval Neville's Inn complex. (The Sphere)

including Grimes and Audrey Williams, were making notes about the sites at various stages, which has contributed to the confusion. There are also problems with the finds since many were discarded during or immediately after the excavation, particularly after incidents with looters who had mixed and scattered finds over the site hut floor. Study of the artefacts that have survived suggests that the site must have been badly disturbed or poorly excavated, since there are very few uncontaminated assemblages. A further problem, common to many RMLEC sites, is that a series of temporary levels were used across the excavations, but the height or position of the main site datum is unknown, hence it is difficult to calculate absolute levels.

Correspondence in the site archive throws little light on the chronology of excavations at Windsor Court and Falcon Square. The Windsor Court material (WFG3) is concerned with the permission required to work there in 1957, while most of the letters in the Falcon Square file (WFG5) deal with the preservation of the fort gate or the wrangling over the loss of several car parking spaces that the preservation of that feature entailed. Excavations began in Falcon Square in 1956 (Fig 44) with cuttings A to G. This was followed by cuttings V, W, X Y and Z in 1957, together with cuttings A and B on the Monkwell Street side of the site. Work also resumed at Windsor Court in 1957 on areas A and B. Thus a series of trenches was opened across the large site and the baulks between them were gradually removed, as can be seen on many of the 200 site photographs, which ultimately show a large open area excavation underway (Fig 43).

Numbered bags of finds have survived from some of the cuttings at Neville's Inn (bag nos 1–65) along with finds from 'miscellaneous pits, wells and vats' as well as from 'cellars and miscellaneous pits' (bag nos 66–102). There are notes on the finds bagged from 300–523, but these can no longer be related to the excavations. Even fewer finds survive from the Falcon Square excavations.

Medieval and later developments on the Neville's Inn site

In spite of the fragmentary nature of the surviving records and finds groups, however, significant results of the Neville's Inn excavations can be discussed, at least in general terms, following the establishment and demise of the Roman fort (Fig 45a). There are no early or middle Saxon finds or features, suggesting that the area was unoccupied during that period. The earliest positive evidence of medieval activity on the site is represented by pits containing pottery dating between 1200–1350, although there is some earlier and some later material (Figs 45b and 46). The most detailed information about these pits comes from the records made at Windsor Court in 1947. In Cutting 1, most of the pits described in the field notes can be identified on plan or section drawings, and here two of the pits contain early medieval sand and shell ware and also early

medieval sandy ware (bag nos 10 and 20), dating to the tenth or eleventh century. In cutting 3 there are two deep pits containing pottery dated 1100–1350. The foundations of the later masonry building might have masked junctions between pits, as there is evidence for an earlier pit group in this trench dating to 1000–1100. In cutting 4 a pre-fourteenth-century pit and a post-medieval pit can be located, while some of the contexts labelled 'miscellaneous' can be identified, such as the fills of the stone-lined well (1240–1350) and some of the cellar deposits from the east side of the site as well as a pit cutting through it, dating from 1630–1700.

The next two phases of occupation relate to the construction and expansion of Neville's Inn itself during the fourteenth century: these phases are amalgamated on Fig 45c. The first phase presumably represents part of the lower levels of the inn used by Ralph Neville until his death in 1367, and comprised a range of small rooms and cellars built largely in chalk with some Reigate stone mouldings (Fig 47). Access to this range appears to be from the south via a flight of stairs from Silver Street, which implies that at least part of the west gate of the Roman fort remained open and in use. These stairs were later blocked up (Figs 48, 49 and 50).

The second phase of medieval construction might represent extensions to the property made by Ralph's son John, who died in 1388. Further rooms and other features were added between the existing building and the City wall (Figs 51 and 52). It is suggested that the construction of a cellar that encroached into Silver Street, marks the stage at which the old west gate in the Roman fort wall was finally blocked. This is a significant event for the topographical development of the area as a whole, and thus is discussed in more detail below.

There might have been some remodelling of the property after the death of the last owner in 1600 but before the Great Fire of 1666. Indeed, much of the fourteenth-century inn might have been demolished and replaced by new buildings, perhaps following the sale of some of the land to the Barber Surgeons immediately to the north in 1605. Ogilby and Morgan's map of 1676 (Hyde *et al* 1992) shows a range of buildings set around a central courtyard, and it might have been fragments of these structures that were recorded by the RMLEC. The excavation plan shows a range of three rooms on the western side of the property and although most of these features appear to be of late seventeenth- or early eighteenth-century date, it is possible that some earlier seventeenth-century elements might have been incorporated (Fig 45d). In his field notes, Grimes comments that 'this wall originally ran along the west side of the building and appears to be of seventeenth century date, judging by its relationship with the Fire period floor' (Fig 53) but there were indications of an earlier shallow foundation trench just to the west of it. Whatever their actual origins, the plan of small units set around a central courtyard survived in this area for some 200 years after the Great Fire, as is shown on contemporary maps. A variety of light industries seem to have been

Fig 45 Phase plans showing development sequence recorded by RMLEC on Neville's Inn site (WFG3-5): (a) Roman fort wall, internal bank to east, line of drains and unblocked west gate; (b) sequence of pit alignments marking back yards of contiguous medieval properties aligned east–west running up to the City wall (shown in black); (c) stone-lined cellar and other subsurface chambers associated with mid fourteenth-century Neville's Inn (in black) shown built out over the former back yard areas to the east of City wall. Later additions (shown hatched) encroached on the internal face of the City wall itself. Both phases of blocking the fort's west gate are shown amalgamated here; (d) subsurface features representing foundations, brick-lined cesspits and vats associated with phases of development from the late seventeenth to the nineteenth century.

established here, for Grimes records evidence of a small blacksmith's shop in the north west corner of the site as well as nineteenth-century circular brick vats (Fig 54). Similar features were recently recorded by MoLAS on the Shelley House site just to the south of Neville's Inn, suggesting similar activities on both sites during that period.

Blocking the West Gate and the implications for medieval street development

Grimes was uncertain as to which period to assign the blocking of the double carriageway of the west gate in the Roman fort wall (Fig 55). There is no doubt that by the fourteenth century, either during the first or second phase of construction of Neville's Inn, access through that gate had been blocked, but the question is whether this took place in the fourteenth century or substantially earlier. However, from study of the site photographs, drawings and field notes it appears that the blocking of the northern carriageway might have been undertaken in two stages. In the first phase, the southern carriageway was completely blocked together with just half of the northern carriageway, effectively converting the wide gateway from a major public access point into what was presumably a private postern. The second phase saw the blocking of the postern.

While it is possible that this all took place perhaps as early as the Late Saxon period, the development of the Neville's Inn complex and the associated street pattern would seem to argue for a fourteenth-century date. The southern edge of the building assigned to the first phase of construction of Neville's Inn (shown black on Fig 45b) is aligned on a point half way across the northern carriageway. On his published plan, Grimes shows this part of the blocking as wider than the rest, and the field records note a difference between the northern and southern make up levels of the blocking here. The photographs also show the northern half topped with a line of larger blocks, a feature absent from the southern half of the northern carriageway (Figs 56–62). The blocking of the southern carriageway, by comparison, appears to be homogeneous and also includes a line of large blocks as the topmost surviving layer. It is therefore suggested that the southern carriageway and the northern part of the northern carriageway were both blocked at the same time, initially leaving a small postern open. This presumably took place in the early fourteenth century contemporary with the construction of the Neville's Inn building immediately to the east. Then the postern was itself blocked during the second phase of building, when the cellar was extended into the street in the later fourteenth century.

If accepted, this sequence of activity has important implications for the development of the street pattern, particularly the course of Silver Street–Addle Street, which is aligned on the west gate of the Roman fort.

In his study of the City street names, Ekwall (1954) notes that thoroughfares referred to as 'street' are usually more important access routes than 'lanes'. In the Cripplegate study area most north–south roads are 'streets' and most east–west roads are 'lanes'. It is suggested in Chapter 5 that Saxon settlement spread north of Cheapside in the later tenth and eleventh centuries, but left many areas in the north of the walled City relatively undeveloped. The excavations at Windsor Court and more recently the work by MoLAS on the Shelley House site to the south of Silver Street, seem to support this general rule. In the earliest phase of occupation noted on the latter site, it is recorded that 'each building lay in an east–west aligned burgage plot approximately the same width as the building, and with yards to the rear. By implication there would have been roads to both the east and the west of the site to allow access to the plots' (MoLAS 1997, 256). The distribution of pits on the Neville's Inn site also suggests that access to the properties was from the east. The main difference between the two site sequences seems to be that there is earlier occupation at Shelley House to the south of the Silver–Addle Street line, suggesting that the east–west route to the west gate of the fort was acting as a significant boundary in the Late Saxon period.

Addle Street was known as Addle Lane until the sixteenth century, suggesting that this east–west route was of lesser importance than the north–south aligned Wood Street, which leads northwards out of the City through Cripplegate itself. The east–west route might have been of more significance initially, however. The origins of the name 'Addle' relate to the etymology of the Late Saxon word 'adel', or 'cow dung': a road called Cow dung Street can therefore be identified as a major drove road for bringing cattle in and out of the City, making use of the wide west gate. It is suggested here that the principal east–west route across the Cripplegate study area might have been known for its full length as 'Addel Street' (with good reason). Although the earliest surviving reference to the road as 'Silver Street' is in 1279 (Ekwall 1954, 76), that name might have been in use during the twelfth century, marking a pronounced change in the character of the area as it was settled by metalworkers. Saxo-Norman crucible fragments have been found on several sites in the area and St Olave's church, on the corner of Noble Street and Silver Street, was the guild church of the silversmiths (Huelin 1996, 22). Significantly, it is referred to as a down graded 'lane' in 1357, by which date the west gate had been at least partially blocked, according to the reevaluation of the RMLEC records of the Neville's Inn site discussed above.

Brewers' Hall (WFG15)

Summary history

One of the earliest written references to the existence of a group of brewers who had joined together to protect themselves and their trade in the City of London is in

N

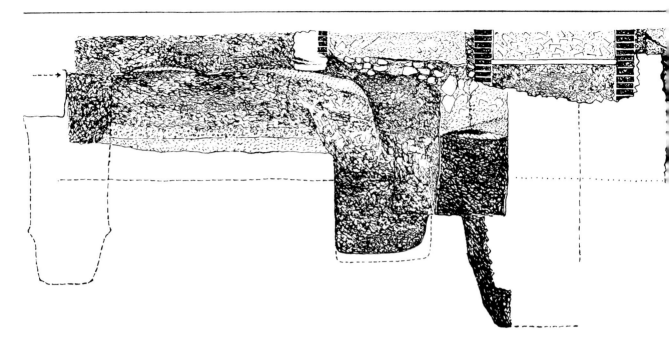

N

Fig 46 Composite north–south section drawn by RMLEC across the Neville's Inn site (WFG3–5), with interpretation drawing below, showing three groups of intercutting pits representing activity in back yards of three neighbouring burgage plots prior to construction of the Neville's Inn complex.

S

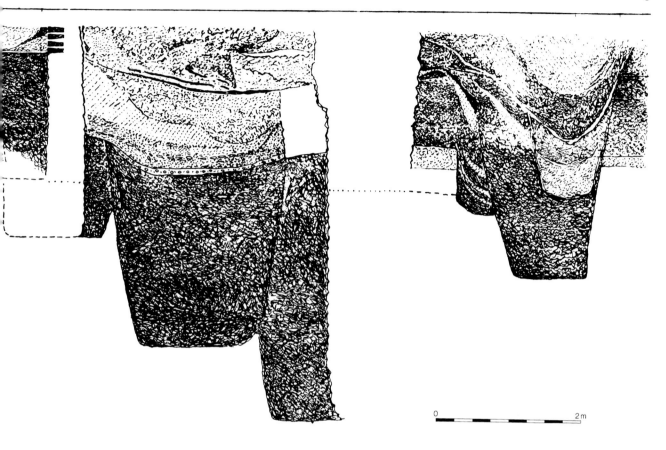

0   2 m

S

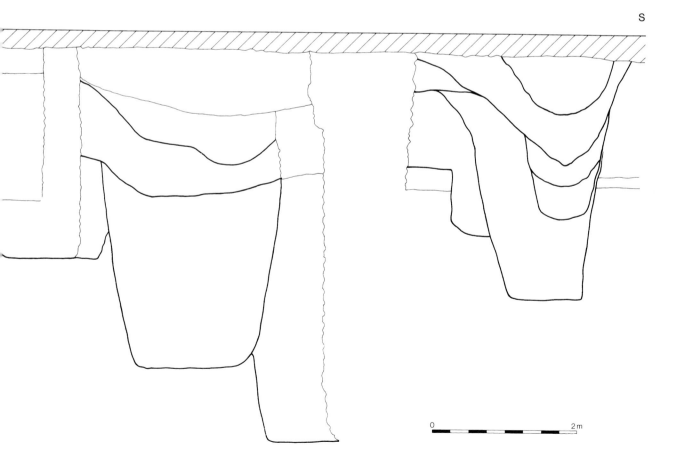

0   2 m

Fig 47 Neville's Inn (WFG3/5): southern edge of the medieval complex revealed by RMLEC in 1956. Note multiphase masonry foundations parallel to the 4 × 1ft scales (c 1.25m) following the alignment of Silver Street heading for the centre of the west gate of the Roman fort, the north turret of which is visible at the top. (GLA GR152)

Fig 49 View of the stone steps revealed by the RMLEC after the blocking shown in Fig 48 was removed, looking north: Neville's Inn (WFG3/5). (GLA GR160; GLA GR145)

Fig 48 Neville's Inn (WFG3/5): the scale in the centre of the photograph rests on the blocked doorway visible in Fig 47. RMLEC excavations, looking southwards. (GLA GR147)

Fig 50 Another view of the stone steps revealed by the RMLEC after the blocking shown in Fig 48 was removed, looking north: Neville's Inn (WFG3/5). (GLA GR160; GLA GR145)

Fig 51 Stone-lined well in Trench 1 recorded by RMLEC on the Neville's Inn site (WFG3/5). (GLA GR654)

Fig 52 Chalk-lined cess pit under excavation by RMLEC on Neville's Inn site (WFG3/5). (GLA GR77)

the City Letter Book of 1292, where it is noted that the Brewers had lodged a complaint against the Sheriffs. The association might have formed in the early thirteenth century according to Stow who states that the Cripplegate postern 'was new builded by the Brewers of London in the year 1244' (Wheatley 1956, 32–3): it is not possible, however, to verify this statement (Ball 1977, 12–15). By the end of the thirteenth century, guilds were beginning to obtain royal charters to protect themselves and becoming more involved with government through the Common Council, which elected City officers. The fourteenth century saw a rapid growth in the importance and influence of the guilds, or 'misteries' as they were known, and conflicts between the groups eventually led to a Parliamentary inquiry into the organisations. Guilds were eventually established on a legal basis in the late fourteenth and early fifteenth centuries through their transformation into incorporated Livery Companies. The Brewers were incorporated in 1437 (Ball 1977, 26–31). It is not known when the Brewers first acquired a hall of their own, but in 1291 they leased land in Addle Street from the Dean and Chapter of St Paul's (Hope *et al* 1982, 105) and the first mention of a 'Brewers Hall' occurs in 1403. The hall was used for members' meetings and also leased to smaller companies, including the Football players! The Minute Book kept by the Company clerk, William Porland, from 1418 to 1441 notes repairs and alterations to the hall and surrounding buildings for example, the construction of a 'Baywendowe' and repairs to the kitchen during the fifteenth century. During the sixteenth century, members of the Company were involved in the foundation of charitable institutions such as almshouses and schools. The 'fayre house' of the Brewers was destroyed in the Great Fire of 1666 along with 44 other livery halls in the City. Although the Brewers had difficulty in raising the money to build a new hall, construction work was completed on the site of the old hall by 1673, at a cost of £5,827 16s 8d (Ball 1977, 81–2). In the mid nineteenth century, the prosperous Brewers bought the freehold of the land in Addle Street and carried out further renovations to the hall, including the rebuilding of one of the end walls (Ball 1977, 100–101). By 1929 the Brewers Hall incorporated a two storied hall while the rest of the building had three stories. The brick walls had Portland stone dressings, the southern wing has been refaced, the loggia filled in and an outside staircase rebuilt (RCHM 1929). This much modified seventeenth-century building was destroyed on 29 December 1940.

RMLEC excavations 1958

Before the construction of a new hall commenced in 1958, the RMLEC conducted excavations on the site (Fig 63). The archive consists of a site notebook, which also includes a finds record, correspondence between Professor Grimes, the Company and the Corporation of London, draft section drawings and plans and eighteen photographs. A brief summary of the results of the excavations was published by Grimes (1968, 170–72). According to the site notebook, largely kept by Audrey Williams, the RMLEC worked at the site from January to early July of 1958. Professor Grimes does not appear to have visited the site frequently, since his notes on the

Fig 53 General view of RMLEC excavations on the Neville's Inn site (WFG3/5) showing many phases exposed simultaneously including a large brick-lined vat or well housing. (GLA GR657)

excavations date to late June. Work moved from east to west and eight trenches were opened (A–H). Across the whole site, the depth of the medieval and post medieval features had severely truncated the Roman deposits and very little information was revealed about this period (Grimes 1968, 35).

Cutting A

Work on site appears to have concentrated largely on cutting A, which ran north–south across the east of the site. There are extensive notes in the field notebooks and all the photographs from the site relate to this trench (Fig 64). Originally it was 45ft long and 8ft wide (*c* 13.7m × 2.4m); it was later extended to 100ft × 17ft (*c* 30m × 5m). Excavation revealed chalk and brick walls running north–south with cellars, floors and a tiled fireplace (Fig 65). The ceramic sequence from this trench is confusing, with pottery ranging in date from the Roman period to the 1800s. The use of temporary levels further complicates the stratigraphic sequence. Grimes' published account of the excavation

in this area is also confused. The plan of the trench shows both the chalk and the brick walls dated to undifferentiated 'pre-Fire' periods, while the text states that the similar alignments of the walls is evidence for the Brewers pursuing 'a policy of economy (after the Fire) by following the original lines and no doubt utilising as far as possible the existing structures, on the east side of the site' (Grimes 1968, 171). It would appear that there are at least five phases of construction in this area:

I   The line of big chalk blocks running east-west in the south of the trench are annotated as 'deep foundations' on the published plan (Fig 66). The top of this wall was 7ft 9in (2.3m) below datum and it is on a similar alignment to the fragments of wall discovered in cuttings D, E and F.

II   To the north of this chalk wall were the remains of two medieval half cellars, cut by a party wall, which had been largely destroyed by the insertion of a modern concrete block. Contemporary ground surface appears to about 7ft (2m) below

Fig 54 Detail to show brick floor recorded by RMLEC on Neville's Inn site (WFG3/5). (GLA GR93)

the modern ground surface. The north–south wall had a blocked splayed window opening (Fig 67) the sill of which was 6ft 4in (1.9m) down (Grimes 1968, 172). In the northern part of the trench, a second north–south chalk wall (with later brick additions) might have been an extension to the north cellar for a staircase, while the northernmost wall might have supported a timber superstructure of another building to the north.

III The insertion of the fireplace south of the medieval cellars must have destroyed much of the south wall of the cellar and the earlier chalk wall. The tile-lined fireplace was made of mixed materials including Kentish ragstone, chalk and flint with external brick facing to the south (Fig 65). The floor of the hearth was at a depth of 5ft 9in (1.7m).

IV The easternmost chalk wall was strengthened by a brick wall (with creamy/buff coloured mortar) that extends southwards and turns westwards, blocking the medieval window.

V Another brick wall (with bright yellow mortar) was built immediately to the west of the first, creating a culvert or channel down the side of the building.

Cutting B

This trench was some 25ft × 4ft 6in (7.6m × 1.3m) and ran north–south across the area used by the Brewers as a walled garden, immediately to the north of cutting A. Excavation in this area produced little in the way of finds or features. Medieval and post-medieval pottery ranging in date from 1200–1800 was recovered from the uppermost two layers of 'garden soil' excavated at depths of 5ft (1.5m) and 7ft 6ins (2.2m) below datum

respectively. A brick floor was also revealed at a depth of 7ft 6in in the southernmost part of the trench. At a depth of 10ft (3m) below the datum, medieval pottery (1400–1450) was found in a soil similar to that of the contexts above it but containing more oyster shells.

Cutting C

Cutting C ran east–west across the western part of the site in the area beneath the courtroom. The trench was originally 40ft 7in × 5ft (12.3m × 1.5m) and appears to have been extended to approximately 70ft × 10ft (21.3m × 3m). There are very few notes relating to the features discovered in this trench, which consist of chalk and stone walls, a 'mortar' wall, postholes and a possible pit. Excavation in this area produced pottery ranging in date from 1230 to 1700. The sequence is difficult to interpret not least because a series of temporary levels appear to have been used to measure the depths of the different layers, thus confusing the stratigraphic sequence. Broadly speaking, the sequence appears to show activity in this area of the site from 1230 to 1360, with further activity during the post-medieval period. It is possible that some of the confusions in the ceramic sequence, for example the discovery of pottery dated 1400–1450 beneath pottery that is a century earlier is due to the presence of a pit that has not been fully excavated or discussed in the field notes. Many of the features revealed in this area, such as the postholes in the northern part of the trench, do not appear to have been fully recorded.

Cutting D

This trench was 47ft × 10ft (14.3m × 3m) ran east–west in the south-west corner of the site. A chalk-lined well was revealed in the west part of the trench with a series of walls and pits in the eastern half. The top of the well was 2ft 5in (0.73m) down from the datum and it was excavated to a depth of 16ft 8in (c 5m). Pottery from the well has been dated from 1150 to 1300, with intrusive sherds dating from 1600 to 1800. Along the east face of the trench a chalk wall 0.7m tall was excavated, the top of which was 9ft (2.7m) from the datum. The ceramic sequence from this trench also appears to be confused. Pottery dated to 1270–1350 was recovered from a succession of contexts at depths of 3ft (0.9m), 7ft (2.1m), 9ft 3in (2.8m) (bag 34D) and 15ft 1in (4.6m). A later entry in the field notebook notes the presence of a dark, sticky black soil over the whole area of the cutting at a depth of 6ft 6in to 10ft (1.9m–3m). This could be the same context 34D noted above but it was given a new number (X1) since the pottery was considerably earlier, dating to 1050–1150. It is possible that bag X1 might relate just to a timber-lined pit in the easternmost part of the trench with a lining of grey clay. To the west was a second pit from which pottery dating from 1150–1300 was recovered, together with intrusive post-medieval material.

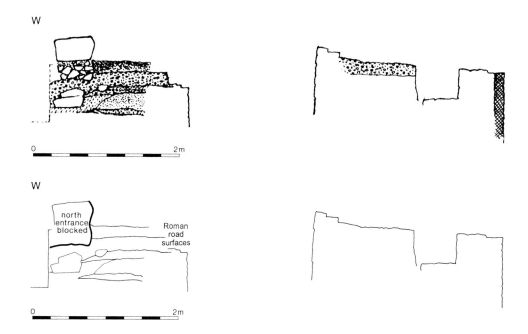

Fig 55 West–east section through the west gate of the Roman fort at Cripplegate, showing the blocking of the northern entrance in rel

Cutting E

Cutting E, to the east of cutting D, was only 18ft × 10ft (5.4m × 3m). In the north of the trench was a chalk wall at a depth of 7ft (2.1m) from the datum. To the south of this was mixed soil and building rubbish down to a depth of 11ft (3.3m), the natural brick earth. Pottery ranging in date from the late Roman period to the twentieth century was recovered.

Cutting F

This trench lay immediately west of cutting E. The robbed out angle of a chalk wall was clearly visible in the north-east corner, set into a sticky black deposit. Williams suggests that the 6ft 5in (1.9m) depth of the black soil from the modern surface might have been the height of the wall prior to its robbing. No finds are recorded from this trench.

Cutting G

No finds have been kept from cutting G and little other information. The angle of a chalk wall with occasional inclusions of Kentish ragstone was found, the north face of which had salmon pink plaster on it. Its base was 6ft 1in (1.8m) below the modern surface.

Cutting H

In cutting H, which lay north of cutting C, Grimes notes the stump of a chalk foundation projecting from the east face and 'a rough wall' below the brick of the north wall of the courtroom, which bounds the south side of this trench. One finds group was recorded spanning the period 1350–1750.

Medieval and later developments on the Brewers' Hall site

The construction phases represented on the Brewers' Hall site are complicated and their interpretation is made more difficult by a field record of variable detail. The following sequence is tentatively suggested (Fig 63):

Phase M1 Although the lower levels have been truncated by later occupation, there is no evidence for occupation or use of this area in the immediate post-Roman period. Late Roman (late fourth/early fifth century) ceramics, however, were discovered in cuttings A, C and E. Cutting D provides evidence for Late Saxon use of the site: the timber-lined pit can be compared with those found on the Milk Street and Watling Court sites, two more recent Museum of London excavations in the Cheapside area. These were dated 1050–1180 (Schofield *et al* 1990, 173), which correlates with the pottery believed to have come from the pit at Brewers' Hall.

Phase M2 The chalk-lined well and the second pit (Fig 63a) both contain pottery dating from 1150–1300. Again, evidence from Watling Court can be used in comparison with Brewers' Hall; a chalk-lined well with an internal diameter of about 0.85m was provisionally dated to the early fourteenth century at Watling Court (Schofield *et al* 1990, 172). The well at Brewers' Hall appears to be of similar construction phase with an internal diameter 0.90m.

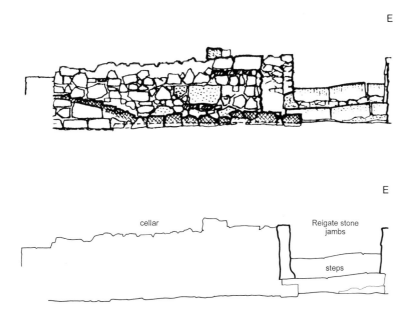

...an road surfaces, with the subsurface remains of a small cellar associated with Neville's Inn to the east (WFG3–5).

Phase M3 The plan of buildings in the Brewers' Hall complex is difficult to determine. In cuttings D, E, F and possibly A are the remains of a chalk building. In cutting D, the wall appears to cut into a 'black sticky' layer dated 1270–1350; the same sequence is noted in cutting F, but no finds are noted. In cutting C, the only structure that can be firmly dated is the slight 'mortar wall', running north–south across the trench; pottery from underneath this wall is dated to 1270–1350. These contexts dating from 1270–1350 are believed to represent domestic occupation of the site. There are no structural remains directly associated with this period.

Phase M4 The fourteenth-century foundations, mentioned above, might, however, be the remains of domestic housing built on the site before the construction of the hall, in view of the depth and size of the chalk foundations in cutting D, it is suggested here that these represent the Brewers' Hall, as constructed in the mid fourteenth century, with its associated outbuildings to the north and east. The walls discovered in cutting A are believed to represent the domestic range of the complex, which clearly underwent a series of repairs and renovations (Fig 63b).

Phase M5 These renovations included the insertion of half cellars (Fig 63c).

Phase M6 It is known that in the building works of 1423, repairs were made to a cloister or tresaunce connecting the Hall to the kitchens and that all of the buildings except the Hall were retiled. The extension of the kitchen area southwards through the addition of the tile-lined fireplace is believed to date from this period. Two sample tiles taken from the fireplace have been broadly dated to between 1270 and 1350–1450

(Ian Betts personal communication). They are pegged roof tiles, which might have been taken from an earlier building on the site and reused in the early fifteenth-century expansion.

Phase M7/8 The addition of brick walling on the eastern side of cutting A is believed to be of pre-Great Fire date (Fig 63e). The presence of a brick floor in the southern part of cutting B, similar to that found at the north end of cutting A (Fig 68), and the chalk wall stump in cutting H suggests that the buildings of the complex extended further north over the site than they did after the 1666 Fire.

Phase M9 The Brewers' Hall complex was rebuilt on a new alignment after the Great Fire rather than following the lines of the original buildings (Fig 63f). It is also possible that the site area was extended southwards. A survey conducted in 1669 by Mills and Oliver shows Addle Street immediately south of the southern boundary of the Brewers' property. The seventeenth-century Brewers' Hall was approached by a small alley off Addle Street, which appears to have been pushed southwards. The area to the south of the courtyard was entirely taken up with deep cellars, which have removed any evidence of occupation or encroachment, and it is probably in this part of the site that the early fifteenth-century almshouses were constructed.

Barber Surgeons' Hall (WFG2)

Summary history

The guilds of the Barbers and the Surgeons initially existed as separate entities until the late fifteenth century. Until this time the Barbers appear to have been

Fig 56 General view of excavations looking north across blocked entrance to northern turret base (GLA GR248)

the more powerful group; the guild might have come into existence as early as the thirteenth century, and in 1308 Richard le Barbour was elected to supervise the barbers of the City. The guild was incorporated in 1462 and in 1540 the Company of Barbers and the Guild of Surgeons were joined by an Act of Parliament (Hope *et al* 1982, 108). 'This act partook of a twofold nature, for while it united the two crafts or mysteries as they were called, yet it separated them. The barbers were not to practice surgery other than bleeding or drawing teeth, while the surgeons were not to practice the art of barbery or shaving' (Lambert 1890, 131). The companies were separated again in 1745 and in 1752, the new Surgeons' Hall was completed in

Newgate. This Company was dissolved in 1797 to be replaced by the Royal College of Surgeons. After World War II, the company based in Monkwell Street again adopted the title of 'Barber Surgeons'.

The first reference to the existence of a Barbers' hall is found in a list of City Company halls, which was initially dated to 1381 (Norman 1903, 135). It has been proved that this list refers to Company halls in existence in the reign of Richard III (1483–5), not Richard II (1377–99) as previously thought (Beck 1970, 16). The records of the Brewers, based in nearby Addle Street, make reference to leasing their hall to the Barbers nine times in 1422–3 (Unwin 1966, 181). The Barbers first built a hall of their own in the

Summary of dating evidence for Brewers' Hall site (WFG15). See also Company Records and City Letter Books

	features	ceramics	documentary references
Roman		1–4C	
Mid Saxon			
900–950			
950–1000			
1000–1050			
1050–1100	(D – pit)	(A,D)	
1100–1150	(D – pit)	(A,D)	
1150–1200	(D – pit / well)	(B,D)	
1200–1250	(D – pit / well)	(B,D)	1244 Secondary (Stow)
1250–1300	(D – pit / well, D & C – occ layer)	(A,B,C,D)	1291 Primary (Land leased)
1300–1350	(D & C – occ layer)	(A,B,C,D)	
1350–1400	(D, E, F, A – chalk building; C – mortar wall)	(A,C,E,H)	1376 Primary (Gild members at Common Council)
1400–1450	(A – extension to kitchen)	(A,B,C,E,H)	1403 Primary (First record of 'Brewers Hall' 1437 Primary Brewers incorporated 1418–40 Primary (Porland's Minute Book)
1450–1500		(B,C,E)	1468 Primary (Coat of arms granted) ★
1500–1550		(A,B,C)	1544 Primary (Coat of arms granted) ★
1550–1600		(A)	1560 & 1579 Primary (Charter granted) ★
1600–1650		(A,C,D)	1603 Primary (Stow's survey) ★
1650–1700	Post Fire rebuilding	(A,C,D,H)	★
1700–1750		(A,B,D,H)	★
1750–1800		(A,B,D,E)	★
1800–1850		(E)	★
1850–1900		(E)	★

★ *see also* R R Sharpe (ed), 1899–1912 *Calendar of Letter-books preserved in the archives of the City of London: A–L*, London

Fig 57 The shovel lies just outside the south-western corner of the turret, leaning against which is the line of large blocks representing the blocked gateway. (GLA GR285)

Fig 58 The vertical scale closest to the camera lies against a west–east section cut by the RMLEC through the deposits blocking the gateway into the fort. The other scale stands within the chamber on the northern side of the Roman gateway, beyond which (to the north) the base of the City wall can be seen. (GLA GR188)

Fig 59 To the east of the vertical scale is the east–west section cut by the RMLEC through the deposits blocking the west gate of the Roman fort: note the line of large blocks sealing the stone fragments. (GLA GR287)

Fig 61 The 1ft scale (c 0.31m) rests on the lower rubble fill of the west gateway into the Roman fort after it had been half-sectioned by the RMLEC and the upper line of large blocks removed. (GLA GR165)

Fig 60 Blocking of west gate from the east, showing line of large blocks over slighter rubble base. (GLA GR217)

Fig 62 The 1ft scale (c 0.31m) rests on the fills of a beam-slot that ran north–south across the western gateway into the Roman fort. (GLA GR240)

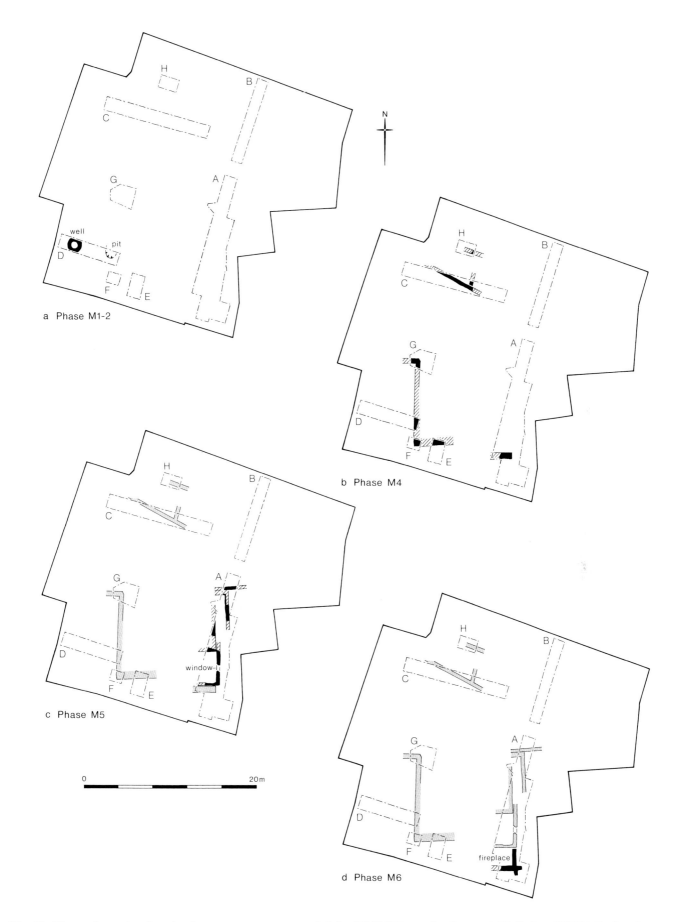

a Phase M1-2

b Phase M4

c Phase M5

d Phase M6

Fig 63 Phase plans showing development sequence recorded by RMLEC on the Brewers' Hall site (WFG15) showing: (a) isolated features that ante-date the construction of medieval hall; (b) to (d): features associated with the development of the medieval hall (cont'd overleaf)

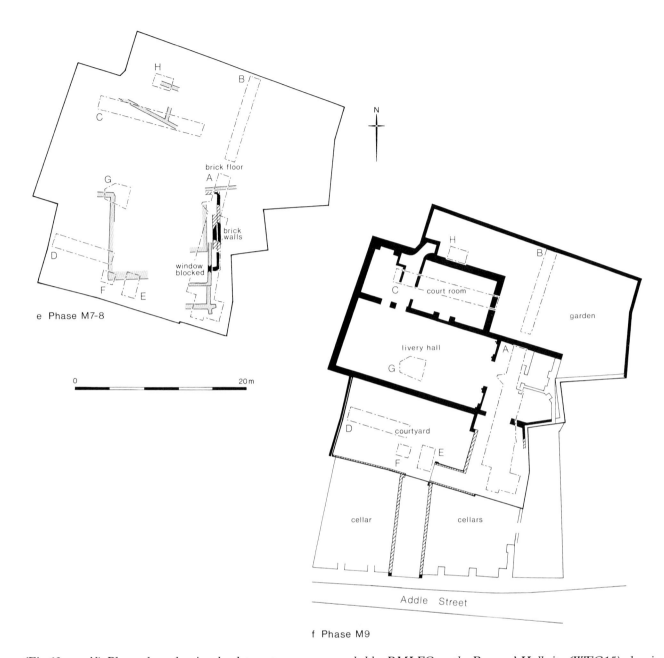

(Fig 63 cont'd) Phase plans showing development sequence recorded by RMLEC on the Brewers' Hall site (WFG15) showing: (e): features associated with the development of the medieval hall; (f) major redevelopment of site after Great Fire of 1666, with hall set back from Addle Street frontage.

fifteenth century, after acquiring land from Sir William Oldhall and John Lavenham (Beck 1970, 15). Very little is known about the plan and development of this building, but it is likely that it lay further to the east than the post-medieval buildings that succeeded it because of the regulations concerning the City wall and the defensive area that was maintained immediately behind it. For example, the City Letter Books for 5 October 1434 state: 'whereas every tenement situated near the walls or gates of the City should be distant from them 16ft at least, according to the laws and customs of the City, the said intermediate space being the common soil of the City' (Dyson 1993, 7). As the need to maintain this defensive strip lessened, the land was let to tenants owing adjoining properties.

The land behind Barber Surgeons' Hall (including Bastion 13) was first let to Lord Windsor, who owned nearby Windsor Court (Neville's Inn WFG3), and in 1605 the lease was bought by the Barber Surgeons, who extended their buildings up to the City wall (Beck 1970, 17). In 1636, Inigo Jones designed an anatomical theatre attached to the main hall buildings. He also designed a Court Room for the Company. The hall was badly damaged in the Great Fire of 1666: the Ogilby and Morgan map of 1676, which shows the extent of the fire in this corner of the City, indicates that the fire swept across all the site apart from the westernmost section, next to the City wall. The roof of the anatomical theatre caught fire, but the building itself was saved. The rebuilding of the hall cost £4292.

Fig 64 *General view of RMLEC excavations at Brewers' Hall (WFG15), showing walls in north end of Trench A. Scales 3 × 1ft scales (c 1m). (GLA GR378)*

Fig 66 *The 3 × 1ft scale (c 1m) rests on chalk foundation to south of tile-built hearth revealed by RMLEC in Trench A on the Brewers' Hall site (WFG15). (GLA GR377)*

Fig 65 *Tile-built fireplace next to 3 × 1ft scale (c 1m) exposed by RMLEC as south end of Trench A on the Brewers' Hall site (WFG15). (GLA GR376)*

Fig 67 *RMLEC excavations at Brewers' Hall (WFG15). The 1ft scale (c 0.31m) rests on the sill of a blocked window beyond which a later wall has been built. (GLA GR386)*

Fig 68 The 3 × 1ft scale (c 1m) rests on the brick floor exposed by the RMLEC at the north end of Trench A on the Brewers' Hall site (WFG15). (GLA GR388)

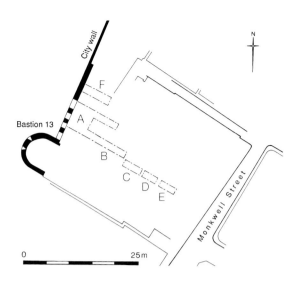

Fig 69 Barber Surgeons' Hall (WFG2): plan showing layout of RMLEC trenches A to F in relation to line of City wall and Bastion 13.

The theatre survived until 1784, when it was demolished and houses built on the site (Wroe-Brown 1998). In 1864, the main hall and kitchen wing, along with three houses belonging to the Company on Monkwell Street, were demolished and the land sold for warehouses. In 1940, all the buildings on the site were destroyed by bombs. A new Company Hall was rebuilt to the east of the post-medieval building and opened in 1969.

RMLEC excavations 1958–9

Before the construction of the new company hall commenced in 1959, the RMLEC conducted excavations on the site (Fig 69). The archive consists of a site notebook, which also includes a finds record, correspondence between Professor Grimes, the Company and the Corporation of London, draft section drawings and plans and 17 photographs. To complement these field records, students from the Institute of Archaeology, University College London recorded the surviving elevations of the seventeenth-century hall during 1996, and the results of this survey have been incorporated in the report. The results of the excavations on the site of Barber Surgeons' Hall were not fully published by Grimes in his 1968 volume; the features revealed were discussed in relation to the City wall (Grimes 1968 64–91) but the development of the hall itself was not.

It would appear from the site notebook that Grimes did not make any notes during the excavations, as all of the entries are in Audrey Williams' hand. The RMLEC had previously carried out some

work on this site, since the occasional reference to an 'earlier cutting' is found on some of the drawings, but there are no notes relating to this. The main phase of work began in August 1958 and continued until June 1959 (Figs 70 and 71). Cuttings A and B, running east from the City wall were opened first with cutting C, to the east of this again opened by December. The two external cuttings (outside the City wall) were also first opened during December. Work continued in the external trenches and then in cutting F during the first six months of 1959. In addition to excavations inside and outside the City wall, the photographs from the site also show that the RMLEC excavated inside Bastion 13. There are no notes relating to these excavations and only one drawing.

Medieval and later developments on the Barber Surgeons' Hall site

Grimes himself noted that the 'results of the work (at Barber Surgeons' Hall) were not spectacular but very useful' (Grimes 1959, 1). The excavations in cuttings A and F revealed the bank sequences associated with the building of the City wall, while the external cuttings showed the depth and make up of the Roman fort wall (Shepherd forthcoming). For the post-Roman period, the results of the excavations are difficult to interpret because of the size and location of the trenches and the limited scope of the surviving finds assemblage that comprise few uncontaminated medieval contexts. Nevertheless it proved possible to suggest eight general periods of post-Roman activity, which can be summarised thus:

Phase M1 Minimal Late Saxon occupation of the area inside the City wall. No structures associated with this period and only residual pottery.

Phase M2 Pottery dated 1150–1250 recovered from 'garden' deposits next to the City wall. No structures dated to this period except possibly the stone-lined well in Bastion 13.

Phase M3 Pottery dated 1270–1350, sealed by a chalk wall, which might represent part of the medieval hall or the property boundary of the site. A later brick wall seals this chalk wall.

Phase M4 Pottery dated 1350–1500 to the east of the chalk wall mentioned above. The brick wall referred to above might also date from towards the end of this phase, preceding the extension of the hall buildings into the area behind the City wall.

Phase M5 Early seventeenth-century expansion into the area behind the City wall, with the court room and anatomy theatre constructed to the designs of Inigo Jones.

Phase M6 Rebuilding after the Fire of 1666, reusing the surviving standing remains.

Phase M7 Nineteenth-century alterations, parts of the site sold off for warehousing.

Phase M8 Post World War II rebuilding.

Fig 70 Barber Surgeons (WFG2): George Faulkner excavating for the RMLEC below the floor of the ruined seventeenth-century hall, the west wall of which was built directly over the City wall. (The Sphere)

Fig 71 Barber Surgeons (WFG2): the RMLEC team of George Faulkner (foreground), Tim Thomas (centre) and Ernest McGee (background) open up a trench across the remains of the seventeenth-century hall. (The Sphere)

Phase M1

Limited Late Saxon occupation of the area inside the City walls is indicated by the presence of residual Late Saxon pottery. Early medieval sand and shell ware (1000–1150) was found in seven contexts (bag nos: A1, A2, B6, B11, B18, B28, F1). Three other types of ceramics dating to 1050–1150 were also found: early Surrey ware (bag nos A1, A32, A33, A34, B28, C35), early medieval shelly ware (bag nos A1, A2, A13, A32, A33, A34) and local grey ware (bag nos A1, A2, A32, A33, A34, B15, B28).

Phase M2

Inside the City walls, pottery dating from 1150 to 1250 was recovered from the uppermost levels of the north extension of cutting A (bag nos A32, A33, A34). The associated deposits are variously described as 'mixed soil' and 'blackish, softish soil'. This part of the site was an open area or garden until the extension of the hall in the seventeenth century.

Phase M3

Further evidence for the westernmost extent of the pre-seventeenth century Barbers Hall was found in cutting B, some 6m east of the City wall. The remains of a chalk wall with buff mortar were discovered with a later brick wall built on top, representing part of the property boundary of the medieval hall. The wall seals a layer containing pottery dated to 1270–1350 (bag No B15).

Phase M4

To the east of the M3 wall pottery dating from 1350–1500 (bag no B6) was recovered from immediately beneath a burnt brick layer, which might represent rubble from the hall's destruction in 1666. In cutting C, to the east again of cuttings A and B, the excavator notes the presence of medieval pits, but these were not excavated. The discovery of these pits further supports the notion that the original Barbers' Hall was built some distance away from the City wall, possibly fronting on to Monkwell Street. Maps of London produced in the mid sixteenth century, such as the 'Agas' woodcut and in Braun and Hogenberg's *Civitates Orbis Terrarum* also show a large garden in this area, with Bastion 13 and the City wall unencumbered by buildings.

The trenches dug outside the City wall produced largely post-medieval pottery, (seventeenth to twentieth centuries) with two of the lower layers producing pottery dating to the fourteenth century at the latest (bag nos 5, 6 external). The medieval pottery might be associated with the ditches constructed outside the wall, prior to the use of the area as a graveyard for the nearby church of St Giles.

Phase M5

The post-medieval building sequence of Barbers Surgeons' Hall can be interpreted from documentary sources and from the surviving fabric. It is known that once the Barbers leased the land behind their hall from the City in the early seventeenth century, they extended their buildings up to the City wall, using Bastion 13 as the dais for the Livery Hall. Photographs of the excavations in Bastion 13 show that the foundations of the bastion were revealed, as were the remains of a substantial stone foundation, which might be a part of the extension into this area in the early seventeenth century. The photographs also show a stone-lined well that might predate the construction of the hall. It is suggested here that parts of Inigo Jones' work on Barber Surgeons' Hall are still visible today.

Phase M6

The fact that the anatomical theatre just to the north of the hall complex survived the Great Fire (Fig 72a) and the demarcation line of the fire destruction shown on the 1676 map, lend weight to the hypothesis that parts of the hall buildings nearest to the City wall remained standing after the fire, and thus were able to be reused during rebuilding. Also, the amount of money spent on the rebuilding suggests some reuse of standing remains since the Barber Surgeons spent only £4292 in comparison with the £5827 spent by the Brewers during their more comprehensive rebuilding. Jones' Court Room annexe used the City wall as its west wall and the surviving windows from this period have been preserved, along with a later window put in during the nineteenth-century reorganisation of the complex (Fig 73a). The distinctive red brickwork of Jones' windows survives to a height of 3.2m externally and 4m internally. In addition to the brickwork, an original Portland stone window dressing survives on the external face. The door that led into the hall from the Court Room lobby is also still visible, with the red brickwork surviving to a height of 5m (Fig 73c and d; Fig 72a). The survival of features built during the period immediately preceding the Great Fire of 1666 is extremely rare in London, and the remains on this site can thus be compared with features such as the lower stages of the tower of All Hallows Barking church, built in 1658–9.

Phase M7

The stone threshold of the Court Room lobby door is visible on both sides of the wall and the entrance has been blocked by yellow stock bricks, which must date from the nineteenth-century alterations, as do the modifications to the windows in the west wall mentioned above (Fig 73a and b). The split from the Surgeons in the mid eighteenth century was marked by the conversion to warehousing of much of the southern half of the property, including Bastion 13 (Fig 72b).

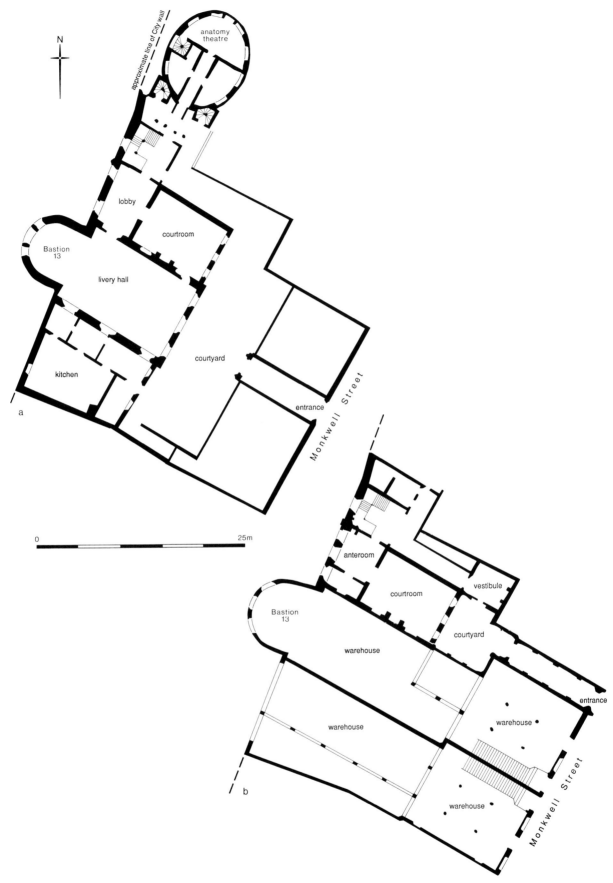

Fig 72 Plans of Barber Surgeons' Hall (WFG2) showing: (a) late seventeenth-century layout of the Barber Surgeons' Hall with Bastion 13 incorporated into the livery hall with the oval anatomy theatre to the north of the courtroom; (b) nineteenth-century layout of Barbers' Hall, following mid eighteenth-century split from the Surgeons, resulting in demolition of the anatomy theatre and conversion of much of the property into warehousing.

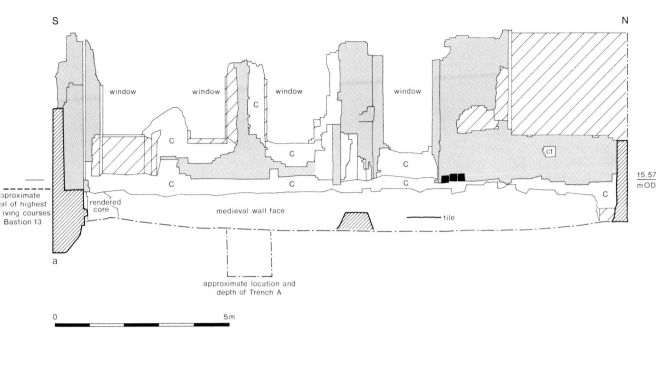

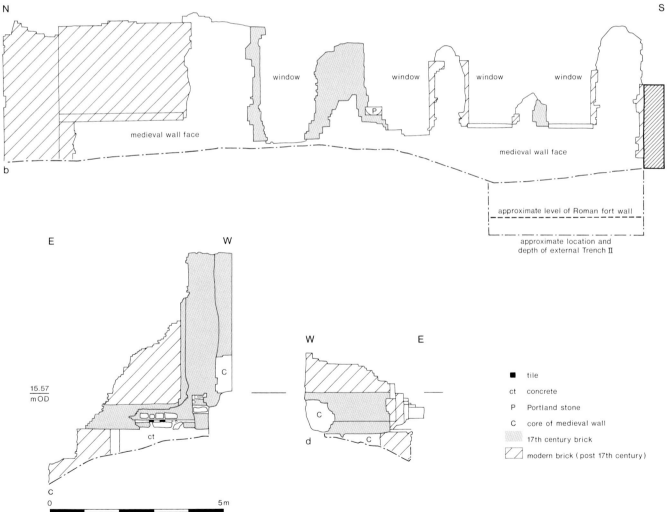

Fig 73 Barber Surgeons' Hall (WFG2): substantial remains of the seventeenth-century hall still survive incorporated within the City wall, as recorded by UCL in 1996: (a) internal east-facing elevation, showing location of lowest cutting within RMLEC Trench A; (b) external west-facing elevation, showing approximate location of RMLEC Trench II, which was excavated to expose the western face of the wall; (c) north-facing elevation; (d) south-facing elevation.

Phase M8

Ironically, it is possible that whatever remained of the medieval Barber Surgeons' Hall might have been destroyed by the mid twentieth-century rebuilding. The present day building is much larger than the post-Fire hall, standing some 8m from the City wall and 5m from the line of Monkwell Street at its south-east corner. The medieval Barber Surgeons' Hall also probably fronted on to Monkwell Street, well away from the City wall, and some fragments of it might have survived below ground after the Great Fire, given that the new hall was built further to the west. The RMLEC, however, did not watch the excavation of that part of the site during the 1960s redevelopment.

Company Halls

The formalisation of the City's trade and craftworkers into distinct companies or guilds can be traced back at least to the early twelfth century, since a guild of weavers is recorded as an authorised society in 1130, for example (Page 1923, 101). Such organisations would require places to meet and conduct their business, and initially this need was served by premises owned by individual members or periodically rented. As the guilds increased in prosperity, power and prestige in the fourteenth century, so to did the need to acquire more permanent and appropriate accommodation. This was precisely the period in which the lords and ladies who had built substantial town houses in the City, usually in the form of a large open hall set within a courtyard complex, were finding the demands of eating in the communal great hall increasingly unfashionable. The desire for greater privacy within the upper echelons of society led directly to the design and construction of new types of multi-roomed, multistoried buildings in which the open hall was no longer required. This was a clear break with a long lived medieval concept, since the plan of the open hall saw the lord occupying the raised dais at one end while his retinue occupied the space in the body of the hall around the shared open hearth: the building plan thus reflected both the hierarchy and the shared obligations of that society (Wood 1965). Just as the aristocracy sought greater privacy in their domestic arrangements, the City guilds were increasing in wealth and power by acting communally. They thus adopted the now abandoned great halls either directly, by taking over a lordly mansion, or by design, by building a new hall to a similar pattern. The guilds could therefore be seen as adopting a role in the life of the City not dissimilar to that once held by a lord and his retinue, in which the mutual benefits and obligations of a particular grouping were inextricably linked. The difference here was that the guilds comprised freemen and not feudal retainers. The result was that the great hall survived in use in the London townscape, as the architectural symbol of feudalism became the symbol of free

enterprise. This then, was the physical expression of 'the enlargement of the idea of community by the principle of Fellowship', which was learning how to displace lordship, that once crucial element of social union (Unwin 1908, 16).

Evidence of such developments has been described above on the Barber Surgeons' and Brewers' Hall sites, as recorded by the RMLEC. It is perhaps worth noting here that Guildhall itself, which lies on the eastern edge of our study area, also shares that history. The shell of the present great hall is substantially mid fifteenth century in date and is set over two undercrofts of differing dates, one to the east and one to the west (Barron 1974). One of the earliest masonry buildings there might have been thirteenth century in date, and occupied the site of the present West Crypt below Guildhall. It was not dissimilar in size to Brewers' Hall, being some 15m wide and might have been as much as 25m long. The ground floor of that building still survives, much altered, but has now become an undercroft. That it was not designed as a subsurface chamber is clear from the recent excavations, which show that the level of the contemporary external yard surface was close to the present day floor level, which, significantly, is higher than the level of the fifteenth-century East Crypt floor, which was clearly designed as a basement. The West Crypt therefore incorporates the shell of at least the ground floor of a two storied, much modified, masonry building, which was further extended to twice its length between 1411 and 1430, becoming the much grander Guildhall we are familiar with today. One of the catalysts for that extensive development has been thought to be the rebuilding, which began in 1394 in the reign of Richard II (Saunders 1951, 71–86), of the great hall at the Palace of Westminster: the construction of such a stunning structure for the King seems to have encouraged the City to build a great hall of their own. In such ways were architectural ideas and pretensions diffused through contemporary London society.

A settlement development pattern for medieval Cripplegate

Study of the medieval buildings, pits and pottery recovered from the RMLEC excavations in the Cripplegate study area has produced significant patterns that are of importance to our understanding of settlement development in this part of medieval London, and some of the wider topographical implications of this research will be discussed in more detail in Chapter 5. Such a statement would come as a surprise to the RMLEC, since their assessment of the research potential of the medieval buildings they excavated was more pessimistic. On most of the sites where relatively extensive excavation was conducted to establish a sequence of occupation and associated development (rather than just to investigate the date of the defences), it was observed that the medieval ground surface had often been truncated by subsequent activity and that much of the area available for excavation was disturbed by pits, cellared features or masonry foundations. This was seen as a problem and a disappointment at the time: Grimes records that, in the Cripplegate area, 'cellar floors and natural surface frequently coincide' and concluded that 'the ground level was relatively higher in Cripplegate and that the accumulations upon it were less deep' when compared to his work elsewhere in the City (Grimes 1968, 4). Since so few complete building plans were indeed recovered by the RMLEC and since the dating of the pottery from the pits seemed imprecise, Grimes was rather dismissive of the value of his work when related to the early medieval City. With the obvious exception of sunken-featured buildings (see Fig 42), he went so far as to argue that 'archaeological excavation therefore cannot be expected to augment or extend knowledge of the medieval house' beyond producing 'some information about details of construction and the like' (Grimes 1968, 163–4).

A reassessment of the RMLEC investigations suggests that it is possible to extend our knowledge of the development of burgage plots and street frontages in the area over the medieval period. This has been achieved principally by noting the date, density and orientation of pit alignments, standard techniques that have now been used on many City sites such as those in the Billingsgate and Cheapside areas (Horsman *et al* 1988, 110–16) but not previously applied to the RMLEC data. Unfortunately it is now no longer possible in every case to be certain which of the surviving pottery assemblages came from which particular pit on an RMLEC site. Nevertheless, there is sufficient evidence to support the basic outlines of a broad pattern, which, allowing for some modification between sites, can be summarised thus:

(a) scatter of widely spaced pits (*c* tenth–eleventh centuries)
This phase seems to represent unintensive settlement within broad plots. It could suggest that the initial allocations of property in this area were generous (when compared with the second phase), or that the narrower burgage plots, so characteristic of later medieval town plans, were not developed in the first generation of settlement.

(b) greater density of pits (*c* twelfth–thirteenth centuries)
This phase represents the occupation of narrower burgage plots than in the previous phase, and the contents of the pits is often associated with craft debris. The pits are clearly orientated at right angles to the principal street frontage. The evidence suggests that the long narrow burgage plots have been established by this date, presumably with a residence built up against the street frontage, marked archaeologically on sites where the contemporary ground surface is now truncated

by an unpitted zone, with a yard to the rear. It would seem that the greater population density reflects a subdivision of the primary insulae into a number of sub-tenancies. This need not imply transient or temporary occupants, since the evidence from the Cripplegate area is that the associated parish churches were also established in this phase, rather than in the earlier or later period, as is discussed below (see Chapter 4). This suggests stable, prosperous and pious communities had been established, of a sufficient size and wealth to support a local church.

(c) foundations of substantial masonry buildings (*c* fourteenth–fifteenth centuries)
The partial plans of the large masonry buildings recovered from the RMLEC sites represent as marked a change in the composition of the population as in the fabric of the townscape itself. Secular masonry buildings seem to have been introduced to the City townscape in the twelfth century, notable in the Cheapside, Gracechurch Street and waterfront areas (Schofield 1994, 32), especially following the great fire of 1136 (Rutledge 1994). Many of the recorded examples of these twelfth and thirteenth-century buildings are related to the need for secure fireproof storage, rather than simply architectural embellishment. In the Cripplegate study area that lies outside the principal market quarters, the masonry buildings here are all substantially later. This could suggest that the activities conducted there before the fourteenth century were not those that demanded masonry building, or that the general level of prosperity was lower than elsewhere within the City walls, or simply that the remains of twelfth century masonry buildings lay outside the RMLEC areas of investigation.

The plan of the masonry foundations recorded on the Cripplegate sites implies the amalgamation of neighbouring properties, since the new buildings often extend over more than one of the earlier postulated property boundaries. Such a pattern has been observed elsewhere in the City, as with the construction of the early thirteenth-century Leaden Hall with its gatehouse, courtyard and attendant buildings at the junction of Cornhill and Gracechurch Street (Samuel and Milne 1992, fig 21). In the case of Neville's Inn and both the Brewers' and Barber Surgeons' Halls in Cripplegate, these masonry buildings all date to no earlier than mid fourteenth century. Thus it could be argued that the property amalgamation that preceded their construction might have been precipitated by a period of depopulation, perhaps that occasioned by visitations of plague. The outbreak recorded in 1349 is known to have taken a heavy toll of the overcrowded City, as the mass graves excavated on the Royal Mint site graphically demonstrate (Grainger and Hawkins 1988). For the Londoners who survived, their material prosperity might have been greater than before, or that unoccupied land within the City was bought up cheaply by those from outside.

In sum, the development pattern discerned from the pits and footings, although it can be ascribed slightly different dates on different sites, arguably mirrors a more general process of settlement and urbanisation in this part of London. That pattern, which is further discussed in relation to the street plan in Chapter 5, seems to represent significant changes in landuse, prosperity and settlement density as well as in the identity and disposable wealth of the occupants in each distinct phase. Thus the study of the medieval backyard as recorded by the RMLEC has arguably proved to be as informative as the fragmentary remains of the contemporary buildings themselves.

4 Parish church

Church archaeology in the City

The rather chequered progress of archaeological interest in the City's 100 medieval parish churches has been discussed in detail elsewhere so need not be repeated here (Cohen 1995; Milne 1997, 1–7; Schofield 1994, 25–9). What needs stressing is that when Professor Grimes began his programme of excavations on the sites of bomb damaged parish churches in London (Fig 74), it marked another pioneering precedent for British medieval archaeology. Although the larger monastic houses could boast a long history of archaeological investigations, few parish churches had been subjected to the rigours of a systematic research excavation. The publication of the summaries of his work on St Alban's and St Bride's (Grimes 1968, 182–209) were therefore widely seen as landmarks in the development of church archaeology not just in the City, but in the country (Rodwell 1997, 5).

The lead was not always followed in London after the demise of the RMLEC and in 1973 it was declared that 'very little reliable work has been done on churches in general' (Biddle 1973, 81). Arguably it was not until the 1990s that research on this crucial aspect of medieval life began to be published in the detail it deserved.

For this chapter, the records collated by the RMLEC on the sites of St Mary Aldermanbury, St Alban's and St Alphage were re-examined as was such pottery as had been retained. As a consequence, a substantially revised interpretation is offered by Nathalie Cohen for the sequence at St Alban's (WFG22) to contrast with the 1968 interim report. Hitherto unpublished RMLEC material is presented in the account of St Mary Aldermanbury (WFG22a), a major site that was excavated after Professor Grimes' last published report on London material had gone to press. The results of more recent recording exercises, which

Fig 74 Ruins of St Mary Aldermanbury (foreground) and St Alban's, looking west c *1960.* (Guildhall Library)

complement the work of the RMLEC at St Alphage (WFG17 and 18), are also included, dealing with one church that was built directly onto the medieval City wall as well as another building that served as a parish church after the sixteenth century, but was formerly the chapel of a medieval hospital, the Elsing Spital. The latter account is another hitherto unpublished report.

St Mary the Virgin, Aldermanbury (WFG22a)

By the end of 1962, the main excavation programme of the RMLEC was over. The laborious task of post-excavation analysis had begun and the supply of digging tools and other equipment disposed of. Four years later Professor Grimes wrote to C Henderson, the treasurer of the RMLEC. 'You will be surprised to know, that the RMLEC is shortly to be involved in yet another excavation in the City: the site of St Mary Aldermanbury church, the superstructure of which has recently been carted off for reconstruction in America'. The site would, he estimated, last for three to four months and cost about £1000 (WFG 22a COR 9/11/66). In the event, the work lasted for more than a year, cost three times that sum and provided as many problems and more as the excavation of St Alban's had. The work was conducted in 1967–8, and was thus completed too late to appear in his famous book summarising the work of the RMLEC (Grimes 1968). Since the report that follows is the first detailed account of the project ever published, it will be given rather more extended treatment than some of the other excavations considered in this volume.

Summary history

The church of St Mary the Virgin lay just to the north of the junction of Love Lane with Aldermanbury. It is within the area of the Roman fort and although it is close to the line of the east wall, it is on a significantly different alignment to it. There are a number of published studies that consider the documented history of the church, including those by the church warden P Carter (1913), an article published just after the Blitz had destroyed the building (Goss 1947) and the most recent account, prepared some 25 years after the church had been rebuilt on a new site in the USA (Hauer and Young 1994). The earliest surviving documentary reference to the church itself dates to 1181, although there is a reference to one Robert the Priest of *Aldermannesberi* that must be earlier than 1148 (Goss 1947, 151). The church clearly started its life as the proprietary chapel associated with the soke or manor of Aldermanbury. Although the right to appoint the priest, the advowson, was sometimes held by the dean and chapter of St Paul's (eg between 1360 and 1374) and sometimes by the Hospital of St Mary Elsing (as in 1331), it was usually retained by the owners of the soke.

This is explicitly stated in 1247, where the grant states that 'all the messuage in Aldermanbury ... together with the advowson of the churches of St Mary Aldermanbury, St Mary Magdalene (Milk Street) and St Michael Bassishaw, which were appurtenant to the manor' (Goss 1947, 119). In 1156 Henry II confirmed 'all the liberties and customs of the soke (ie Aldermanbury) to Reiner de Aldermanbury, son of Berengar', which suggests that the customs must have already been established when Berengar held the soke, which he did from perhaps as early as the 1120s. That in turn implies that the advowson (and therefore the church) might also date back to at least the early twelfth century (Goss 1947, 119–22). Clearly archaeology has a role here to illuminate the question of the origins of this church, which are certainly earlier than the oldest surviving reference, and might arguably be substantially so.

There are many bequests to establish or maintain chantries at St Mary's, which suggests a modest level of prosperity and expansion for the later medieval building, since some of the chantries would need additional chapels as well as additional priests. The earliest mentions are in 1251 (Adam de Basing), 1273 (William de Kingeston) and 1275 (Thomas de Basing), which records that money was to be provided to maintain a chapel, a clear indication that a chantry chapel had already been built by the late thirteenth century. References to chantries continue from 1280 (Isabella Bokerel), 1311 (William de Carleton), 1335 (Henry de Bydyk), 1357 (Henry de Chadesdene), 1367 (William de Bristowe), 1399 (Simon de Wynchcombe), 1431 (John Constantyn and Dennis Towers) to 1446 (William Estfield), which mentions the altar of St George (Goss 1947, 150).

John Stow described it in the late 16th century as being a 'fair church, with a churchyard and cloister adjoining' (Wheatley 1956, 262). The latter feature, unusual for a City parish church, presumably served as a covered walkway joining the nave and northern chapel to the capital messuage of Aldermanbury owned by the holder of the advowson. As such, it served as an explicit indication of the proprietorial origins of this particular parish church. A number of notable monuments were recorded by Stow, including one for Sir William Estfield, who had been elected Mayor in 1438. He had been a notable benefactor of the church, being responsible for the building of the steeple 'with five tuneable bells' (Wheatley 1956, 263) as well as the chantry of 1446. The great window at the east end of the church was reglazed in 1571 and a charnel house is mentioned in 1575 (Carter 1913, 107): such repositories for disturbed burials are documented in several City churches from at least the fifteenth century (Harding 1992, note 53).

One of the neighbourhood's more illustrious inhabitants was the dramatist William Shakespeare (1564–1616), whose London residence for some 14 years was a house on the corner of Silver Street and

Monkwell Street. Two of his near neighbours and actor friends, John Hemmings and Henry Condell, were responsible for printing the first folio edition of his plays. Their names are recorded in the parish registers of St Mary the Virgin, the church where they were married and where their children were baptised.

The church was rebuilt 'at the parish charge' (Carter 1913) in 1633, but was burnt out in the Great Fire of 1666. The shell was then demolished and rebuilding began in 1671, to a design by Sir Christopher Wren executed by Joshua Marshall and his team. Work was largely completed on the church by about 1675, with the steeple added in 1680–81. Among the craftspeople involved with the church was Grace Smith, one of several women mentioned in the accounts of the rebuilding of London's churches (Jeffrey 1996, 271).

The new design was then subjected to a series of rebuildings and modifications. These involved a new floor in 1777, the addition of a gallery for the choir at the west end in 1797, changes and replacements of the windows in 1777, 1830 and 1863 (including the removal of all Wren's tracery); the movement of the vestry in 1729, the organ in 1863 and the pulpit in 1810; the addition of a stone pulpit and stone reredos in 1863, as well as a completely new roof in 1808. There were also substantial restorations and renovations between 1890 and 1898 (Carter 1913, 3). By the early twentieth century, there was therefore very little left in the church, beyond the exterior walls themselves, that could really be related to Wren's designs.

It was that much modified building that was reduced to a burnt out shell once again following the firestorm on 29 December 1940, when an incendiary bomb exploded in it (Fig 75). A young soldier called Noel Mander was an eye witness to the tragedy: he watched helplessly as the church burned, unable to get into the building to save any of the effects as the doors were securely locked. He recalled hearing the bells crash down the tower and the sound of the organ burning: 'the hot air blowing through the organ pipes almost sounded as if the poor old organs were shrieking in agony at their destruction' (Hauer and Young 1994, 355).

The church dismantled: 1961–3

Although the roof and all interior fittings had been destroyed, the upstanding masonry walls survived as a gaunt ruin for more than 20 years (Figs 76 and 77). It was then decided that the church should be dismantled and shipped to Fulton, Missouri, in the United States of America. It was seen as a gift to that nation for all its help to London during the recent war, and as a tribute to Winston Churchill who had delivered his famous Fulton speech about the Cold War and the Iron Curtain in 1946. Between 1961 and 1963 the walls were carefully dismantled, numbered and then shipped across the Atlantic. The rebuilding process began in

Fig 75 St Mary Aldermanbury (WFG22a): the burnt out church in 1956 showing tower at west end, looking south-east towards site of present day Guildhall Library. (Guildhall Library)

1964, but continued with increased vigour following Winston Churchill's death in January 1965, and was completed in 1967, after which the interior was completed and fitted out by May 1969 (Hauer and Young 1994, 384–5).

There was no archaeologist present during the demolition work in London, even though the RCHM report on the church had claimed that the tower was broadly of fifteenth century date. Professor Grimes openly admitted that he paid no interest in that stage of the work (WFG 22a COR 8/5/67), although he was actually recording the neighbouring church of St Alban's Wood Street, some 50m to the west, in 1962 as the work at St Mary's progressed. The architect responsible for the project, Marshall Sisson, retrieved from the rubble a number of architectural fragments that he considered to be of medieval date. He discussed their future study and fate with Professor Grimes in 1966 (WGF 22a COR 27/1/66), and although no subsequent report on the items has been traced, they were taken into the London Museum's collection, of which ten fragments were located thirty years later. These are:

24071   carved limestone moulding from a window or tracery

24075   moulded block of oolitic limestone with possible mason's mark

24076–7 two rectangular oolitic limestone blocks with candystick moulding

24081   carved and decorated Reigate stone fragment, possibly from capital

24083   two marble fragments with smooth concave surface and leaf design on reverse

24085   moulded limestone block decorated with miniature applied columns

24090   Purbeck marble? Fragment of decorated sculpture with a floral tracery pattern

24091   Oolitic limestone with some detail

24092   Possibly Caen stone boss with flower motif

Of these, three are presumably medieval (nos 24081, 24090, 24092) while the rest are in fact of seventeenth-century date, as was a plaque recorded in 1966 (but now lost) inscribed *May 1st MDCLXXIII This vault was built at the charge of John Emey, bricklayer and parishioner* (1673) (GM Acc No 24067).

Archaeology at St Mary the Virgin, Aldermanbury

It was in 1965 that the idea of an excavation on the cleared site was first mooted, following discussions between Canon Mortlock, the rector, and Ralph Merrifield of the Guildhall Museum. In November of that year Professor Grimes accepted the invitation to undertake the project. A protracted correspondence began, which concerned the exhumation of the many anticipated burials: these would have to be removed before the archaeological investigation could commence (WFG22a COR 1/1265 to 25/10/66). These negotiations were complicated by the change of ownership of the site halfway through the discussion, for the diocese sold the site to the Corporation of London for use as a public open space in August. Grimes designed a work programme around the schedule initially presented to him, in which he was to start work in October 1966 and agreed to leave the site in March 1967, although he asked for the possibility of a short extension to be considered, as 'one can never know what problems

Fig 76 St Mary Aldermanbury (WFG22a): nave, south aisle and east end of the burnt out church looking south, on the eve of demolition. (Guildhall Library)

Fig 77 St Mary Aldermanbury (WFG22a): the church awaits demolition and transportation while post-war London rises to the north in c 1962. (Guildhall Library)

might present themselves in the course of archaeological investigations' (WFG 22a COR 3/10/66). Problems did indeed arise (not all of the RMLEC's own making) and the research continued into 1968, more than a year later than planned, which embarrassed Grimes as much as it exasperated the Corporation of London.

As for the standard of the work undertaken, it was recently summarised thus: 'the excavation was carried out by a gang of five labourers, supervised by an ex-army captain who professed an interest in archaeology but had no previous experience. Recording was basic and largely conducted on Thursday afternoons when the director paid his weekly visit to check on progress and to take away any artefacts' (Rodwell 1997, 5). The report that follows is an assessment of such field records and associated data as survive, from which others may judge Dr Rodwell's statement.

The progress of the archaeological excavations can be reconstructed in outline from the comments in the site notebook (with dated entries from May 1967 to April 1968), from scrutiny of the main site plan, dated February 1967 to February 1968, and in the associated correspondence, which suggests work began in February 1967 and was completed in April 1968. There certainly does not seem to have been any major conceptual change in his methodology since his first major church

investigation at St Bride's in the 1950s: as with his other church projects, there was no attempt to mount an open area excavation or even to dig limited areas in plan, few elevations were drawn and next to no graves were excavated archaeologically. The contemporary work at Winchester on St Mary in Tanner Street where the open area method was used does not seem to have influenced the RMLEC approach, for example (Biddle 1966, 317; 1967, 262–3; 1968, 263–5).

Instead, the interior of St Mary Aldermanbury was emptied of its burials without an archaeologist in attendance: according to some 'skeletal remains were shovelled into sacks.., and lead coffins were rolled up by the labourers and transported to a scrapyard on Friday afternoons in order to provide cash for the weekend' (Rodwell 1997, 5). Then, working from that much reduced ground surface a series of trenches were dug within or in between the vaults and tombs, after which the sections were examined (Fig 78). Some attempts were made to identify some of the more notable burials, such as the infamous seventeenth-century Judge Jeffreys and also on the memorial for Robert Askes, a benefactor of Haberdasher's Askes' school (WFG22a Cor 6/2/67), but without notable success.

Grimes also rejected the idea of using volunteers for the project, a practice that had become increasingly common elsewhere in the City during the 1960s: the remains of the neighbouring church of St Michael Bassishaw was recorded with the help of the City of London Archaeological Society in 1965 for example (Marsden 1968): the RMLEC argued that the presence of burials provided too many complications (WFG22a Cor 6/11/65). Grimes also seems to have rejected the concept of student excavators drawn from the Institute of Archaeology, of which he was then the Director. He preferred to use his standard team of some four to five workmen supervised by one archaeologist or chargehand, which he would visit occasionally to take responsibility for much of the recording.

Grimes had originally intended to employ his wife Audrey as the supervisor: she had worked most successfully in that role on, for example, the St Bride's and Walbrook sites in previous years. She felt quite understandably, however, that 'she had done all that should be expected of her in that way' (WFG22a Cor 9/1166) and was, as it turned out, facing serious illness. Grimes was therefore obliged to find a new supervisor, but replacing Audrey would be difficult, since she was very good at dealing 'with your workmen', as William Henderson reminded the Professor (WFG22a 14/11/66). Laborious enquiries were then made to trace one of the RMLEC chargehands (with whom Grimes had not been in contact for a decade) to see if he would undertake it. Mr Samuel Thomas of Poplar, London E14 replied that he was not in good health, but had a good job at Guildhall working with the surveyors, and was therefore unable to accept the offer: nevertheless, he asked to be remembered to Mrs Grimes

Fig 78 St Mary Aldermanbury (WFG22a): the RMLEC did not adopt open area excavation techniques for their work in 1967–8, as is shown by this view of a deep trench excavation in progress in the nave, looking east. The seventeenth-century arcade piers for south aisle are visible to right, set over earlier foundations for the medieval church. (GLA GR592)

(WFG22a Cor 13/12/66). The job was then offered to one WT Eadie, the ex-army captain who professed an interest in archaeology. The post was due to start 'after Christmas, for about three months, for a small wage of £12 per week' (WFG22a Cor 20/12/66). Eadie stayed with the project to the end, after which he then helped move the finds from the RMLEC store in the Guildhall Art Gallery basement to the new store in Bonhill Street in June 1968.

As for the tools and equipment needed for the excavation, they had to be borrowed from the Ministry of Public Buildings and Works, to whom a request was sent in December 1966 for four barrows, four picks, four shovels, two spades, four buckets, trowels, brushes, dust pans, two brooms, 40ft of barrow planking, two tarpaulins and a movable shelter (WFG22a Cor 13/12/66). They arrived in time for work to begin on 13 February 1967, when Grimes recorded that 'in addition to the navvy labour, I am taking on a couple of people who will be paid on an hourly basis: Mr Eadie, chief assistant, and Mr Land, a senior student, less continuous presence' (WFG22a Cor 13/2/67). The very next day the Corporation wrote asking for confirmation that the RMLEC would have left the site by 31 March as promised: Grimes wrote back explaining that he had not been able to start work the previous October as anticipated, as the Corporation had not erected the hoarding around the site until January 1967, and therefore he asked for a 21 week extension to make up for lost time (WFG22a Cor 14/3/67). In the circumstances, the Corporation consented, while expressing concern (WFG22a Cor 18/4/67): it was an inauspicious start to the RMLEC's last major excavation.

Test pits recorded in the centre of the nave by early May 1967 had exposed Roman levels 0.6m thick some 3m below the floor of the church. Others showed that although the seventeenth-century arcade was supported on an earlier foundation on the south side, Wren's building did not follow exactly the line of the medieval church in other places (WFG22a Cor 8/5/67).

According to the first dated entry in the site notebook (19/5/67), his archaeological investigations had moved to the south-east corner, where they continued into July of that year. At that point, the site had to be closed down until October to enable Grimes to direct his summer school for the Institute of Archaeology in Wales, a previous commitment from which he could not be disengaged. Things were not running smoothly, for he had written to the Corporation of London on 10 July requesting another extension, since the work had proved more difficult than expected, bad weather in May had adversely affected progress, and he had had to spend some time looking after his wife, who was now suffering from serious heart illness. The extension was duly, if reluctantly granted, to 30 November, with the comment that the Corporation had no wish 'to grant any further extension beyond that date' (WFG22a Cor 11/9/67). In his acceptance letter, Grimes ruefully commented that 'for my own sake, I very much hope that I shall be finished in time' (WFG22a Cor 14/9/67).

In October the site was reopened, with work beginning at the west end of the nave, after which the northeast chapel was investigated. All this was not without further problems, however. The framed shelter, which had been provided by the Ministry of Public Buildings and Works (MPBW) to cover the deepest trench, had been destroyed by the wind, the site was in a sad condition because of the rain, and Grimes felt that he should 'take on another man to quicken things up as much as possible' (WFG22a Cor 7/11/67). He was also obliged to ask for yet another extension, this time until 31 January 1968 (WFG22a Cor 22/1/68).

Work then moved over to the area around the tower, but the deadline was missed again. According to the site notebook, he was recording on the north side of the tower on 4 March 1968, the south side a fortnight later, after which he examined the south-west angle of the earliest church and then the north wall foundations, the last dated entry being the 1 April 1968. On the 25 of that month he reported to the Corporation that 'at last my work is finished at St Mary Aldermanbury: not that I could not have done more, but that the time has come when I should call a halt'. He was 'grateful for the patience and forbearance in allowing me to go on so long' (WFG22a Cor 25/4/68). Thus ended the RMLEC's last major archaeological intervention in the City, in the same month that Professor Grimes' long awaited volume, *The Excavation of Roman and Medieval London*, was finally published.

The surviving records that this year-long programme produced include a scale plan of the site, more than 30 finds groups for which the location of the majority had been plotted on sketch plans, summary reports on the clay pipes and medieval floor tiles, a transcription of some of the coffin plates, and a detailed correspondence file. There is also the all important site notebook, written in his own hand, often in pencil. This records 11 dated site visits between May 1967 and April 1968, one each in May, June and July before the site closed for the summer school; one in the following December, three times in January and in March 1968, and finally one in April of that year. There were clearly other visits not recorded in the book: one such was compiled on the back of a set of minutes of a committee meeting held on 6 February 1968, but not otherwise dated. There are also undated entries in the notebook itself, which presumably record progress in October and November 1967, for example. Taken together, they show that Professor Grimes visited the site between one and three times per month, but not apparently always on a Thursday, as suggested elsewhere (Rodwell 1997, 5): the recorded visits took place on three Mondays and Wednesdays, on two Fridays and once on a Thursday, as well as on a Saturday and even on a Sunday. This rather irregular pattern could suggest he was responding to the actual pace of the work, rather than simply to his own regular (if busy) schedule: the £7 spent by Eadie on telephone calls during the final period of the excavation (WFG22a 14/3/68) suggests that Professor Grimes also offered direction for the project from his office at the Institute of Archaeology in addition to his site visits.

The costs of digging St Mary's increased as the programme had extended. The AGM of the RMLEC in July 1968 was duly informed that the excavations were now complete, but at a cost of £3038 14s 9d. Since the Ministry had only contributed £750 towards that sum, the Council were out of pocket by more than £2000. To put these sums into perspective, it is worth recording that Martin Biddle's 1968 season at Winchester cost £19,500 (Biddle 1969, 295), while Brian Philp's five month excavation of a site on the London forum in 1968–9 was just £1500 (Philp 1977, 4). Some idea of the costs involved at St Mary Aldermanbury can be gained from the few references to the accounts in the correspondence file. The work in November 1967, for example, had produced invoices for £29 10s from J Sinnott; £105 10s from

Professor Grimes (it is uncertain how many site visits this represents, since there are no dated entries in the notebook for November) and £138 7s 3d for WT Eadie. For the period from December 1967 to 8 March 1968, by contrast, Eadie was paid but £96 2s 4d: this smaller sum for a longer period perhaps reflects the RMLEC's practice of not paying their staff if time was lost for bad weather or bad light. Other items that required payment on the same bill included £1 6s 8d for a hammer and chisel and 2s for band aid: these items might not be unconnected (WFG22a 14/3/68).

In the event, the MPBW were prevailed upon to provide further funding, other sources, including the Americans in Fulton USA (who got the fabric of the church) having proved unfruitful. By September, the MPBW grant had been raised by £1250, to a total of £2000 (WFG22a Cor 24/9/68). There then followed a series of requests from the MPBW to the RMLEC for a fifty word summary of the site for their records (WFG22a Cor 1/11/68; 5/11/68; 1/1/69): it is not clear if one was ever sent, but a brief note did appear in *Medieval Archaeology* (Wilson and Hurst 1969, 251). No interim report of any substance (beyond the summaries discussed below) seems to have been published or prepared, although a simplified phase plan apparently based on the work of the RMLEC was displayed at the Fulton site (Hauer and Young 1994, Fig 2.3).

Archaeology of St Mary the Virgin, Aldermanbury

The report on the AGM in July 1968 also included a summary of the results of this work. Grimes explained that although the Wren superstructure had been removed to Fulton, the bases of the church walls had been left in place: these rested upon the chalk and gravel foundations of the medieval church. He commented that the precise dating of the pre-Wren features was difficult in the absence of architectural details, and went on to describe the development sequence:

The church appears to be of three compartments, but the situation at the East end is difficult to unravel because of the eighteenth-century brick vaults, which could not be removed. Since the first mention of the church was in 1181, the first building was presumably twelfth century, but this was replaced by an open 'hall-type' church with a western tower, probably of the fourteenth century. The walls of this later church carried the Wren church (RMLEC AGM 5/7/68).

The summary published in *Medieval Archaeology* furnished the additional information that the northeast and south-east chapels had been added to the primary vessel of nave and chancel (Wilson and Hurst 1969, 251). Further information is provided in a letter to the architect Marshall Sisson written in 1975, in which Grimes restates his comment that, unlike the neighbouring church of St Alban's, no medieval superstructure survived on the site above ground level in the post-Fire reconstruction of St Mary's. This comment

also applied to the western tower, about which Grimes was happy to contradict the report published by the RCHM in 1929. He was convinced that, although the late seventeenth-century tower incorporated much material recycled from the medieval church, none of that medieval stonework was in its primary position. He also reiterated in passing that the 'original' church was of twelfth-century date (WFG22a Corr 21/11/75).

Overlying the Roman features there were thus four basic phases relating to the church of St Mary's, which were identified and dated by Professor Grimes as below:

1: Nave and chancel established 'presumably 12th century' (RMLEC AGM 5/7/68).
2: Addition of Chapels at east end
3: Enlargement of Nave and addition of external western tower 'probably of the 14th century' (RMLEC AGM 5/7/68).
4: Comprehensive levelling of the medieval superstructure to ground level after the Great Fire of 1666: major rebuilding utilising earlier features as foundations.

The development of the church

Study of the records suggests that a more complex development is represented by the foundations and features recorded on this site (Fig 79).

Phase 1 (Fig 79a)

The first church seems to have been of masonry construction, comprising a nave that was twice the length of the chancel, being *c* 19.3m long × *c* 5.82m wide internally (Fig 80). At the west end of the nave was an additional strongly built foundation defining a cell some 3.5m × 4m internally with a chalk and gravel footing up to 1.7m wide on the northern side. This might represent the footings of a small tower (Fig 81). All these elements, including the nave and 'tower' were clearly contemporary, as the site photographs show. The foundations were usually some 1m wide, and were of chalk rubble alternating with layers of gravel 100mm to 150mm thick (Fig 82).

Dating: early to mid twelfth century (see 'Discussion of dating' below)

Phase 2 (Fig 79b)

The complex of walls built around the eastern end of the church clearly represent more than one phase of development, since differing alignments were in evidence, although the same type of foundations were used. There was, however, insufficient detail recorded to allow for a full phasing of the developments represented. There is evidence that at least one flanking chantry chapel was added to the chancel. The foundations for Chapel 1, set on the north-east side, was at least 5.6m long and some 3m wide internally, with foundations of undressed chalk rubble, alternating with thinner layers of gravel.

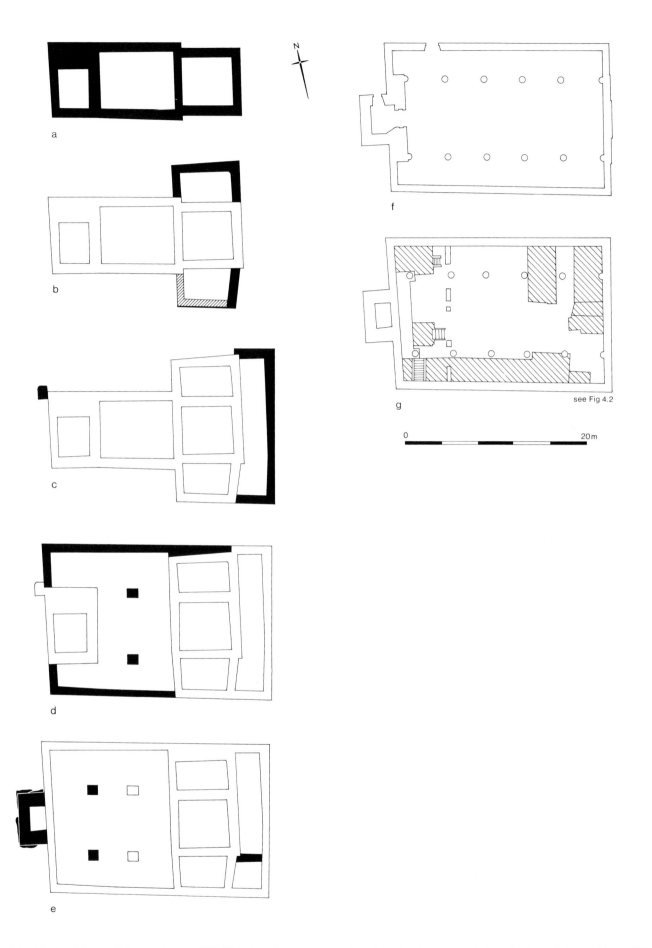

Fig 79 St Mary Aldermanbury (WFG22a): plan sequence showing development of church from (a) to (e) twelfth–seventeenth century; (f) late seventeenth century; (g) location of late seventeenth–nineteenth century vaults.

Fig 80 St Mary Aldermanbury (WFG22a): junction of foundations of twelfth-century nave with chancel. The 3 × 1ft scale (c 1m) is aligned north–south, resting on the south-eastern corner of the foundations on the nave's southern wall. A surviving pillar of medieval masonry rises above the junction supporting the pier base used in the late seventeenth-century building. (GLA GR516)

There might have been a similar chapel, Chapel 2, set to the south-east, but this area had been badly disturbed and obscured by later vaults. Nevertheless, the footings of earlier walls, which were exposed here, presumably represent the chapel's foundations or associated vaults. Chantry chapels are a common feature in City parish churches, and it is known from the documentary record, for example, that bequests were made by Adam de Basing and William de Kingston to establish chantries at St Mary's in the thirteenth century.

Dating: although more than one phase is represented here, it is argued that all must be later than Phase 1 on stratigraphic grounds but earlier than Phase 4, in which a different foundation type is employed. A date probably in the late twelfth or thirteenth century is suggested.

Phase 3 (Fig 79c)

A wall running north–south was set to the east of the
original chancel wall, and seemingly also to the east of
the chantry chapels just described. The foundations
were recorded directly beneath the footings of the late
seventeenth-century church wall, while both the internal and external faces of the north-east corner were
examined, showing that the eastern and northern walls
were of one build here. The foundations were again of
chalk rubble alternating with layers of gravel, and thus
must be earlier than the walls set on arched foundations discussed in Phase 4. This is a somewhat unusual feature not closely paralleled in City parish churches.
It might relate to the cloister or covered walkway mentioned in John Stow's sixteenth-century description of
the church, or it might represent extensions to the new
chapels themselves.

At the other end of the church, just beyond the west
wall, a substantial foundation or buttress more than 1m
wide was recorded, projecting well beyond the north-
west corner of the tower it is thought to be associated
with. It seems to have been added to the west wall, and
therefore might represent remedial action reflecting
structural instability at this corner of the tower
(Fig 83). Significantly, this tower seems to have been
rebuilt to the west in Phase 5, which suggests it might
have been in danger of collapse or might have actually
fallen down prior to its rebuilding.

Dating: later than Phase 1 but earlier than Phase 5;
probably mid to late thirteenth century.

*Fig 81 St Mary Aldermanbury (WFG22a): the 3 × 1ft
scale (c 1m) rests on massive medieval foundation,
presumably for a tower, with the rebuilt internal face of the
west wall of the church rising above it. View is looking
north-west. (GLA GR542)*

Phase 4 (Fig 79d)

The church was considerably enlarged with the construction of a new north and south walls, the new open
plan 'hall' church described by Professor Grimes. The
foundations of the north wall were of random ragstone
rubble with occasional chalk blocks set over foundation
arches: there was an irregular offset some 0.3m above
the arch voussoir. The northern end of the new west
wall was also set on subsurface foundation arches. The
mixed stone and chalk footings of the new south wall
were observed running beneath the later seventeenth-
century wall, and seemed to butt against the west wall
foundations.

Dating: later than Phase 1; earlier than Phases 5
and 6; probably late fourteenth or fifteenth century.

Grimes' description of the church as an open hall
assumed that the old nave had been demolished and
that the new building had no aisles in it. It is suggested
here, by contrast, that the building possibly had at least
one if not two aisles. These would have been formed by
the partial demolition of the Phase 1 nave, with the old
northern and southern walls pierced to form the new
arcade of two arches beyond the Phase 3 tower. The
northern aisle might have been 3.7m wide, while the
southern aisle was a narrower 2.4m. The bay divisions
defined by the arcade were probably reflected in the

*Fig 82 St Mary Aldermanbury (WFG22a): foundation of
gravel and chalk used in the north-west corner of the first
masonry church. (GLA GR519)*

Fig 83 St Mary Aldermanbury (WFG22a): foundations below the external junction of the west wall of the late seventeenth-century church (externally faced with ashlar blocks) and the north wall of the tower (with doorway). The 3 × 1ft scale (c 1m) is aligned north–south, resting on a medieval foundation that underpins the medieval tower foundation that is itself below the base of the late seventeenth-century tower. (GLA GR565)

Fig 84 Medieval arched foundations below south side of footings of late seventeenth-century tower, clearly showing that the medieval tower was demolished to ground level after Great Fire of 1666. (GLA GR568)

spacing of the doors and windows in the new northern and southern walls. If that was the case, then there might have been visible on the south wall three windows lighting the nave (given that the main entrance was through the tower), with two more windows for the chapel at the east end.

It is assumed that the new northern and southern walls were contemporary, but the possibility remains that the aisles might have been opened out at different dates: that could explain the differing widths of the two aisles.

Phase 5 (Fig 79e)

Tower 2
It seems that the first tower was demolished and replaced by a second tower, this time set outside the west end of the church. The remains were recorded directly below the footings of the third tower on this site, the late seventeenth-century structure built after the Great Fire (Fig 84). The second medieval tower was 1.7m east–west × 2.5m north–south set over a substantial arched foundation up to 1.4m wide (Fig 85). The tower was clearly not built at the same time as the west wall, since its foundation arch butted up against the wall foundation. This tower presumably represents the one described by Stow as having been built with funds provided by William Estfield in the fifteenth century (Wheatley 1956, 263).

Dating: fifteenth century.

Fig 85 Medieval arched foundations revealed on eastern side of late seventeenth-century tower. (GLA GR506)

Tiled floors The fragmentary remains of a slumped sequence of tiled floors were recorded in the church on 14 March 1968, right at the end of the excavations. The latest of the pavements clearly represented the surface of the chancel at the time of the Great Fire, which

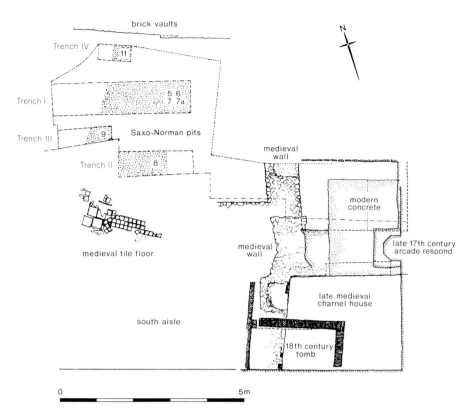

Fig 86 St Mary Aldermanbury (WFG22a): multiphase plan drawn by RMLEC showing part of east end with sequence of medieval walls and later features revealed within body of late seventeenth-century church. Note irregular nature of archaeological excavations: only a small proportion of site (Trenches I to IV) was excavated to a level substantially lower than the medieval church, revealing Saxo-Norman pits.

was 1m below the floor of the late seventeenth-century church. The surface comprised a mixture of tiles of differing dates, extending for some 2m north–south × 0.8m east–west, cut away in the east by a grave containing a lead coffin. The exact position was not recorded on the main site plan, which had just been inked up in February, a few weeks earlier, and not subsequently amended. A plan was drawn in the field (Fig 86) and the photographs show that the surface was on the southern side of the chancel close to the southern wall (Fig 87). The floor tiles from these excavations, which remain in the Museum of London's collections, include three Flemish tiles of late fifteenth to mid sixteenth-century date, 20 fourteenth-century Penn tiles and some thirteenth-century 'Westminster' and Chertsey types. This dating confirms the suggestion of several different phases of reflooring within the church during a 300 year period. The designs represented have been listed by Dr Ian Betts (1994, 138) and need not be repeated here.

Charnel House The base of a brick-floored charnel house at least 1.5m deep and some 2.5m across was recorded in the extreme south-east corner of the church. It had been formed by excavating the soil within the corner of the building, utilising the existing foundations to the north, south and east as its walls, and adding a new wall to the west. The latter was roughly dressed on its

eastern face but not on its western side, where a later brick vault had been built against it. The pit had been filled with long bones, reflecting token reburial of bodies disturbed by a major rebuilding programme (Fig 88). No attempt was made to sample or record this skeletal material, some of which had been stored in antiquity within the excavated alcove beneath the foundation arch on the north wall.

Dating: this feature must be later than the Phase 3 and 4 walls against which it was built, but was clearly earlier than the Phase 6 developments. The red brick floor was probably of sixteenth-century date, and thus the feature might be the charnel house mentioned in the church records of 1576 (Carter 1913).

Working from the archaeological evidence, the Phase 5 church on the eve of the Great Fire therefore seems to have comprised an external western tower, a nave with aisles to the north and south founded on the alignments of the Phase 1 walling, beyond which lay a deep chancel with flanking chapels and a charnel house. The pronounced development of the east end beyond the Phase 1 chancel arch clearly represents a history of medieval patronage and endowments. This can be contrasted with the rather more modest development of the nave to the west, suggesting that the late medieval population of the parish might have enjoyed a relatively greater growth in prosperity than in numbers.

Fig 87 St Mary Aldermanbury (WFG22a): medieval tiled floor. The 3 × 1ft scale (c 1m) is aligned east–west, lying next to fragment of tiled floor slumped below its contemporary level into an underlying grave in the east end of church. It is itself cut by later burials in lead coffins to the east. The floor level of late seventeenth-century church is represented by pier base for south arcade just beyond scale. Internal face of south wall of the church is visible beyond that. (GLA GR516)

Dating: later than Phase 4; earlier than Phase 6: fifteenth to sixteenth century.

Contemporary memorials displayed in the church included those to Simon Winchcombe (1391), Robert Combarten (1422), John Wheatley (1428), John Middleton (1428), Sir William Estfield, Mayor (1429), John Middleton, Mayor (1472), John Tomes, Draper (1480), William Bucke (1501), Sir William Browne, Mayor (1507), Dame Margaret Jennings, wife of Stephen Jennings, Mayor (1515), Dame Mary Gresham, wife to Sir John Gresham, Mayor (1538), Elizabeth Davy (1569), Thomas Godfrey, Remembrancer (1577), Ralph Woodcocke, Grocer and Sheriff (1586), Thomas Digges and his wife Agnes, daughter of Sir William Sentlieger and granddaughter of Lord Abergavenny (1595). Among the seventeenth-century memorials were those to Mary Briggs (1610), Thomas Hayes (1617), David Briggs (1626) and Robert Offley (1631).

Some grave slabs were broken up and reused in the core of the building reconstructed after the Great Fire: of these some can still be seen today (Fig 89) in the park laid out around the consolidated ruins of the church (Bertram 1987, 144–6).

Phase 6 (Fig 79f)

The documentary records and the archaeological evidence combine to demonstrate that the church damaged in the Great Fire was subsequently levelled and rebuilt effectively from ground level. Considerable use was made of the medieval wall footings as foundations (Figs 90 and 91), and hence the new church was of a very similar size to the late medieval one, at 22.3m long × 14m wide. The new walls were up to 11.7m tall, and the tower rose some 28m. The plan of the late seventeenth-century church, however, was more symmetrical than its predecessor, and therefore not all of the wall phases directly overlay each other. The northern arcade was set to the north of the Phase 1 footings, for example. The plan of the internal arrangements of the Phase 6 church was also rather different, comprising a much longer nave separated from the north and south aisles by a four-arched arcade with a fifth bay over the chancel.

Dating: later than Phases 4 and 5; earlier than Phase 7: late seventeenth century.

Contemporary memorials displayed in this church included Walter Pell, Alderman and Merchant Taylor (1672), John Emey, Bricklayer and Parishioner (1673), John Chandler (1686), Richard Chandler (1691), Mary Hack (1704) and Anne Betton (1713). In addition, the infamous Judge Jeffreys, George Lord Jeffreys, Baron of Wem, was buried in a vault under the communion table in 1693.

Late 17th-century tower

The RCHM survey published in 1929 assumed that much of the second medieval tower had survived the Great Fire and was incorporated in the rebuilt church subsequently. The records compiled by Professor Grimes, however, make it quite clear that the late medieval tower was demolished together with the rest of the fire damaged shell before the late seventeenth-century reconstruction began (Fig 92). For example, evidence of a narrow band of 'occupation soil' was observed separating the surviving top of the medieval stone tower footings from the lowest course of Wren's tower, with its distinctive harder mortar (WFG22a: Site Notebook 21/1/68). The fabric of the later tower comprised stone reused from the old building (see Fig 75), and it was this fact that presumably misled the RCHM surveyors and subsequent commentators (eg Jeffery 1996, 271; Schofield 1994, fig 78).

Phase 7 (Fig 79g)

Some of the major modifications in the eighteenth and nineteenth century have already been mentioned: among the features represented on the site were the brick footings of the choir gallery built in 1797 across the west end of the church. The other major features were the range of burial vaults, which were cut into much of the eastern, western and southern sides (Fig 93).

Fig 88 St Mary Aldermanbury (WFG22a): token reburial of human longbones in a late medieval charnel pit in the south-east corner of the church. (GLA GR548)

Study of the dates on the plates fixed to the coffins shows that one of the vaults was in use from at least 1728 to 1812, while the vault in the north-east corner of the church contained coffins dated from 1745 to 1839. All burial vaults within City churches were sealed up by 1850.

Dating: later than Phase 6; earlier than Phase 8: *c* 1700–1940.

The RMLEC recorded some of the coffin plates from two of the vaults, as summarised below:

Vault 1
Miss Anne Strode d. 1745 aged 28
Mrs Catanach d. 1779
Mrs Hannah Fryer d. 1784 aged 38

Mrs Ann Ryder d. 1789 aged 33
Miss Sophia Forbes d. 1793 aged 13
Mrs Rebecca Lawrence d. 1795 aged 74
Sir John Swimmerton Dyer d. 1801 aged 63
Harriet Newcoomb d. 1809 aged 19
Master John Telford d. 1813 aged 14
Miss Helena Babington d. 1814 aged 4
Master George Byrn d. 1816 aged 6
Miss Eliza Byrn d. 1821 aged 12 weeks
Sam Trist d. 1822 aged 74
Richard Babington d 1823 aged 3 days
James Hall d. 1827 aged 69
Mrs C Tayle d. 1828
Benjamin Taylor d. 1831 aged 80

Miss Eliza Oliver d 1831 aged 7 years 10 months and 9 days
William Ireland d.1838 aged 52
Miss Julia Wollaston d. 1839 aged 11 months

Vault 2
Samuel Lamb d. 1728 aged 6
Joseph Bagnall d. 1729 aged 67
William Bagnall d. 1734 aged 38
B Callamy d. 17*2 aged 56
Rev Callamy d. 1755 aged 57
Hugh Granger d. 1762 aged 82
William Partridge d. 1764 aged 63 (he also had a commemorative plaque on the church wall)
** d. 1764 aged 67
Mrs Sarah Calamy d.1764 aged 55
** d. 1769
A Prans*ard d. 1769
Somerset Phillips d. 1775 aged 81
Master John Brown d. 1782 aged 13
Edward Austin d. 1809 aged 62
Mrs I* M* d. **11 aged 35
Rebecca Wendy d. 1811 aged 56
Sophia P* d. 1812 aged 53

Phase 8: Fulton and London

Phase 8a The majority of the surviving late seventeenth-century superstructure is now reconstructed in Fulton Missouri, in the United States of America (Hauer and Young 1994). It comprises the original facing stones and some of the rubble core, much of which was material reused from the earlier medieval church. The restoration is an accurate reflection of the external appearance of the late seventeenth-century church, with the exception of the modern addition of an additional window set into the west face of the tower. There is now an open undercroft beneath the building, housing a museum, in place of the enclosed vaults and tombs that lay below the nave floor on its original site. The church at Fulton is an active centre of worship, being used for weekly services, Harvest Festival, Nine Lessons and Carols, a Morning Prayer service using the 1662 Book of Common Prayer, and has become the most popular chapel in outstate Missouri for weddings. The climate in that state, however, sees a temperature range from minus 18C in winter to 32C in summer, and this has caused some deterioration to the Portland Stone while the interior plasterwork has been damaged by moisture. Remedial works began in 1996 and by May 1997 the problem seems to have been resolved (Hauer 1997). The former City parish church is therefore enjoying an active life as a much loved college chapel, community centre and tourist attraction on its new site.

Phase 8b The foundations, meanwhile, are now displayed in situ in the City of London, laid out as a small park. It is possible to trace the plan of the late seventeenth-century external walls as well as the position

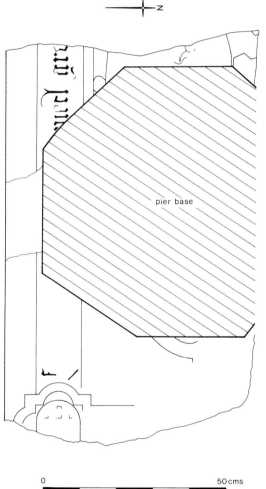

Fig 89 St Mary Aldermanbury (WFG22a): fragments of late medieval grave slabs reused in surviving late seventeenth-century arcade foundations recorded in 1996 (after N Constantine, for LARF).

of the arcade bases defining the two aisles. Traces of earlier late medieval material are also visible, most noticeably in the form of late medieval grave slabs reused as foundation packing beneath the pier bases on the southern arcade (See Fig 89), for example.

Fig 90 The 3 × 1ft scale is aligned east–west against the levelled south wall of the medieval church, over which a late seventeenth-century pier base sits. (GLA GR594)

Discussion of dating

The rebuilding after the Great Fire of 1666 provides one readily identifiable horizon on the site, while the foundations types used to support the medieval walls were also broadly datable. Two types were identified, the earlier one using alternating bands of chalk rubble and gravel, the later one using arched subsurface foundations. These suggest a general date range for the associated developments from the twelfth to the fifteenth century. As for the foundation of the church itself, study of the ceramic evidence proved constructive. Some 61 groups of pottery were recovered from the excavations, and these were identified in the field by a mixture of numeric and alphanumeric codes (eg 18, 18a, 18b, 18c etc). Although a general location was recorded for some of these groups, there are insufficient surviving data to provide detailed contextual or stratigraphic information. Nevertheless, the assemblages have recently been re-examined by the Museum of London Archaeology Service, and their study shows that although much third and fourth century Roman pottery was found, there is no medieval pottery that can be dated earlier than AD 950. It therefore seems unlikely that there was any substantial occupation or activity here in the middle Saxon period. Such ceramic evidence as there is shows that, of the 22 small

assemblages of medieval pottery recovered, almost 70% have now been dated to somewhere in the period 950–1150, although all of this might have been deposited in the eleventh century. The remainder of the medieval period is much more scantily represented in the ceramic record, with only seven other groups, three dated 1150–1200 (nos 11, 12 and 14c), three of early thirteenth to mid fourteenth-century date (nos 3e, 17 and 18b) and one 1400–1500 (no 18).

It is suggested here that the larger collection of medieval pottery (nos 2, 12a, 13, 13b, 15a, 16, 16b, 18a, 18d 18e, 18f, 18g, 18h, 19c, 19d and 20) comprises material from pits or other occupation features representing activity earlier than the construction of the church. Its foundation would therefore be dated to the early twelfth century on this ceramic evidence, a date that is quite consistent with the type of foundations used and the general plan form. Such a date is not inconsistent with the documentary record and serves to confirm the initial suggestion made by Professor Grimes himself.

The significantly smaller pottery assemblages recovered from the site dating to the period 1150 to 1500 therefore represent disturbances associated with the later development of the church itself or associated burials. Such an interpretation of the ceramic evidence is in keeping with the now all too common picture drawn

Fig 91 Section through south wall of twelfth-century church capped with reused late medieval grave slab over which sits a column for the southern arcade of the late seventeenth-century church. (GLA GR515)

Fig 92 St Mary Aldermanbury (WFG22a): base of tower of late seventeenth-century church on which 3 × 1ft scale rests (c 1m) looking north. The foundations rest on the remains of the medieval tower, demolished after the Great Fire of 1666. (GLA GR516)

from other church excavations, which suggest that large contemporary ceramic assemblages are rarely recovered from features directly associated with the construction and development of the building foundations.

1:     Pottery representing medieval activity before church was built

     Medieval pottery groups AD 950–1150:
     Bag nos 13b 15a 18a 18d 20

     Medieval pottery groups AD 1000–1150:
     Bag nos 2 12a 13 16 16b 18e 18f 18g 18h 19c 19d

2:     Pottery representing medieval activity after church was built

     Medieval pottery groups AD 1150–1200:
     Bag nos 11 12 14c

     Medieval pottery groups AD 1200–1350:
     Bag nos 3e 17 18b

     Medieval pottery group AD 1400–1500:
     Bag no 18

St Alban's, Wood Street (WFG22)

Summary history

The church of St Alban was located on the east side of Wood Street (Fig 94), on the corner of Love Lane. Little Love Lane ran to the north of the churchyard. Addle Street, to the north of the site, is said to have been formerly called 'King Adel Street,' justifying a tradition connecting the church with the tenth century Saxon King Athelstan (Jenkinson 1917, 178). A more prosaic derivation, however, suggesting that it actually meant 'Cow–dung Street', is discussed in Chapter 3. The church is the only one in the City of London dedicated to Alban who was martyred by Diocletian in *c* 209. The abbey of St Alban's, in Hertfordshire, was founded by King Offa in 793, and it is this connection with Offa and the tradition that his royal palace was located within the Cripplegate fort area that has led to the suggestion that the church is of eighth-century date. It was believed that the church was originally Offa's private chapel (Dyson and Schofield, 1984, 294; Hobley 1988, 73). With regard to the dating of the church to this period, it has been noted that none of the other churches (in England) dedicated to St Alban exhibit early fabric: 'the spread of his dedications throughout the south midlands may owe as much to the territorial claims of the great Benedictine abbey as to the efficacy of visits to the shrine after the new translation in 1129' (Butler 1986, 46).

The church was owned by St Alban's Abbey until 1077, when it was transferred to the patronage of the Masters, Brethren and Sisters of the Hospital of St

Fig 93 St Mary Aldermanbury (WFG22a): eighteenth and nineteenth-century brick-lined vaults cutting through earlier medieval foundations in the south-east corner of the church, looking west. The scale is 3 × 1ft (c 1m). Note the pile of human long bones disturbed by the RMLEC excavations discarded on the spoil heap. (GLA GR516)

James, Westminster, who owned it until 1477. From then until the seventeenth century, the Provost and Fellows of Eton College were the patrons of the church (Daniell 1907, 113). In 1670, the parish of St Alban's was united with that of St Olave, Silver Street (which had been destroyed in the Great Fire) and in 1894, the parishes of St Mary Staining and St Michael, Wood Street were also joined to the united benefice. The patronage was owned alternately by Eton College and the Dean and Chapter of St Paul's (Clarke 1898, 50).

Very little is known about the early construction history of the church. Just before the church was rebuilt in 1633, Anthony Munday recorded his impressions of the building: 'Another character of the antiquity of it is to be seen in the manner of the turning of the arches in the windowes and heads of the Pillars. A third note appears in the Romane bricks here and there inlayed among the stones of the building' (Munday 1633, 308). It has also been suggested that the two western bays of the south aisle appear to have been cut off, and that the area subsequently used for commercial purposes was once part of the church grounds (Tabor 1917, 60). The church was rebuilt in 1633–4 to designs by Inigo Jones after it became dangerously dilapidated (Daniell 1907, 114) but was subsequently burnt out in the Great Fire in 1666. The extent of the damage caused by the fire is not clear but it is possible that only partial rebuilding was needed to restore the church as only £3165 0s 8d was spent during the period of restoration (1682–7). This figure can be compared with the accounts from other churches restored by Sir Christopher Wren after the Great Fire (Weaver 1915): for example, £11,430 5s 11d was spent at St Bride's (1671–1703), £7455 7s 9d at St Michael Paternoster Royal (1686–94) and £4687 4s 6d at St Swithun's (1678). During the nineteenth century the Gothic style church was restored, the interior being 'inordinately altered and modernised... no pains seem to have been spared to render a once interesting and dignified interior as commonplace as possible' (Daniell 1907, 114–15). In 1858, an apsidal chancel was added to the east end of the church by Gilbert Scott. St Alban's was destroyed in December 1940 (Figs 95 and 96) and only the tower, now privately owned, survives today (Cobb 1989, 176).

RMLEC excavations 1962

Twenty years after the destruction of the church in World War II, the RMLEC began making enquiries as to the possibility of excavating on the site. Grimes (1968, 204) notes that 'the excavation of the church in 1961–2 was carried out in circumstances that were not entirely satisfactory'. The correspondence in the site archive reveals the full extent of the frustrating and prolonged negotiations that took place before excavation began, and the difficulties encountered on site. With the Ministry of Works, the Corporation of London and the Church all involved, difficulties soon arose regarding responsibility for the removal of rubble from the area, the demolition of the church superstructure and the disinterment of burials. Grimes maintained that it was not the responsibility of his team to clear the site of rubble and human remains, and stressed the need for this to be carried out in advance of archaeological investigation. Although Grimes began negotiating to work on the site early in 1960, by October 1961 the human remains still had not been removed from the site. The City Engineer, Francis Forty, commented in a letter to Grimes 'it is a perfectly maddening situation. One seems unable to get any movement out of the other side (ie the Church)'. In February 1962, the situation had still not advanced: 'Work is, and becomes, increasingly difficult on practically anything now because of the multiplicity of persons of one sort or another involved. However, that seems to be the modern trend' (Forty to Grimes, 06/02/62). There were also problems with financing the site, as the RMLEC was at this point coming to the end of its work and its excavation budget: 'the time is fast approaching when our last grant from the Ministry will be exhausted...so that in any further work that we do we

shall be spending our own money without hope of recovering any part of it from an outside source. The present position is that we are really marking time and waiting to tackle St Alban's in Wood Street. The delays in this seem to have been endless' (Grimes to Denham, 21/03/62). The situation was made even more desperate because the site had already been sold for redevelopment, and there was a limited amount of time available for excavation; the building of the new police station was due to begin there in August.

The removal of the bodies was finally carried out in April 1962 and excavation started in the churchyard in early May. Problems with the clearance of the church itself continued throughout May, although the site notebook records that by June, work had progressed to the northernmost part of the church. The RMLEC remained on the site until 15 December 1962 as the developers left some areas open for further investigation. The site notebook shows that Professor Grimes visited the site on average once a week: once in May 1962, four times in June, five times in July, four times in August, five times in October, six times in November and once in December. On 17 March 1963, he made the final entry in the site notebook after a visit to the site during redevelopment. Letters in the correspondence file indicate that Grimes was interested in examining the area to the south of the tower (formerly called 36A Wood Street) where cellars were being cleared in late 1964, however, there is no record of any corresponding visit.

The site archive consists of one site notebook, two finds records books and the associated artefacts, correspondence incorporating the work at St Alban's, St Swithun's, Cannon Street and on the City Wall at Noble Street, section drawings from the churchyard and north transept, and several plans of the church and churchyard. There are also 67 photographs of the excavations.

Generally, work on the site appears to have moved from north to south. Only four of the cuttings have been numbered (1, 2, 3 and 5) and these were all located outside the main body of the church; cutting 1 in the western part of the north east chapel, cutting 2 in the churchyard directly north of the chapel, cutting 3 in the eastern part of the chapel and extending eastwards beyond it and cutting 5 to the east of the apse. From the photographic record, it can be seen that long narrow trenches running east–west were also opened in the north churchyard area (Fig 96). It is assumed that trenches were opened in the same way in the main body of the church itself. Although most of the photographs show large areas of the interior stripped, they were presumably taken after the intervening baulks had been removed. Indeed, although most of the images are undated and unlabelled, a significant proportion seem to have been taken near (if not at) the end of the project.

For the first month of the excavation, attention was focused in the churchyard to the north of the church, gradually moving eastwards into the north-east chapel and the area north of the apse during June and July.

Excavation in these areas produced evidence of Roman occupation on the site in the form of a series of walls running north–south as well as pits, ditches and a road (Grimes 1968, 35–7). From the end of July to mid August, investigations were carried out around the tower at the west end of the site, revealing the foundations of the tower, the remains of a post Fire burial vault and further Roman features. Moving eastwards during

Fig 94 St Alban's church (WFG22): west end of burnt out church prior to demolition, looking eastwards across Wood Street. (Guildhall Library)

Fig 95 St Alban's church (WFG22): south side of burnt out church prior to demolition, showing blocked south aisle wall: Wood Street to left. (Guildhall Library)

Fig 96 St Alban's church (WFG22): RMLEC excavations in the northern churchyard revealed the remains of Roman buildings and Late Saxon pits. The vertical 3 × 1ft scale (c 1m) stands below the junction of the medieval north aisle wall (supported by timbering) and the projecting north-east chapel. (GLA GR784)

late August, the Roman features to the east of the apse were excavated and the south-eastern corner of the late medieval church was examined. Professor Grimes was away in Wales on field courses and also visited Italy in late August and September, and his notes resume in early October when the north wall of the church was examined. During the rest of October, the south wall of the nave was excavated (Fig 97), and areas to the south and east of the tower were cleared. In November, the south chapel and south aisle were excavated and further work was carried out in the north aisle. Work appears to have continued until the last possible moment in the south aisle during early December, and Grimes revisited this area when he returned to the site in March 1963.

Archaeology of St Alban's

The evidence for Roman occupation on this site has been discussed by Grimes (1968, 35–7) and those features have also been re-evaluated as part of the publication of the Grimes London Archive by the Museum of London (Shepherd forthcoming). The following summary of the development of the medieval church building is based on Grimes' published comments (1968, 203–9) and examination of the unpublished archive. All imperial measurements have been converted to metric, and relative levels discussed where it proved possible to establish what was being used as a datum in 1962. The finds from St Alban from the post-Roman period were extremely sparse. Only four contexts, all of which were outside the main body of the church, produced artefacts of this period.

Fig 97 St Alban's church (WFG22): RMLEC excavations in south-western angle of nave of the late medieval church, showing structural succession. The 3 × 1ft (c 1m) scale rests against the later medieval pier foundation above which are the footings of the late seventeenth-century church, which are laid over the remains of the south wall of the early medieval church, to left of scale. Just visible at base of photo to right of scale is the top of a Roman wall. (GLA GR752)

The finds are catalogued by bag number and are discussed below. Grimes' published sequence of the development of the church shows six construction phases from its postulated eighth–ninth century origins to the Wren rebuilding after the Great Fire (Fig 98):

Phase 1   'simple nave' with chancel at east end, possible porticus or tower to west: dated to eighth or ninth century

Phase 2   north and south chapels added to chancel and west tower is built/consolidated: dated to fourteenth or fifteenth century.

Phase 3   chapels extended west forming north and south aisles: dated fourteenth or fifteenth century

Phase 4   north transept added: dated to fourteenth or fifteenth century

Phase 5   brickwork in south aisle identified as part of the Inigo Jones rebuild of 1633–4

Phase 6   church as rebuilt by Wren after Great Fire of 1666

A substantial revision of that sequence is offered here (Figs 99 and 100), and can be summarised thus:

Phase I   nave only early / mid eleventh century
Phase II   chancel added mid eleventh century
Phase III   tower added to NE corner late eleventh / early twelfth century
Phase IV   north aisle added thirteenth century
Phase V   south chapel added fourteenth century
Phase VI   south aisle added / tower moved to west end fifteenth century
Phase VII   north transept added late fifteenth century
Phase VIII   Inigo Jones rebuild early seventeenth century
Phase IX   Wren rebuild post 1666
Phase X   apse added 1858

Phase I

Grimes dated the first church to the eighth–ninth century through comparison with the church of All Hallows Barking, near the Tower of London and

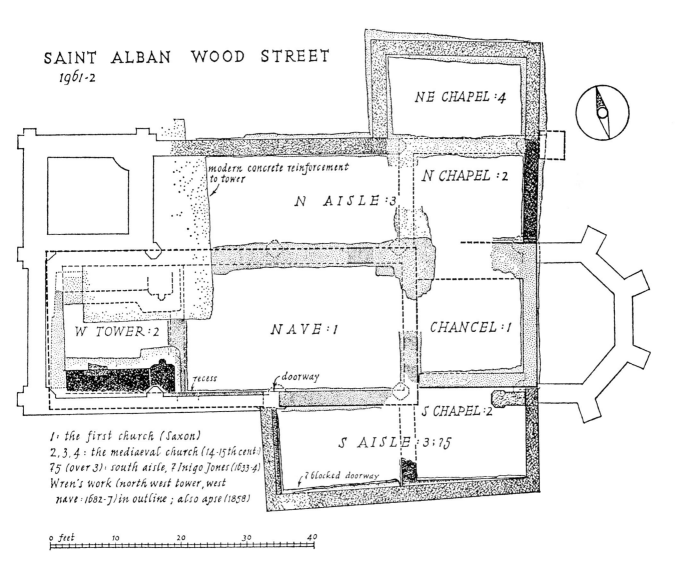

SAINT ALBAN WOOD STREET
1961-2

NE CHAPEL :4

modern concrete reinforcement to tower

N CHAPEL :2

N AISLE :3

W TOWER :2

NAVE :1

CHANCEL :1

recess

doorway

S CHAPEL :2

S AISLE :3;?5

?blocked doorway

1: the first church (Saxon)
2,3,4: the mediaeval church (14-15th cent.)
?5 (over 3): south aisle, ?Inigo Jones (1633-4)
Wren's work (north west tower, west
  nave: 1682-7) in outline; also apse (1858)

0 feet   10   20   30   40

Fig 98 St Albans (WFG22): phase plan of sequence drawn up and published by Professor Grimes (1968, 205: fig 50).

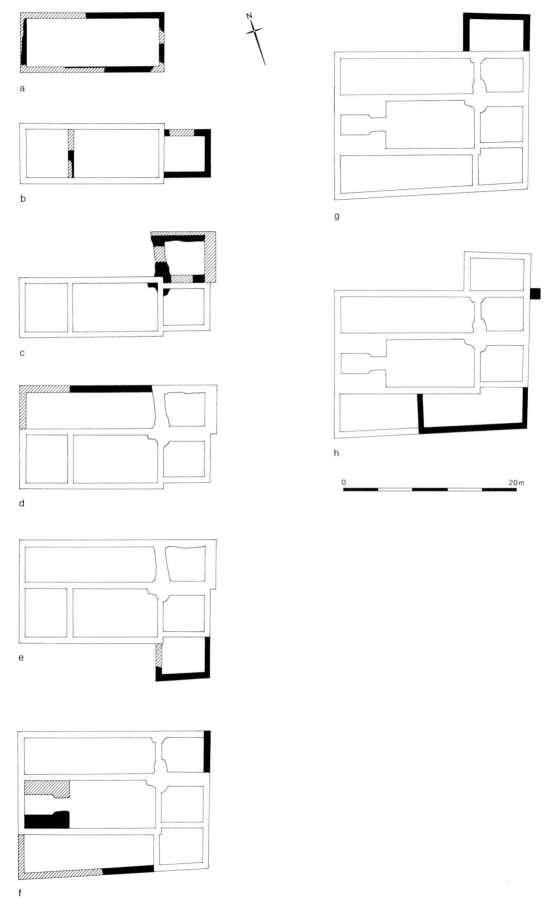

Fig 99 St Albans (WFG22): plan sequence to show suggested development of church based on walls and foundations recorded by the RMLEC.

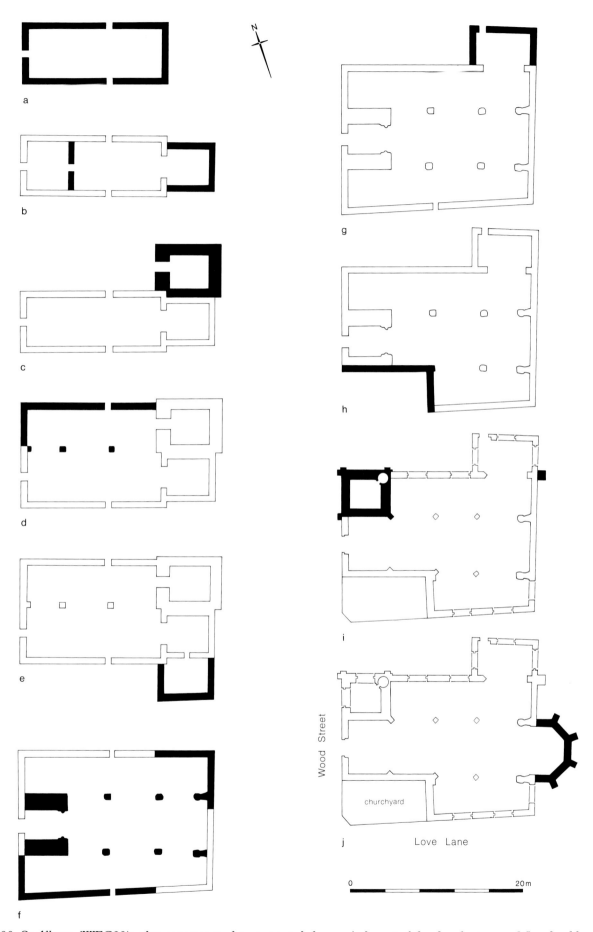

Fig 100 St Albans (WFG22): plan sequence to show suggested changes in layout of the church at ground floor level based on the structural sequence shown in Fig 98.

used Matthew Paris' assignation of St Alban's as
Offa's chapel to support his conclusion. In the light
of recent investigation, both of these assumptions can
be challenged and the date of the foundation of the
church revised. During the 1920s, an undercroft was
constructed beneath the nave and chancel of All
Hallows Barking and during the excavations, foundations of ragstone and reused Roman rubble and
worked stone were discovered under the chancel.
The destruction of the church during World War II
revealed an arch constructed of similar materials at
the south-west corner of the church and another
fragment of similar masonry on the north-west corner. These features indicate the dimensions of the
first church on this site, and it is these features and
proportions that Grimes uses in comparing the two
churches, commenting on the similarity of plan form
and wall thickness. All Hallows Barking was originally dated to the eighth–ninth century, but this date has
now been revised, and it is more likely that the first
church dates from the late tenth century at the earliest (Haslam 1988, 43; Cohen 1994, 26–9). In addition to this, it will be demonstrated below that the
materials used to construct the two churches are different, and that more convincing comparisons can be
found for St Alban's in terms of size, plan and construction types. Grimes' assumption that St Alban's
can be identified as Offa's chapel can be discounted
by the lack of evidence for any settlement, royal or
otherwise, in the Cripplegate area during the mid
Saxon period.

Two further pieces of evidence can be presented to
support a Late Saxon foundation date for St Alban's.
The loomweights excavated in the churchyard (see
below) are of late Saxon type and were sealed by a
deposit containing Late Saxon Shelly ware (dated
950–1050). It is extremely unlikely that these
loomweights could have been buried in consecrated
ground and so their deposition must pre-date the
building of the church. The first phase of church construction at St Alban's is more closely comparable to
developments at the churches of St Nicholas Acon
(Marsden 1965, 185–6) and St Bride's, (Milne, 1997)
rather than All Hallows Barking. The nave at St
Alban's measures 17.64m × 7.01m and the foundations are of ragstone, chalk and reused Roman rubble,
laid in gravel. These dimensions and make up are very
similar to those found at St Nicholas Acon (where the
first phase church was 10m, as surviving, × 8m), and
at St Bride's, which measured 18m × 7.4m. Both of
these churches have been dated to the early to mid
eleventh century, and it is this date range that is suggested here for the construction of St Alban's.

Phase II

Two other developments at St Alban's have also been
ascribed to the first phase of building by Grimes: the
north–south cross wall in the western part of the nave

and the extension of the chancel. Both of these features
are made of similar material to the nave foundations,
and Grimes regarded them as 'structurally though not
necessarily chronologically, later' than the nave. The
north–south cross wall has been interpreted as the
foundation of a tower. In spite of the medieval and
post-medieval disturbance in this area, the surviving
dimensions of this wall postulated as the east wall of an
Anglo-Saxon tower seem far too slight to have
supported such a feature. It might be that, instead, this
represents an entrance porch or vestibule leading into
Wood Street, in addition to the door discovered on the
south side of the church (Grimes 1968, 206) (Fig 101),
or a temporary feature marking an internal division of
the church. It could be suggested that this wall
represents the original west wall of the first church; but
the fact that the south wall of the nave
continues behind the late medieval foundations to the
west of the cross wall lends no weight to this suggestion
(Grimes 1968, 205–6).

Phase III

With regard to the construction of the chancel, Grimes
was unable to explain the peculiar thickness of the
north chancel wall (Figs 102 and 103). The make up
of the wall is similar to that of the nave (chalk, ragstone
and reused Roman rubble, laid in gravel), and appears
to be of one build. In his published account, however,
he does not mention the corresponding thickness of the
west wall of the 'north chapel'. In the field notebook,
this wall is described as being constructed of large
chalk blocks set in a yellowish, sandy mortar. It is suggested here that the unusual thickness of the north

*Fig 101 St Alban's church (WFG22): RMLEC excava-
tions looking south. The 3 × 1ft scale (c 1m) stands in the
Late Saxon doorway, beyond which can be seen the later
south aisle walls. (GLA GR792)*

chancel wall and the surviving part of the west wall of the 'north chapel' are in fact the remains of a north-east tower built very soon after the chancel. The use of chalk and a yellowish mortar suggests a construction date in the late eleventh to early twelfth century.

There are several facts to support this suggestion. There is no reason for the north chancel wall to be of such massive construction because of any underlying features that might have led to problems with subsidence. In fact, excavation in this area showed that the church walls at this junction lie almost directly on top of

Fig 102 St Alban's church (WFG22): north and south corners of nave and chancel wall foundations revealed by RMLEC excavations. Scale 3 × 1ft (c 1m). (GLA GR804)

Fig 103 St Alban's church (WFG22): detail showing north-east corner of nave revealed by RMLEC excavations. Scale 3 × 1ft (c 1m). (GLA GR802)

Roman masonry. According to Grimes' published plan, it also appears that the east wall of the 'north chapel' was rebuilt, possibly during the later medieval period. At the junction of this wall with that of the later chapel to the north, a buttress has been added. This buttress is dated to the seventeenth century on the plan of the church, which appears in the Royal Commission on the Historical Monuments volume (1929); inferring that it was either added by Wren after the Great Fire, or by Inigo Jones during repair work carried out before the Fire. Whether this buttress dates to the pre or post-Fire period, the reason for its construction could very well be because these thinner walls were subsiding into an earlier foundation trench, that is, the deep foundation trench needed for a tower. In his field notes, Grimes comments that the foundation of his 'north chapel' wall was 9ft (2.7m) below the modern ground surface.

The location of a tower on the northern, rather than on the western, side of the church perhaps requires comment. The confines of the land owned by the church and the constraints of the surrounding street pattern are prime reasons for the building of the tower on the north rather than the west side of the church. Unable to build into Wood Street, St Alban's extended northwards. Although this development is by no means a common one, comparisons can be found in the City of London. At the church of All Hallows the Great, bounded on three sides by roads and with a disputed southern boundary (see Schofield 1994, 83–4), the pre-Fire building had a tower in the centre of the north side of the church, while at St Nicholas Acon, the possible foundations of a tower can be seen in the north-east corner (Marsden 1965, 185–6). Grimes' own excavations at St Bride's revealed the existence of a twelfth-century tower located in the centre of the south side of the church, later moved to the west end (Milne 1997), and further excavations of City churches might expose other early church towers in similar locations. Even among those towers sited at the west end, arguably the more common location, there is great variety of position: some are placed in the centre, some at the north and some at the southern corners. In sum, it might be that the builders of churches in the earlier medieval period were more constrained by the physical limitations of the church site rather than standardised methods and forms of church construction.

Phase IV

Grimes dates all his phases 2, 3 and 4 to the fourteenth and fifteenth centuries and comments that there is no evidence of Norman work. He believes that the two chapels are built first, (although they are not necessarily contemporary), and the west tower is consolidated during this phase. The chapels are then extended into aisles (Phase 3) and in Phase 4, the north-east chapel is added. It is suggested here that the chancel was added to the nave soon after its construction and a north-east tower built in the late eleventh or early twelfth century. After this, rather than the construction of the south chapel, it is suggested that development continued on the north side of the church with the addition of the north aisle. Grimes' field notes describes the make up of the north aisle wall as follows:

'[the] upper part is composed mainly of chalk rubble in the core, with ashlar clunch on inner face originally rendered in a thin yellowish plaster still surviving in places below Wren's floor line, with a thicker pale plaster below. There are irregular brick patches in various places towards the west (tower) end on the inner face. Externally the wall was also rendered in a thick greyish plaster (?nineteenth century as surviving) false-pointed. The face beneath is largely knapped flint closely set to the top of the chamfered plinth, but stone material also occurs and again there are brick patches. Below the plinth is dressed rubble of Kentish rag, resting on a double offset foundation the upper part of which is a line of heavy ragstone blocks the lower, to the base chalk entirely. The offset is a simple chamfered block, of Reigate stone, weathered and battered. Very plain with traces of a later plaster rendering, but there are one or two good pieces to show the original sectioning'.

The varied make up of this wall indicates several periods of rebuilding. The chalk and ragstone wall with its Reigate stone plinth represents the first phase of the north aisle, built butting up against the north-east tower.

Through comparison with other church excavations in London, the use of chalk or ragstone with yellow mortar/plaster has been tentatively dated to the mid twelfth to early thirteenth century (Cohen 1994, 46–53) and the presence of Reigate stone further suggests a construction date in the thirteenth century. Reigate stone was used in large quantities in London from the eleventh century onwards, initially on royal projects, for example at Westminster Abbey and in large public works such as London Bridge in 1176 (Clifton-Taylor 1972, 117). The use of this stone in a parish church such as St Alban's would not have occurred during the earliest period of the use of the stone when it was in demand by royal and secular authorities, but might have been more freely available when supply increased, possibly to compensate for the lack of Caen stone imported after the loss of territory in Normandy in the early thirteenth century (Tatton-Brown 1990, 76). It is suggested here that the external flint facing represents fifteenth-century work and the internal and external brick patches the repair work of the mid seventeenth century (see below).

Phase V

The techniques used in the construction of the south chapel are very different to those found on the north side of the church. Grimes' excavations revealed two well built ragstone arches in the south and east walls of the south chapel (Figs 104 and 105). Foundation arches have been found on several church excavations in the City, for example at All Hallows Gracechurch (Bloe 1948), St Dionis Backchurch, St Stephen Coleman (Cohen 1994, 51–2), St Michael Bassishaw (Eeles 1910; Cohen 1995, 315–20) and St Bride's (Milne 1997, 38). This technique was widely employed in London in both domestic and religious buildings during the fourteenth century and the first half of the fifteenth century (Schofield et al 1990, 167) and it is this period that is suggested here for the construction of the south chapel. The pattern of the streets surrounding the church provide further evidence regarding the development of the building. Since construction on the south side of the church would have encroached on Love Lane, it is more likely that the church would have been extended onto the available land to the north first. The construction of the south chapel and its later extension into an aisle changed the alignment of Love Lane.

Phase VI

The fifteenth century saw further adaptations to the church. The western wall of the south chapel was largely removed and the south wall was extended the full length of the church to create an aisle (Fig 106). The north-east tower was taken down and the east wall rebuilt, and a new tower was built within the old wall of the Saxon nave at the west end. Other renovations, such as the facing of the north aisle wall with flint, might also have been carried out at this point. All this rebuilding produced a large church with a regular, well proportioned plan: a nave and chancel with arcaded aisles and a central western tower. The respond for the easternmost point of the arcade on the south side of the church was revealed during excavation (Fig 107); it coincided with a small group of medieval tiles, believed to represent the floor level of the

Fig 104 St Alban's church (WFG22): east end of south chapel showing foundation arch as revealed by RMLEC. Scale: 3 × 1ft (c 1m). (GLA GR768)

Fig 105 St Alban's church (WFG22): arched foundation supporting south wall of south chapel, revealed by RMLEC. (GLA GR777)

Fig 106 St Alban's church (WFG22): detail showing junction of south chapel and later south aisle wall revealed by RMLEC. Scale 3 × 1ft (c 1m). (GLA GR788)

late medieval church. A further indication of arcading is revealed only in the photographic record (Fig 108). This photograph, probably taken near the beginning of excavations within the body of the church, shows a large, roughly circular mass of stonework, which corresponds with the position of the late seventeenth-century pier in the centre of the south wall of the church. The mouldings of the blocked door in the south aisle suggest a late medieval date as does the surviving pier of the tower arch jamb at the west end of the church (Fig 109). A date of construction in the fifteenth century is suggested by Stow's record of the then surviving monuments in the church (Wheatley 1956, 265–6). The long list of prominent citizens buried there in the fifteenth century, which includes three mayors, suggests that St Alban's was increasingly patronised during this period.

Phase VII

In the fifteenth century there might also have been the addition of the north-east chapel. Grimes made very little comment on this feature, other than to note that it appeared to be late medieval in date and abutted the north aisle wall (Grimes 1968, 208).

Phase VIII

Grimes' phase five concerns the early seventeenth-century repairs carried out by Inigo Jones. It is difficult to differentiate between Jones' work of the early seventeenth century and Wren's of the later seventeenth century, but while it is known that the church was 'dilapidated', it is suggested here that the church could only afford more minor repairs and alterations before the Great Fire. Jones might have been responsible for the brick patching found internally and externally on the north aisle wall, the construction of the buttress on the east side of the church, and the truncating of the south aisle together with the blocking of the door leading into it. It might be that the church, no longer patronised by the wealthy as it was during the fifteenth century, was obliged by the early seventeenth century to sell property in order to afford repairs. Thus the south aisle was shortened and the land sold off for commercial purposes. The Ogilby and Morgan map of 1676 confirms that this happened before the Great Fire as it shows two separate units on the south-west corner of the St Alban's site.

Phase IX

Grimes' final phase 6 is the Wren rebuilding after the Great Fire of 1666. In common with Wren's work on many of the City churches, substantial amounts of the

Fig 107 St Alban's church (WFG22): east end of south chapel showing foundation arch and scar of arcade respond foundation revealed by RMLEC. Scale 3 × 1ft (c 1m). (GLA GR763)

pre-Fire stonework appear to have been incorporated in the rebuilding of the church. The work was carried out for a comparatively small sum, and Grimes' excavations showed that Wren largely followed the late medieval ground plan of the church, deviating only at the west end, where he moved the tower from the centre to the north-west corner. In addition to reusing the foundations of the church, photographs of the bomb damaged church taken during the 1950s reveal a considerable amount of upstanding medieval walling incorporated into the super-structure of the building (Fig 110).

Finds from the St Alban's site

Bag no 3 Only one sherd of post-Roman pottery was recovered from a north-east (unnumbered) cutting in the north churchyard. It came from the base of a much disturbed deposit of black soil, which also contained a considerable amount of Roman pottery. The sherd has recently been identified as a strap handle with applied thumbed impression, possibly of Thetford ware, and dated to 900–1100.

Bag no 15 The largest and most closely dated assemblage of bun-shaped loomweight fragments yet recorded from the City was recovered by the RMLEC from a square pit that lay to the north of St Alban's church in cutting 2. There is one complete example, which was consolidated after excavation, and evidence of at least sixteen more. All are made from the locally occurring brick earth. Since many of the fragments were charred they might represent the remains

Fig 108 St Alban's church (WFG22): general view of RMLEC excavations looking south towards Love Lane, showing south wall of nave with pier base to west. (GLA GR794)

of a burnt loom, a circumstance shared by other examples from London (Pritchard 1984, 65). The weights from the St Alban's site came from a layer in the pit containing sherds of Late Saxon Shelly ware dating from 950–1050 (bag no 16). This suggests that the associated loom went out of use no later than the early eleventh century. According to the field notes, fragments of daub were found with the weights, but these were not retained by the RMLEC. Those fragments might have represented the structure that housed the loom, a building that would have been dismantled before St Alban's church was constructed.

Bun-shaped loomweights have been found on many London excavations, usually only in groups of two to four, but often without associated dating evidence or from unstratified contexts (Boddington and Rhodes 1979, 29–30; Pritchard 1984, 65–6; Wheeler 1935, 154–5). The group from the St Alban's site are therefore an unusual and important find, presumably representing a burnt loom that had been in use in the neighbouring property

<6> three conjoining fragments; no inclusions; partly charred
<7> complete loomweight broken in three pieces, now restored; flint and pebble inclusions; partly charred

<8> two conjoining fragments, attempt at consolidation visible; very occasional flint inclusion
<9> two conjoining fragments; small flint inclusion; very slightly charred
<10> four conjoining fragments, consolidated; very occasional small flint and quartz grain inclusions
<11> two conjoining fragments; quartz grains visible
<12> two conjoining fragments; no inclusions
<13> one fragment with quartz grains; slightly charred
<14> one fragment with quartz grains; occasional flint and pebble inclusions
<15> one fragment with quartz grains; very occasional inclusions of small pebble; possible brand mark?
<16> two conjoining fragments with quartz grains; very roughly made
<17> one large piece and seven conjoining fragments; quartz grains and very occasional flint inclusions; slightly charred
<18> one fragment; very occasional pebble inclusions; slightly charred
<19> one fragment with quartz grains
<20> one fragment; very occasional pebble inclusions with possible indications of organic temper in section; possible brand mark on side; faint finger impression; joins with <23>
<21> eight non-joining small fragments

Fig 109 St Alban's church (WFG22): late medieval pier and tower foundations revealed by RMLEC. (GLA GR756)

<22> one fragment; very occasional pebble inclusions; evidence of attempted consolidation but does not seem to join any other fragment in surviving assemblage; groove caused by vertical thread visible on both sides

<23> one fragment; very occasional pebble inclusions; slightly charred; joins with <20>

<24> one fragment; occasional pebble inclusions; evidence of attempted consolidation but does not seem to join any other fragment in surviving assemblage

Bag no 16 From the upper part of the 'square' pit. The sherds are of Late Saxon Shelly ware.

Bag no 36 Two sherds of Early Surrey ware and Early Medieval Sandy ware were recovered from a possible pit to the north of St Mary Aldermanbury, to the east of St Alban's, by contractors working on the site. The exact location of the finds was not inspected because it had been destroyed.

St Alphage and Elsing Spital (WFG 17 and 18)

The report on the work at St Alphage (WFG17 and 18) is more of a standing buildings survey than an excavation and will be presented in three parts. Consideration will first be given to the original site of the late Saxon church, which was initially built onto the City wall while the second section briefly deals with its relocation in 1538, when it occupied part of the priory and hospital of St Mary Elsing after the Dissolution (Fig 111). The third section looks at the evidence for the Elsing Spital itself, which was founded in the fourteenth century. Although the RMLEC did not actually excavate on the sites of either the church or the priory as far as is known, Professor Grimes did uncover part of the only surviving wall of the Late Saxon church in 1949, and ensured its survival as a visible ancient

Fig 110 St Alban's church (WFG22): interior of burnt out church looking towards east end with medieval masonry visible in north aisle wall. (Guildhall Library)

monument. He was also retained as the Corporation of London's consultant during the period when the tower of the medieval priory (also confusingly known as St Alphage) was saved from demolition in the early 1960s.

The first church of St Alphage

The church of St Alphage (or Alphege) was dedicated to a Saxon saint (954–1012) who once served as a monk at Deerhurst in Gloucester. He would therefore have been familiar with some of the buildings that were the subject of the major archaeological and architectural study of that famous site (eg Rahtz 1976; Rahtz et al 1997). He later became the Bishop of Winchester (AD 994–1006), and would have officiated in the minster excavated in the 1960s (Biddle 1970) in another ground breaking archaeological project. His next post saw him elevated to Archbishop of Canterbury in 1006: part of the Saxon minster church over which he would have presided has also been excavated, following the recent investigations below the floor of the nave. In 1012 the Archbishop was brutally murdered by Danes at Greenwich, reportedly on

the site over which the first church dedicated to him was raised. On the instigation of a contrite King Cnut, the body of the martyr was moved from St Paul's in London to Canterbury in 1023 following his canonisation, and was then interred on the north side of the high altar.

The existence of a City church dedicated to St Alphage is implied in a reference dated to 1068 in which William the Conqueror confirms that the gift of the advowson lay with St Martin le Grande (Baddeley 1922, 29): the church was certainly established by the early twelfth century, according to the muniments of Westminster Abbey (1316, no 138: Schofield 1994, 92). The earliest documentary reference to a rector serving the church is to one Osbert the Priest, who had been appointed to that post by 1137 (Baddeley 1922, 30). The church itself was built 'near unto the wall of the City by Cripplegate' (Wheatley 1956, 264). There are few surviving written records to illuminate its history and development, but chantries are mentioned in 1349 (William Payn), 1385 (Edmund Harengeye) and 1450 (John Graunt); there were chapels to St Katherine and St George, and two chaplains serving there in 1379 (McHardy 1977, 22), as well as a steeple

Fig 111 The northern facade of the second church of St Alphage, built in 1913, masked the remains of a fourteenth-century tower that was burnt out in the 1940s and partially demolished shortly after this photo was taken in 1960. To the right is part of the City wall onto which the first church of St Alphage was built in the eleventh century. (Guildhall Library)

that incorporated a bell frame and bells worth £20 in the early sixteenth century (Baddeley 1922, 23–4). By 1536 the church was in such poor condition that the parishioners petitioned parliament to be allowed to move into part of the adjacent priory (St Mary Elsing), which, together with all such institutions, were dissolved by order of the King. This wish was duly granted, and the chancel of the hospital chapel was converted to serve as the new parish church.

The old church on London Wall was then dismantled (or rather the southern, eastern and western walls were demolished) and many of the building materials, fixtures and fittings were sold to defray the cost of the rebuilding programme. A lease dated to 1587 makes mention of a 'tenement lately erected... between the gate called Cripplegate on the west, one parcel of ground now used for the churchyard of St Alphage ... to the east ... the Wall ... on the north part and the Queen's highway on the south part', which some have argued might represent the bounds of the church (Baddeley 1922, 24). That property, however, probably lay to the west of the church, since another lease signed in 1588 records the transfer of the parcel of land that specifically comprised 'the ground and soil of the old parish church of St Alphage'. In this document the site of the church does not seem to have been built on by the late sixteenth century, since it is described as 'sometime parcel of the ground and soil of the old parish church of St Alphage... lately broken down and now or late used for a carpenter's yard' and was subsequently leased to another carpenter, one Peter Cobb (Westman 1987, 22). This situation finds confirmation in Stow's survey, which, when recording the site of the church, notes that 'the plot thereof (was) made a carpenter's yard with saw-pits' (Wheatley 1956, 264). The plot was measured as being 65ft (20.15m) long against the City wall to the north, 62ft (19.20m) along the street frontage on its southern side and 27ft (8.40m) wide at each end (Baddeley 1922, 24).

Archaeology at St Alphage

In 1949 when the remains of brick walls from the early nineteenth-century buildings had been cleared from the northern face of the City wall during the RMLEC investigations of the Cripplegate buildings and St Alphage sites (WFG17 and 18), a substantial exposure of medieval masonry was eventually revealed (Figs 112 and 115). Part of this stonework clearly represents the north wall of St Alphage's church, a blind wall in which courses of ragstone and knapped flint together with putlog holes and a plinth course have all been observed. The church therefore incorporated the City wall into its fabric, a feature observed in other London churches such as St Martin's at Ludgate, or at All Hallows on the Wall, for example.

The visible medieval masonry on the north face of St Alphage is clearly of at least two main phases (Fig 116), with undistinguished stonework marking the lower levels, but with the more decorative fourteenth-century flint-banded walling rising above that to a level

Fig 112 The remains of the church of St Alphage, as first revealed after bomb damage on the Fore Street site (WFG17), looking south-east before the ground level was lowered and later brick walling removed. (GLA GR410)

higher than the adjacent fifteenth-century brick crenellations. This shows that the roof and tower of the church must have ultimately projected visibly above the general line of the top of the town wall. Given that the eastern limit of the church was so clearly identifiable, it then proved possible to suggest the extent of the original church on the ground, working with the dimensions given in the 1588 document (as is indicated in Fig 117).

Fig 113 Detail showing medieval masonry with knapped flint courses on the north face of St Alphage, after clearance of bomb rubble (WFG17). (GLA GR412)

Fig 114 Part of the medieval masonry on the north face of St Alphage (WFG17), partially obscured by later brick walling. (GLA GR411)

Fig 115 Removal of the brick wall seen in Fig 114 reveals further medieval masonry from the north face of the church wall (WFG17). (GLA GR413)

The exposed north facing elevation of the church was drawn up with the help of the Corporation of London's surveyors and the results promptly published (Forty 1955), while Professor Grimes reproduced a similar illustration in his own report (Grimes 1968,80, fig 19; see also Fig 10). In addition to the work of the RMLEC and the Corporation of London, who subsequently conserved this section of walling as an ancient monument, a study was also made by the Museum of London's archaeological team in 1986. This was part of a major scheme in conjunction with the Corporation to manage its historic sites, and incorporated a photogrammetric survey of the wall. The report on that work published by Andrew Westman extended the observations of Professor Grimes (site code APG86; Westman 1987): the interpretations he presents are not challenged here, and are summarised below.

The church seems to lie over the projected site of a Roman interval tower, which would have been some 3.4m square (Grimes 1968, 3–4). There is no direct evidence to suggest that remnants of such a tower (given that it did exist) influenced the positioning of the church or its own tower. Indeed, the fact that the line of the north wall of the church perceptibly diverges from the alignment of the City wall itself suggests that the defences were in need of substantial repair in this area at the time when the church was erected. The lowest surviving visible section of the Late Saxon church wall comprises dressed ragstone rubble laid in rough courses with frequent reused tile fragments. It extends for some 15m east–west and stands up to 2m high,

with no evidence for doors or windows. Unlike the medieval City wall to the east, which had a pronounced batter before it was cut back by a later cellar, the face of the Late Saxon church wall is vertical.

Above that rubblework and rising to a height of more than 4m the wall has been substantially refaced or heightened with courses of close jointed ragstone ashlar separated by courses of knapped flint. Professor Grimes noted the similarity of the fourteenth-century St Katherine's Chapel in the infirmary at Westminster Abbey with the wall at St Alphage, commenting that the structures must have been built with the same hand (Grimes 1968, 81). Although that might be pressing the parallel too hard, there seems no reason to suggest that the two structures were not broadly contemporary. Once again, there is no evidence for windows let into the City wall here, and thus the church would only have been lit from windows in its southern and eastern walls, given that a tower occupied most of the west end.

The second parish church of St Alphage

The old parish church had become ruinous by the early sixteenth century. When the neighbouring priory and hospital was dissolved in 1536, the parishioners of St Alphage successfully petitioned parliament to be allowed to take over the tower and chancel 'of the said church of our Blessed Lady the virgin called Elsing Spital' (Baddeley 1922, 23). Some modifications followed, and a new parish

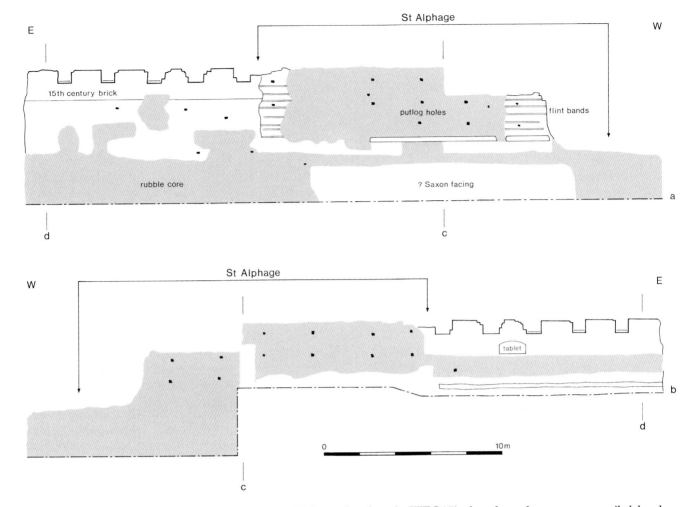

Fig 116 Surviving section of the City wall in St Alphage churchyard (WFG17), based on the surveys compiled by the RMLEC and the Corporation of London: (see also Fig 10) (a) external elevation, showing part of north wall of St Alphage church extending for c 15m east–west butted up against City wall with fifteenth-century brick crenellations to east; (b) internal elevation, with most of faced masonry removed.

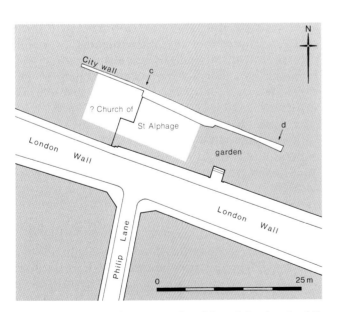

Fig 117 Plan showing suggested position of the church of St Alphage from the eleventh to the sixteenth century, in relation to 1940 street plan. The north wall of the church had been built onto the City wall itself: see Fig 116.

church was established. The situation recorded here is thus similar to that for the neighbouring priory church of St Bartholomew the Great in West Smithfield or Christchurch Greyfriars in Newgate Street for example, where the nave of the conventual church was demolished but the crossing and chancel were modified to serve as post-Dissolution parish churches. Unusually for a church within the City walls, St Alphage survived (just) the Great Fire of London in 1666, although the rectory was destroyed. Nevertheless, the church was rebuilt in 1777 (Fig 118), although the base of the tower and other fragments of medieval walling were still incorporated in the new structure. In 1913 a grandiose Gothic facade was built onto the London Wall frontage (Fig 119), but did not ultimately increase the viability of this church, which was serving an ever dwindling number of parishioners. Just ten years later, the parish was finally amalgamated with that of St Mary Aldermanbury (Carter 1925). The nave of St Alphage was then demolished, leaving just the ancient tower and the vestibule.

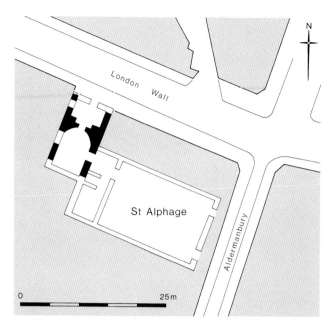

Fig 118 Location of the surviving tower and vestibule of St Mary Elsing (shown in black) in relation to the parish church of St Alphage as rebuilt in the eighteenth century and the streets as they were in 1923. The church was subsequently declared redundant and the nave demolished (WFG17).

From parish church to ancient monument

Thus by 1923 little of the second parish church of St Alphage remained, beyond those elements of the much earlier priory building, which had been incorporated into the church. The Blitz saw that much modified tower burnt out though still surviving as a roofless standing structure (see Fig 119). When Francis Forty gave the Bannister Fletcher lecture to the London Society in 1956, he mentioned the tower of St Alphage, claiming that 'little if anything agreeable to the eye now remains'. Nevertheless he had been persuaded that the remains were of some merit, since he also reported that they were 'being protected' even though they stood on the very northern edge of the new wide Route 11 (the street now called London Wall), which was then under construction. In 1958, following the City's acquisition of the site, officials from the Corporation and from the London County Council recommended that the height of the tower be lowered to 18ft (*c* 5.5m), but this was clearly not done. Consequently, in 1960, a Dangerous Notice was served upon it (Ellen Barnes personal communication: EH File no LRF 3689): the last photographs of it were taken in March of that year (see Fig 111). A meeting of the Town Planning Committee on 25 April 1961 rejected the proposal from the site developers to demolish the ruins 'since the remains of the church as now standing are scheduled as an Ancient Monument, they must be preserved at all costs' (CoL Town Clerks Files 1958–64 Ser: ITP/RU4/CPT no 3 1960–61). Some demolition was undertaken subsequently since the early twentieth-century Gothic facade was removed, as were the later

brick additions that had, until then, masked much of the medieval stonework. Acting on the advice of their consultant, the Corporation ensured that the remains were retained in the new development on the northern side of Route 11. The line of the proposed road, however, could not be compromised and the southern end of the church had to be demolished. There was, however, a redesign of the line of the elevated pedestrian walkway to accommodate the surviving top of the flint-faced tower. Thus retained, the subsequent consolidation of the monument involved the addition of a concrete buttress, the insertion of at least one steel girder into the tower and substantial repointing.

St Mary Elsing

The surviving tower was once part of the priory and hospital founded by Sir William Elsing, and dedicated to St Mary, from which components the names of St Mary Elsing or the Elsing Spital were derived. It was one of a number of such institutions that were established in and around the City to support the sick and the poor (Rawcliffe 1984). Stow's survey records that the hospital was founded in 1329 'for sustenation of one hundred blind men' although Elsing's will mentions 'poor blind of both sexes' (Baddeley 1922, 200). The site extended from Aldermanbury in the east to Philip Lane in the west, fronting the City to the north and land belonging to the Brewers Company to the south (Baddeley 1922, 200; Carter 1925, 40: see also Fig 120). The new hospital was not built on an empty site but where there 'was of old time a house of nuns; which house being in great decay..' (Wheatley 1956, 263): arguably traces of that older convent might have been identified in the surviving fabric of the medieval tower, as is discussed below.

The hospital's modest complement of 32 beds was soon increased to 60 and by 1342 had become an Augustinian priory for regular canons. It has been argued that a small order of lay sisters might also have been resident applying their skills in caring for the poor and infirm, since a will of 1372 refers to 'sisters' and a 'house in the close that was assigned to them' (Page 1909, 537). In addition to that building and the chapel, Stow records that there was a cloister, houses for the prior and for canons and other lodgings, as well as accommodation for the poor (Wheatley 1956, 264).

Then, '...after two centuries of beneficent work the hospital was taken into the rapacious maw of that king who despoiled so many other kindred institutions throughout the country' to quote Sir John Baddeley's description of the dissolution of the priory in 1537 (Baddeley 1922, 201). Although much of the precinct fell into private hands, the east end of that priory church was sold for £100 to the parishioners of St Alphage to serve as their new parish church. The deeds proclaimed that:

'...the said parishioners may from henceforth have hold, occupy and enjoy to them and to their successors forever the church chancel with two

Fig 119 Part of the northern facade of St Alphage, which opens onto the old street called London Wall, was rebuilt in 1913. This is one of the last photographs of it, taken just prior to demolition in March 1960. (Guildhall Library)

SPECIMENS OF ANTIENT ARCHITECTURE
Exhibited in the Porch and Belfry of St Alphage London Wall:
FORMERLY THE CHAPEL OF ELSYNGE SPITAL.
With a Plan of Sion College and the Vicinity.

AN ARCH ON THE EAST SIDE OF THE PORCH.

AN ARCH IN THE WEST FRONT OF THE PRESENT BELFRY.

Plan of Sion College and the Vicinity

London, Published January 1813, by Robert Wilkinson, No 58 Cornhill.

Fig 120 'Specimens of Antient Architecture exhibited in the porch and Belfry of St Alphage London Wall, formerly the chapel of Elsing Spital, with a plan of Sion College and the vicinity': *early nineteenth-century illustration.* (Guildhall Library)

aisles on every side of the quire of the said church of our blessed Lady the Virgin called Elsing Spital within your said City of London, together with a chapel of John the Baptist next adjoining to Our Lady Chapel in the same church with the steeple of the same, lately belonging to the same priory' (Baddeley 1922, 23).

An account of the sale records that the chapel dedicated to John occupied what later became the vestibule of the parish church (Carter 1925, 29; Camps-Linney 1997, 12). Part of that therefore remains in the surviving monument. The Lady Chapel was probably in the south aisle just beyond the crossing (ie the mirror image of the chapel to John the Baptist). It was not included in the sale, and was demolished together with the north aisle (which became a range of private houses) and other parts of the building.

The fate of the rest of the hospital after the Dissolution seems to have been less drastic, and is described by Stow. Rather than wholesale demolition: 'the prior and canon's house with other lodgings were made a dwelling house; the churchyard is a garden plot, and a fair gallery on the cloister. The lodgings for the poor are translated into stabling for horses' (Wheatley 1956, 264). The properties were subsequently purchased in 1631 by the founders of Sion College who seem to have adapted many of the standing buildings: thus the broad outline of the medieval priory plan can be traced in the plan of the college, which survived until 1885 (Baddeley 1922, 201: see Fig 120).

The archaeology of St Mary Elsing

Thus a substantial section of walling from the medieval chapel survived the Dissolution, the Great Fire, the Blitz and subsequent urban renewal. It is indeed fortunate that the Corporation of London were persuaded to retain the tower after the war, since its subsequent study has suggested that it is a structure of some interest. The monument comprises the lowest two stages of the tower of the former priory chapel of St Mary Elsing standing some 8m tall and c 4.5m × 5m internally in plan, together with fragments of a vestibule to the north (Figs 121 and 122). At ground level, all that survives are two north–south walls of varying thickness and some 11m long, which are joined together by the pair of 5m high arches supporting the tower. Access is via a gate (usually locked) in a high fence on its northern side.

Although there are published accounts of the documentary history of the Elsing Spital (eg Baddeley 1922, 22–31; Carter 1925), little attention has been paid to the standing fabric, beyond the unillustrated description provided by the Royal Commission on the Historical Monuments of England, which was published after the body of the church had been demolished but before the tower had been burnt out in the Blitz (RCHM 1929). Since neither plan nor elevation of the standing remains could be located in the surviving papers of the Grimes

London Archive, it was decided that a fresh survey should be undertaken. This was achieved during a one week period in June 1996 with a team from University College London directed by the author with the assistance of Nathalie Cohen and Mike Webber. A plan was drawn up at 1:20 and outline elevations prepared. It was not possible to complete stone by stone drawings of all elevations in the time available, but a comprehensive photographic record was prepared by Kate Morris and Ken Walton from the Institute of Archaeology. By combining the data from the photos and the drawings, the basic elevations subsequently drawn up by Chrissie Harrison were used for the provisional phasing of the monument summarised below. A more detailed study of the history of the church was undertaken by Jane Camps-Linney as part of her undergraduate research at the Institute (Camps-Linney 1997): much of the information in this and the preceding section is a paraphrase of her research.

The recent study of the surviving remains of the tower and transept of the priory church has clearly shown that more than one phase of building is represented. It is suggested here that the construction of the early fourteenth-century priory chapel might have incorporated the remains of an earlier building, some of the evidence for which is described below. This is followed by summary descriptions of other main features related to the medieval monument.

Possible pre-priory building

The plan of the monument shows that the complex represented is not all of one build since the main eastern wall is slighter than the main western wall, being only 1m wide to the north of the tower (Fig 123). The elevations show that it has clearly been thickened and refaced below the tower itself. Study of the main east facing elevation on the eastern side of the tower where the thinner wall has not been refaced shows that the lower courses of walling comprise courses of ragstone rubble while the upper work is faced with knapped flint (Figs 124 and 125). There is an arched doorway some 1.75m wide cut through the wall with dressed quoins (Fig 126), and there are rebates on the eastern face, presumably to accommodate a door. The head of a blocked arch is visible 2m to the north (Fig 127) and this might be part of the same blocked feature visible on the opposite side of the wall, where a fragment of hood moulding is visible, cut by the large altar or tomb recess on the west facing elevation of the main east wall (Fig 128).

Interestingly an etching of the southern elevation of the church drawn up in c 1747 before it was substantially rebuilt shows that the threshold for the southern entrance was notably sunk below the contemporary ground level and that a blocked window or door is visible just below the level of the sills of the contemporary (possibly late medieval) windows (Baddeley 1922, 25). Again, the coursing is very different above and below the sill level. There therefore seems to be a case for suggesting that parts of the western and southern walls of

Fig 121 West side of St Alphage London Wall, showing the porch and belfry (part of the medieval Elsing Spital) exposed when buildings to the east were demolished in August 1880. (Guildhall Library)

a substantial masonry building were incorporated directly into the plan of the early fourteenth-century chapel, the internal floor of which was at a higher level than the original building. Other interpretations are of course possible: the blocked window apertures might represent lights for a crypt beneath the chancel, for example, although there is no trace of the roof level associated with it. Another suggestion is that the earlier building represents the earliest development of the new hospital, and that the tower and associated features were components of a major expansion.

On balance, it seems that the western wall and tower (which are all flint faced) were built over and against the levelled remains of an earlier building. Given that the general style and the mouldings on the arches would support a broadly fourteenth-century date for the tower itself, it would seem reasonable to suggest that the tower was built as part of the initial construction of the early fourteenth-century chapel, ie the work initiated by William Elsing from c 1330. If that is accepted, then the ragstone rubble walling represents part of a building that occupied the site before

it was purchased by Elsing. It could even be part of the earlier house of nuns that Stow noted as being in a decaying state, for example.

Spiral stairs

The next major phase saw the tower constructed against the western end of the earlier building. Significantly, the southern end of that wall is notably wider on plan than the northern, showing that it had been thickened and refaced during the rebuilding. The tower was supported on arches (Fig 129 and 130) and had an enclosed spiral stair rising clockwise from within the crossing in its north-east corner, lit by narrow windows (Fig 130). There was also evidence of a second stair, this time opening out into the nave or infirmary hall, but surviving solely as a scar on the west facing elevation of the west wall (Figs 129, 131 and 132). Although it is hard to be certain, this stair seems to have risen anticlockwise, judging by the orientation of the rubble scar. It therefore seems that both stairs could have been contemporary

Remains of the Priory of Elsing Spital, 1879.

Fig 122 The base of the medieval tower that formed the entrance to the later parish church of St Alphage, looking south, as drawn in 1879: the floor level shown here masks the plinths supporting the arch: compare with the present day view Fig 136. (Guildhall Library)

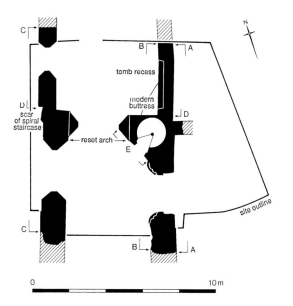

Fig 123 Plan of the surviving remains of the tower of St Mary Elsing (WFG17) as they are today (shown in black) with the edge of the sunken area around the monument shown in outline, based on survey conducted by UCL in 1996.

(rather than the survivor being a replacement for the scar), since the eastern one was for ascending, the western for descending.

Internal features

Other features associated with the priory chapel include the 'chancel arch', which has a cinquefoil headed niche set into the tympanum on its west facing side (Fig 133). This would once have accommodated a statue, presumably one showing Mary with the Holy Child on her left arm and a flowing branch in her right hand, since this is the composition shown on the seal of the priory (de Gray Birch 1887, 640 no Lxviii; Glendinning Nash 1919, 7), which is held by the British Museum. The form of the arch and its associated mouldings are broadly of fourteenth-century date.

Set to the north of that arch in the vestibule that formed part of the medieval chapel dedicated to John the Baptist is a recess with chamfered jambs and a seg-mental-pointed head some 2.25m long × 1m in height, now partially obscured by a concrete buttress. It is clearly a later addition to the wall into which it has been set, since it cuts through the blocked arch or hood moulding just visible beyond its northern edge (Figs 134 and 135). The recess might have been for an altar or more likely a tomb: indeed it has even been suggested that it marks that resting place of the founder of the hospital, William Elsing himself (Glendinning Nash 1919, 10).

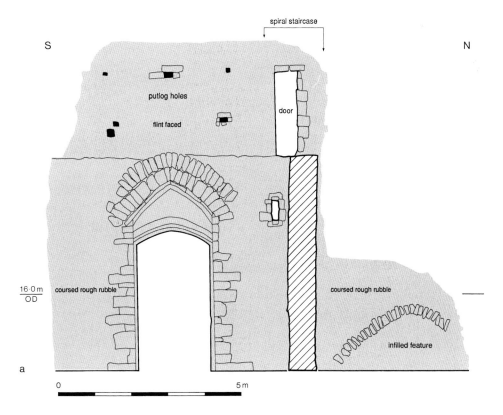

Fig 124 The surviving remains of St Mary Elsing (WFG17), surveyed by UCL in 1996: east-facing elevation of east wall, showing remains of possible pre-priory building below flint-faced addition to structure.

Fig 125 St Mary Elsing: view of east wall, facing east in 1996. The lower ragstone rubble walling has been heightened in the early fourteenth century with the addition of the flint-faced tower. The 1m scale rests against the stub of north wall of the late sixteenth-century parish church. (Ken Walton, *London Archaeological Research Facility*)

Fig 126 St Mary Elsing: mouldings at base of doorway with 5 × 100mm scale, recorded in 1996. (Ken Walton, *London Archaeological Research Facility*)

Fig 127 St Mary Elsing: blocked arch in east wall with 1m scale, recorded in 1996. (Ken Walton, *London Archaeological Research Facility*)

Structural problems

There is also evidence of structural problems, in that plinth heights and coursing in the columns are not consistent, suggesting either subsidence, setting out problems perhaps arising from the attempt to incorporate part of an older building into the east end of a new construction, or major repairs to a steeple that was prone to instability: indeed, a combination of all three is possible (Figs 136, 137 and 138). There is documented evidence for such structural modifications: the upper sections of the medieval steeple had been removed by 1718, following complaints from parishioners who also described leaning walls and sunken pillars (Carter 1925, 4), for example. The complaints bemoaning the danger of attending services in a church that was so old and ruinous continued until 1775, after which a major rebuilding of the main body of the church took place, although the lower stages of the much repaired medieval tower survived more or less intact (Baddeley 1922, 26).

Infirmary Hall and Chapel

It is assumed that the priory church would not have had a parochial nave, but was served simply by the Infirmary Chapel connected directly to the Infirmary Hall, broadly in the linear style of St Mary's Hospital, Chichester (Gilchrist 1995, 17–18). Certainly the site was too constricted by the presence of the street called London Wall on its northern side to accommodate the

'T'-shaped plan found at, for example, St Mary without Bishopsgate, London (Thomas *et al* 1997, eg 35; Fig 25). A minimal reconstruction would suggest that the Hall had an arcade with two aisles: the arches leading into the north aisle and the central nave still survive (see Fig 129). The entrance into the chapel itself had a statue niche above it, while the tomb recess to the north was presumably for the founder, Sir William Elsing, set in the chapel of John the Baptist. A tower stood over the junction of Hall and Chapel, and was

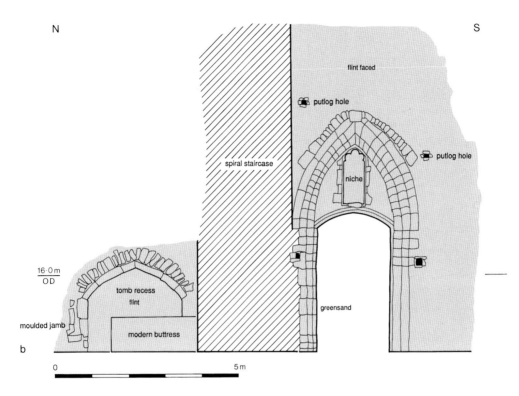

Fig 128 The surviving remains of St Mary Elsing (WFG17), surveyed by UCL in 1996: west-facing elevation of east wall.

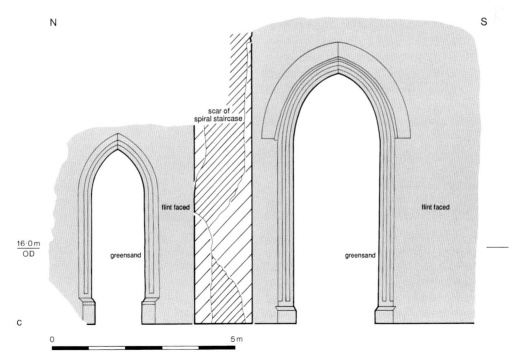

Fig 129 The surviving remains of St Mary Elsing (WFG17), surveyed by UCL in 1996: west-facing elevation of west wall showing scar of spiral staircase.

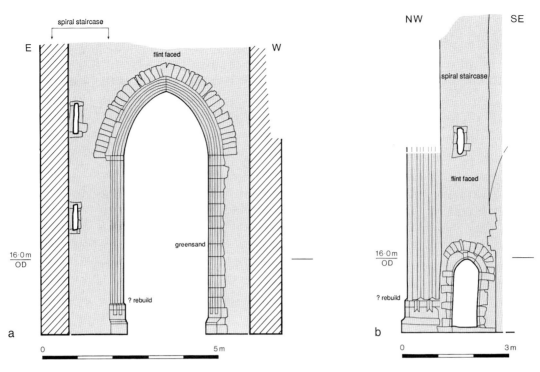

Fig 130 The surviving remains of St Mary Elsing (WFG17), surveyed by UCL in 1996: (a) north-facing elevation of north wall: note uneven heights of plinths; (b) south-west facing elevation of external face of stair turret: note evidence of reset plinth to west.

Fig 131 St Mary Elsing: scar of the spiral stair visible on the outer face of the surviving west wall viewed from above, with doorway to stair in north-east corner in background. (Ken Walton, London Archaeological Research Facility)

Fig 132 St Mary Elsing: scar of the spiral stair visible on the outer face of the surviving west wall, remains of robbed ascending treads just visible. (Ken Walton, London Archaeological Research Facility)

Fig 133 St Mary Elsing: internal view of flint-faced walling above fourteenth-century doorway with restored statue niche in tympanum recorded in 1996. (Ken Walton, London Archaeological Research Facility)

provided with sets of spiral stairs (Fig 139). It is possible that these stairs provided access not just to the belfry but also to a second storey in the Infirmary block or to an upper gallery. Two storey halls are certainly known at St Bartholomew's, Oxford and at SS John the Baptist and John the Evangelist, Sherborne, for example (Gilchrist 1995, 21). The value of such a feature in a hospital for the blind might have been limited, but it might have served to segregate the sexes, given that both males and females were being cared for.

It is unfortunate that more cannot be said of the plan of this part of the Elsing Spital. Its arrangements must have differed from other hospitals where those who were too ill to move would be positioned in the infirmary hall so that they could still see the elevation of the body of Christ during the masses performed in the chapel. Since the raising of the host by the priest was such a crucial part of the medieval service for the sighted faithful, the blind inmates of the Elsing Spital would presumably have needed special provision to enjoy the full benefit of the mass. The ringing of the sacring bell at the start of the mass would no doubt have taken on added significance for them (S Roffey personal communication), and a medieval reference to its use is found in the *Lay Folks Mass Book* (Simmons 1879, 38–9): 'A litil belle he wol to us rynge. Thanne

is resounne that we do reuerence To Ihesu criste presence, That may loose of alle balful bondes; Therefore knelynge, hold up thyn hondes And with inclination of thi bodi, Behold the leuacioun reuerently'.

The contribution of the RMLEC to church archaeology in the City

The study of the archaeology of London's parish churches is still in its infancy. In 1996, only four major projects (St Bride's, St Alban's, St Swithun's and St Nicholas Shambles) could be listed as having been 'substantially excavated and reported on in more than outline before 1991' (Schofield 1994, 80). Not only is that arguably too small a sample on which to consider general trends in the development of City churches but, more significantly, all the reports produced before 1996 were only interim summaries. It was not the lack of excavations and observations but the lack of detailed reports that was retarding church archaeology in London. As Martin Biddle noted a quarter of a century ago: 'not only does this mean that much basic material is unavailable, it also means that much of it has never been worked over for publication and its implications made apparent to the excavators or observers themselves' (Biddle *et al* 1973, 37). Wider interpretations made on the basis of interim reports will always be weak, as the study of those four London church summaries all too clearly shows. Of those four publications of pre-1991 date, the phasing of St Bride's has now been reconsidered and substantially revised (Milne 1997, fig 109) as has St Alban's, with dramatic effect (see Nathalie Cohen's report above).

It was the RMLEC that inaugurated research archaeology of the parish church in the City: despite the shortcomings to be expected in 50-year-old fieldwork, the recent re-evaluation has demonstrated that there is much of value in those excavations. Thus it is fitting that the reports on the RMLEC work at St Bride's, St Alban's and St Mary Aldermanbury should be among the first to be published in sufficient detail to allow the wider studies to begin, albeit belatedly. Working with the preferred interpretations of that small group of three RMLEC church projects, a number of useful ground rules can at least be suggested, always taking into account the particular topographical constraints imposed upon an urban church in a populated area, and the specific structural problems each would have been subject to. Although the trends discussed below all need to be tested against further detailed reports as they become available before a more widely applicable picture can be drawn, at least a temporary bench mark can be established.

To begin with, there are the shortcomings of attempting to date the foundation of a parish church by relying too heavily on the particular dedication. Although St Alban and St Bride died in the third and sixth century respectively, both before the arrival of the Augustinian mission in 597, there is now little

Fig 134 St Mary Elsing: the founder's tomb? The 10 × 100mm scale stands below a possible tomb recess on the western side of the surviving east wall. It might be associated with the tomb of Sir William Elsing who founded the hospital in 1329. (Ken Walton, London Archaeological Research Facility)

archaeological evidence to support suggestions of a Celtic or even a mid Saxon church on either site. Indeed, it now seems that both were established no earlier than the late tenth or eleventh century. All three of the RMLEC churches considered here were founded before 1200 and show an approximate correlation with the date of population expansion into the neighbouring area. As such, the churches presumably show that, by that date, the associated localities had already acquired a population that was sufficiently stable and prosperous enough to support their foundation. In the case of St Alban's and St Mary's there is evidence to suggest that the church was not a primary feature of the layout, but had been built over an area of earlier occupation, since pits and occupation debris were recorded from levels beneath the earliest church floor or footings. It would therefore seem that a generation or so passed before the neighbourhood developed the demand or the desire for its own church. Before that date, the inhabitants would have worshipped in St Paul's itself or in a church in one of the older established parishes within the primary settlement to the south of Cheapside.

Of the two pre-Conquest foundations discussed here (St Bride's and St Alban's), the initial plan was that of a simple single rectangular cell without apse or narthex, perhaps representing a proprietary chapel without wider parochial responsibilities. To that plan, additions were made to the east end either in the form of a narrower or square chancel, which, in the case of St Bride's, had an apse added to it. Such extensions seem associated with liturgical change rather than the need to accommodate a larger body of worshippers. As for St Mary's, a post-Conquest foundation, its primary plan seems to have been a rectangular cell with the smaller square ended chancel as at St Alban's, but with what appears to have been a small tower set at the west end.

Towers also appeared at the other two churches, initially at the north-east corner at St Alban's or to the south at St Bride's. In all three cases, new towers were erected at the west end of the churches in the late fourteenth or fifteenth centuries following evidence of repair, collapse or at least partial demolition. If this pattern were repeated on all other City churches, then the remains of more twelfth to thirteenth towers might be anticipated in a variety of locations, not just at the

*Fig 135 St Mary Elsing: remains of a blocked window immediately right of the 10 × 100mm scale: the blocking was subsequently cut by the possible tomb recess, part of which is visible in the top corner. (*Ken Walton, *London Archaeological Research Facility)*

*Fig 136 St Mary Elsing: arch supporting north wall of tower recorded in 1996: note difference in plinth height to east and west: 5 × 100mm scales. (*Ken Walton, *London Archaeological Research Facility)*

west end, as has been shown at St Mary le Bow, for example, or at St Nicholas Acon, where a tower foundation was recorded in the north-east corner (Marsden 1965; 1967). Another possible implication is that where a City church has a tower not centrally situated at the west end, then its foundation is likely to be of pre-fifteenth-century date. Few pre-fourteenth-century parish church towers in the City seem to have had the resilience to survive unscathed following the earthquake of 1382. In his review of parish churches in the City, Dr Schofield proposed that, 'from about 1370, towers were constructed in numbers' (Schofield 1994, 77): study of the small sample of RMLEC church projects suggests that towers are a very much earlier introduction in London churches, but that they were being widely rebuilt from about 1370.

As for the east end, all three of our examples acquired chapels flanking the chancel in the late thirteenth to fourteenth century. At St Brides and St Alban's the development followed the construction of a north aisle, but not at St Mary's. By the mid fifteenth century, the body of all three churches had established a more symmetrical plan with the construction of both north and south aisles running up to or alongside the new western towers. That symmetry was retained at St Mary's up to the Great Fire, but not at the other two

examples, which saw additional building at the east end in both cases as well as a partial demolition of the south aisle at St Alban's.

It has been argued that the relative prosperity of the later medieval parishes can be traced in broad terms by the subsequent phases of embellishment and rebuilding in the churches, together with the provision of major chapels. Working with the archaeological model provided by the RMLEC sample discussed here, for example, the church of St Bride's in its suburban parish seems to have been better endowed than St John the Evangelist (Cohen 1995), which lay well within the walled City south of Cheapside and just east of St Paul's. Perhaps it is worth recording that St John's was not rebuilt after the Great Fire, whereas St Bride's, St Alban's and St Mary Aldermanbury were. In other words, London archaeologists need to sample a representative selection of the 51 churches that were rebuilt after the Great Fire of 1666 (most of which were arguably already among the richer foundations) as well as a representative selection of the 35 poorer sites that were not rebuilt, whose relative poverty might well be reflected in a less complex plan form. In addition to that, it should be noted that both St Alban's and St Mary's lie in parishes that were

Fig 137 St Mary Elsing: base of the main arch on the surviving west wall. Note different plinth heights and coursing either side of the 5 × 100mm scale, as recorded in 1996. (Ken Walton, London Archaeological Research Facility)

Fig 139 St Mary Elsing: the 10 × 100mm scale stands next to doorway into stair turret at north-east corner of tower recorded in 1996. (Ken Walton, London Archaeological Research Facility)

Fig 138 St Mary Elsing: reset plinth below arch supporting north side of tower, internal face recorded in 1996: 5 × 100mm scale. (Ken Walton, London Archaeological Research Facility)

not intensively settled until the later tenth or eleventh centuries: consequently, church sites from within the early tenth-century settlement core to the south of Cheapside should be closely studied to see if an earlier foundation date is more evident there.

The point that there is no necessarily common form for London churches needs stressing: some will be earlier than others, some will show greater development than others. It is thus unhelpful to propose that there is a 'London' style of churches or that there is a common 'urban' type, as some have attempted (eg Schofield 1994, 77–9), since not all City churches were embellished with richly endowed chantry chapels, for example. Each church site will have its own story, reflecting the local circumstances of patronage and prosperity as well as topographical constraint and structural failure, upon which the wider changes in liturgical development are imposed. It is hoped that the publication of these RMLEC excavations and observations have supported that contention and helped progress the archaeological study of the City's parish church.

5 Townscape and topography

Using RMLEC data for topographical studies

The aim of this chapter is to widen the focus of the investigation from individual buildings to the study area as a whole. It is an attempt to use archaeological data gathered 50 years ago to answer questions such as those posed by the eminent historian Professor Brooke 25 years ago: 'if we could tell the history of Aldermanbury, a great slice of London's past would be revealed to us. It is not the name of a ward, not the origin of a ward; its parish is apparently no earlier than the 12th century; it was not even a street name until the 14th century. But it is evidently an ancient district' (Brooke and Keir 1975, 154). But how ancient is ancient? There can be no doubting the importance of the role played by the RMLEC in the development of the concept of multiperiod urban archaeology: but how valid are the results of those 50-year-old excavations, when judged by today's standards?

The RMLEC investigations were not recorded in as much detail nor was the finds collection policy as systematic or rigorous as the later Museum of London excavation programmes. Most RMLEC field plans were simply a plotting of whatever features were visible at that time, regardless of date or chronology: the sections were usually drawn to show whatever features happened to be identifiable on the edge of the cutting. Thus by no means all features encountered were drawn, while the precise location of the finds that survive is often impossible to determine. It is therefore difficult to make direct comparisons between the RMLEC results and those of the later excavation programmes. There are, however, a number of ways in which the RMLEC work can prove to make valid contributions to current studies on its own terms.

Primarily, it is of importance because it opened up a number of crucial debates, providing models that guided the direction of most later work: there are consequently few reports on the archaeology of the City in which Professor Grimes' 1968 volume does not appear in the bibliography. There are also many localised instances where the stratigraphy and the finds can be clearly identified, as in the case of Bastion 14, for example, where thirteenth-century pottery can be shown to have been recovered from above and below the bastion's primary internal surface: such sequences and proven relationships will also remain valuable.

Even if the value of some of the controlled RMLEC excavations as a whole might not stand up to too close a reappraisal, if seen simply as a major sampling programme for a study area such as the 12 acres of the Cripplegate study area, then it has real value today. Indeed, the best use of the RMLEC data is arguable to examine the chronological and topographical development of a wide area, rather than straining the evidence of the 50-year-old records to support a more

detailed analysis of one particular sequence. This chapter adopts that principle, by trying to show that several major questions can be addressed in a valid and effective way, looking principally at the overall distribution of the pottery recovered from those RMLEC cuttings, related to the general occupation context. Questions that could be aired, addressed and arguably illuminated by such an approach include these:

1 the relationship of medieval developments to the underlying Roman fort
2 the archaeological dating and development of street pattern compared with the documented dates of the streets (eg Ekwall 1954)
3 the broad chronology of medieval settlement in the Cripplegate study area compared with that in Lundenwic, in the Alfredian core south of Cheapside, in the recently studied areas just north of Cheapside, and within the site of the amphitheatre
4 the archaeological dating for the foundation of the parish churches in the area, related to the development of the associated parishes or wards
5 how such topographical studies might impact upon the long held suggestion that there was a mid Saxon royal focus within the Cripplegate fort area

The archaeology of micro- and macro-topography

Given that sufficient time and money can be invested in archaeological recording and research, detailed and subtle social, economic and topographical inferences can be drawn. The recent Leadenhall Court project, for example, examined the minutiae of the Roman development on that site, considering the status and ethnic mix of the inhabitants as well as the function of buildings. The work relies on very detailed site recording, systematic finds collection and environmental sampling policy, and substantial resources to study, interrogate and integrate the diverse databases. The lives of 22 short-life buildings, which expanded, contracted, were modified or demolished during a 25 year period, formed the core of the study, an intimate and intensive examination of the City's origins and development. It is not possible to replicate such a micro-topographical study for the Cripplegate area, since the appropriate data were simply not collected.

Examination of the RMLEC sites can support a broader, more extensive macro-topographical study, looking at the development of the street system in the area, for instance. Once the dating of the streets has been achieved, that is to say, the chronological development of the spread of occupation in the area, it might prove possible to show when and how the parishes or wards were established. This might be achieved by noting whether or not they are contemporary with the dated street pattern, or whether they represent earlier or later developments. In this way, archaeology moves from a purely topographical study to an examination of the development of the administrative and religious framework of the medieval City. This task is made easier for the post-RMLEC generation of scholars, since we now know that very little of the townscape is likely to be earlier than *c* AD 900, when a substantial part of the City was laid out anew. Thus the aim of this study of the Cripplegate area is simply to identify the extent and date of the post-Alfredian urban regeneration here, and to take especial note of any elements that can be argued to be significantly and stratigraphically earlier.

Saxon street plans

When Grimes published his study of Roman and Medieval London in 1968, there was a broad consensus that even if Londinium had suffered considerable shrinkage it might never have been completely deserted: continuity of occupation in some tangible form linked the Roman and medieval cities, even though some pronounced differences in street alignments were evident from the RMLEC's work. The medieval town was therefore described by Grimes as 'a more densely occupied city, recreated on the shadow of the Roman street plan, but lacking the guidance of Roman urban administration' (Grimes 1968, 151). He also reiterated the view presented by Wheeler more than 30 years earlier that, after considering the distribution of Saxon finds and church dedications (Wheeler 1934; Wheeler 1935, 185–94), the early or mid Saxon recolonisation of London began in the western half of the City, around St Paul's, and then spread eastwards (Grimes 1968, 153).

Such a view was in fact in defiance of the evidence from his seventeen year research programme. As he reluctantly admitted, even though the majority of his excavations were in the supposedly favoured western half of the City, 'the first clearly defined chronological evidence... in this region is consistently of *later* Saxon date', in spite of the documented establishment of St Paul's minster church and the ordination of the Bishop of London in *c* 604: indeed, 'the archaeological evidence seems to be consistent in showing no sign of life until more than 150 years later' (Grimes 1968, 153–4). More recent research clearly supports those findings of the RMLEC, rather than the weak interpretation he put on it, since it is now known that the mid Saxon settlement of Lundenwic lay to the west of Londinium around the Aldwych between *c* AD 600 and *c* 900 (Vince 1990), after which date the abandoned Roman site was reoccupied by a population making use of whatever remains of the Roman defensive wall survived. The RMLEC sampling programme had correctly identified and dated the chronology of the City's occupation, although Grimes was reluctant to accept his own evidence. To be fair, few archaeologists were prepared to believe the message proclaimed by the RMLEC investigations until 1984 (Cowie and Whytehead 1989; Vince 1984; Vince 1990).

It has therefore been shown that the finds collection policy adopted by the RMLEC, although considered unsystematic and unrefined by the standards of the successor units, was nevertheless subtle enough to identify that which hindsight has shown to be the more representative trends in the broad occupation chronology for this part of London. This fact is of fundamental importance to what follows, for the work of the RMLEC will be used to suggest how the street pattern in the Cripplegate area developed. Once the underlying framework of streets and associated settlement has been dated, then it follows that the foundation of the churches can be more readily dated, once the relationship of the parish boundary to the street pattern is understood, for example. In addition, it follows that the date at which the ward was established might also be better understood, once the streets have been dated.

Fields and streets within the walls (Fig 140)

Serious attempts at reconstructing the topography of the Saxon City began tentatively with Wheeler and were continued by Grimes (1968, 160) who described the town as 'a scattered group of hovels laid out to no ordered plan'. The sum total of available knowledge and speculation on the eve of the establishment of the City's first full time professional unit was systematically mapped out by Martin Biddle together with a declaration that 'the archaeology of Anglo-Saxon London barely exists as an organised field of enquiry' (Biddle 1973, 4.20). Since then, progress has been made and a series of fresh interpretations proposed (eg Brooke 1975; Schofield and Dyson 1980, 30; Tatton-Brown 1986), which were subsequently refined in line with the detailed publication of relevant excavations (Horsman *et al* 1988; Vince 1990). Outside the confines of the archaeological world, however, the City's ancient street plan was still 'generally held to be the archetypal organic city, moulded directly by social and economic process without the imprint of conscious design' (Hanson 1989, 22). As late as 1995, even the Director of the Centre of Metropolitan Studies argued that, although London's street plan was essentially complete by 1200, 'much remains to be done to elucidate the growth of the City within the walls' before that period (Keene 1995, 11).

Recent topographical studies of the intramural Saxon city have been able to identify the core of the earliest settlement area, thanks to an extensive programme of systematic excavations and a much improved knowledge of the date ranges represented by the pottery recovered from those stratigraphic excavations, from pit groups and from deposits associated with coins or dendrochronologically dated material. In 1990 it was argued that the principal area settled by *c* AD 900 lay in a discrete block bounded by Cheapside to the north, Queenhithe to the west, and Billingsgate to the east (Milne 1990: see Fig 140). That core is subdivided into

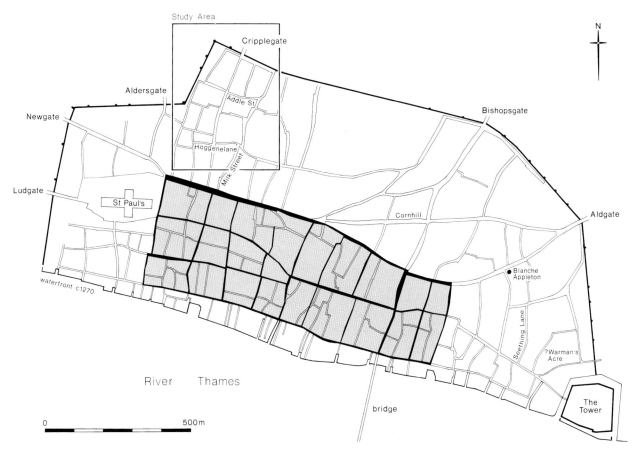

Fig 140 Plan to show extent of planned core of Saxon City in c AD 900 shown in relation to later medieval street plan. Note extensive undeveloped areas between primary core and line of City wall, with lack of intensive settlement in Cripplegate area at this date.

a block of broadly regular insulae by a series of north–south streets running directly from Cheapside to what was then the Thames (ie what is now Upper and Lower Thames Street, sundry encroachments having moved the bank of the Thames southwards). Excavations within that core had shown that the earliest stratified medieval occupation could be dated to *c* 900–950, the first generation or so of the newly replanned settlement, as the work at Bow Lane, Fish Street Hill and Botolph Lane shows (Horsman *et al* 1988, 110–16). This implies that the areas between that occupied core and the line of the (presumably repaired) Roman wall were initially left as fields. They could therefore have served as pasture, allotments, livestock enclosures, or markets. In addition, these areas might have been set aside for the accommodation of families from the hinterland requiring refuge in times of war, or for elite enclosures or estates, or simply for future planned expansions.

That there were fields immediately outside the City walls in the twelfth century is well known, as Fitzstephen's famous description makes clear: 'on the north side too are fields for pasture and a delightful plain of meadow land interspersed with flowing streams... . The tillage lands of the City... produce abundant crops and fill the barns of their cultivators...' (Wheatley 1956, 502). That there were fields worked

by Londoners in the late ninth century is also known, since it is recorded that King Alfred camped with his army near London in 896 'while the corn was being reaped so that the Danes could not interfere with the citizens' harvest' (Garmonsway 1972, 89). But there is some documentary evidence to support the concept of fields actually within the walled area. The matter has been discussed by several commentators including Page, who when describing the thirteenth-century City, claimed that there was still 'a good deal of open land, which, near the Walbrook in Coleman Street and Broad Street Wards, was probably pasture' (Page 1923, 270–71). To suggest that parts of the north-western intramural area were also pasture in the tenth century seems not unreasonable, and is possibly supported by the later place names of Addle Street, which arguably means a cattle drove road being 'the street of cow dung' (Ekwall 1954, 55), as discussed in Chapter 3, the more obvious Milk Street, and Hoggen Lane, the lane of the pigs, are (or were) all to the north of Cheapside (Ekwall 1954).

There are a number of place names that, although the earliest surviving references are eleventh to thirteenth century in date, might allude to the situation in the tenth century on the opposite side of the City beyond the settled area. These suggest an arable regime, and include the well known street name of Cornhill, referring to the fields north-east of the Alfredian settlement where cereals where grown (earliest reference AD 1100), Seething Lane, a lane where corn was threshed (earliest reference AD 1250, but clearly older according to Ekwall 1954, 38) and the explicit Warmanacre, one of the City's few pre-Conquest place names, meaning the tilled acre or field belonging to Warman, which was in what became Tower ward. There is also evidence of an extensive orchard on the eastern hill between Fenchurch Street and Hart Lane, represented by the twelfth-century place name Blanch Appleton (Ekwall 1954, 38). The archaeological evidence also supports the suggestion of agriculture within the walls at various periods, with the almost universal discovery of dark grey silts often representing a horticultural soil overlying the Roman occupation levels but cut or sealed by later medieval features.

Whatever initial roles the intramural late Saxon fields served, they ultimately succumbed to the spread of 'suburban' settlement. All the urban topographer has to do is to date that gradual expansion. Significantly, the excavations of one such area in 1976, that just to the north of Cheapside in the Milk Street area, produced evidence to show that this was a second or third generation expansion, for here the earliest pottery is datable to the mid to late tenth century or later (Horsman *et al* 1988, 23–6). A similar picture was found on the St Alban's House site in Wood Street, excavated a decade later: here the earliest pottery from the large number of pits recorded falls in the period 950–1000 (Chitwood and Hill 1987, 13–16), a finding confirmed by the most recent excavations at 100 Wood Street (MoLAS 1998, 28).

In spite of this brisk start, however, there seems to have been sufficient open ground available up against the town wall itself to allow for the foundation of such large precincts as Holy Trinity Priory in 1108, for example. By contrast, when the Dominican Friars looked for an intramural precinct in the late thirteenth century, the City wall had to be expanded westwards to accommodate them, the population of London having more than doubled in size since the time of Alfred in *c* AD 900.

Dating the Cripplegate streetscape (Figs 141 and 142)

The question to be asked of the Grimes London Archive could thus be easily formulated: what were the dates of the earliest settlement associated with the streets in the Cripplegate area? The answer lay in simply plotting the earliest medieval pottery from all the RMLEC excavations in the area and observing whether the resulting pattern identified:

(a) a pre-tenth-century core (perhaps near the churches of St Alban's or St Mary Aldermanbury), supporting the long lived tradition of an elite estate or King's Hall here

(b) a uniform and early tenth-century date for the whole area, suggesting that it was an integral part of the primary Alfredian core

(c) a uniform but later tenth or early eleventh-century date for the whole area, suggesting that it was a planned expansion of the primary core

(d) a non-uniform date for the settlement, representing a gradual expansion over area either from south to north or from west to east

The evidence when plotted out leant no support to the first three options, but seems to show that development moved from south to north. The insulae abutting the northern edge of Cheapside seem to have been settled by 950–1000 (WFG6; 14; 20; 22; 22a), reaching the line of the drove road, Addle Street by 1000–1050 (WFG21). The insulae to the north of this line were occupied significantly later in the post-Conquest period, *c* AD 1150+ (WFG4) or the thirteenth century in the case of WFG5 and WFG15, while the earliest pottery from the extreme north-west corner of the Cripplegate fort area was late fifteenth century (WFG1).

The pattern suggested above has clear implications for the longevity of the Roman fort. After it had been identified as a direct result of the RMLEC's investigations, it was easy to see how the fort wall had influenced the line of the late City wall, which diverged significantly at the south-west and north-east corner. With hindsight it was also possible to suggest that Wood Street and Silver Street were both roads that had survived from the Roman period, since both clearly respected the line of second-century streets and gates, at least at the respective north and west ends (Grimes 1968, 21–2). Here was an example of topographical continuity, so the argument ran in the days before Lundenwic was discovered, which showed that the fort exercised an influence upon the development of the medieval town, strongly suggesting that the area was continuously occupied for nearly 2000 years.

Detailed study of the RMLEC records has now shown that the eastern and southern walls of the fort, the associated ditch and all the buildings within it had been levelled during the Roman period (Shepherd forthcoming). This can be demonstrated graphically in a medieval context by consideration of the alignments of the churches of St Alban's and St Mary Aldermanbury. The underlying Roman buildings obviously respect the line of the fort walls, whereas both of those churches markedly do not, again showing that the fort walls were not a topographical determinant or constraint at the time the churches were built. Indeed, St Mary's was built but yards from what had been the east wall of the fort, and all too clearly ignores it. Significantly, the church of St Alphage was aligned on the City wall, since the defences here still survived in a tangible form and were actually incorporated in the fabric of the church itself. Since the fort did not even

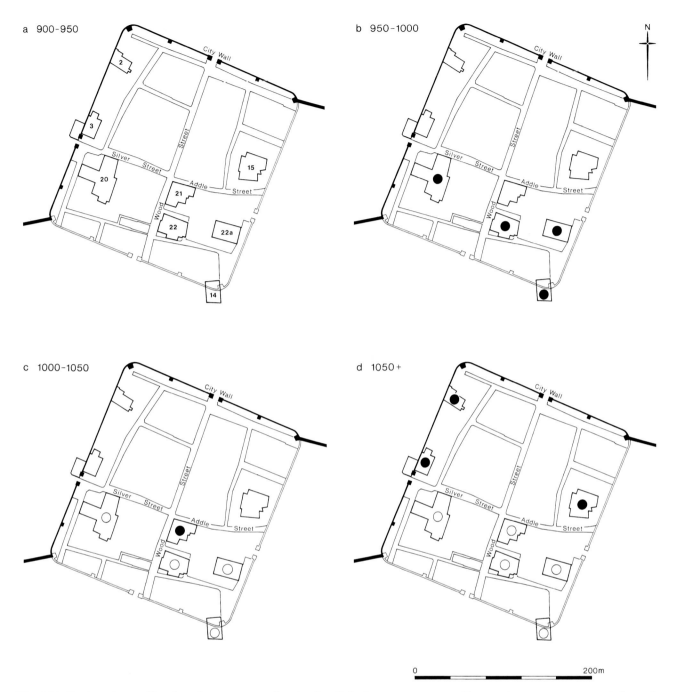

Fig 141 Dating the medieval settlement expansion in the Cripplegate area, according to the pottery recovered from the RMLEC excavations: (a) 900–950: no contemporary pottery from any of the RMLEC sites; (b) 950–1000: sites to the south of Addle Street and Silver Street; (c) 1000–1050 sites up to the Addle Street frontage; (d) 1050+: sites north of the Addle Street–Silver Street.

survive into the fourth century as a significant topographical entity, it can no longer be argued to have served as a settlement focus in the mid Saxon or later medieval period.

The northern and western walls did survive, encased within the later town wall, as did the two associated gateways, blocked or open. It was the survival of the west gate and of Cripplegate itself that dictated the lines of the later medieval streets in the area, not the survival of the fort and its road network.

This is amply demonstrated by the fact that the lines of medieval Wood Street and Silver Street diverge significantly from the older Roman line the further they run from the surviving gates. There is therefore no longer a case to be made for continuity within the Cripplegate area, according to the archaeological and topographical evidence presented here: the medieval street and settlement pattern encroached over a relatively undeveloped area from south to north from the late tenth century onwards.

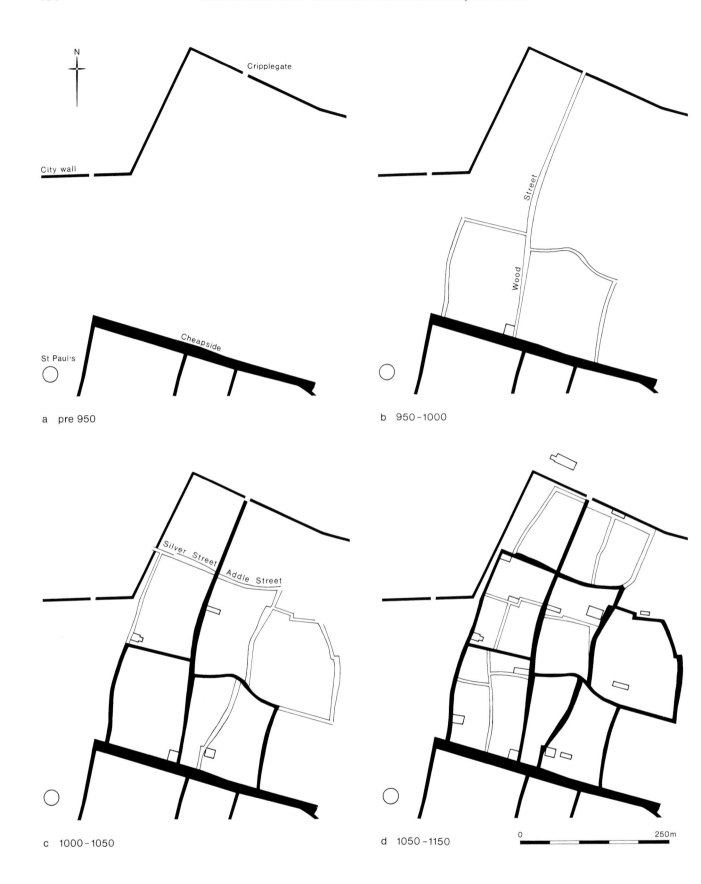

Fig 142 Suggested development of street pattern and establishment of churches in Cripplegate study area: (a) before 950, settlement is broadly confined to the core south of Cheapside; (b) 950–1000: development of Wood Street, as primary north–south thoroughfare in study area, although its northern frontages were not extensively developed initially; (c) 1000–1050: more intensive settlement of the Cripplegate study area, but not north of Silver Street and Addle Street; (d) 1050+ settlement only extends up to the City wall in the north west corner of the study area after the mid eleventh century.

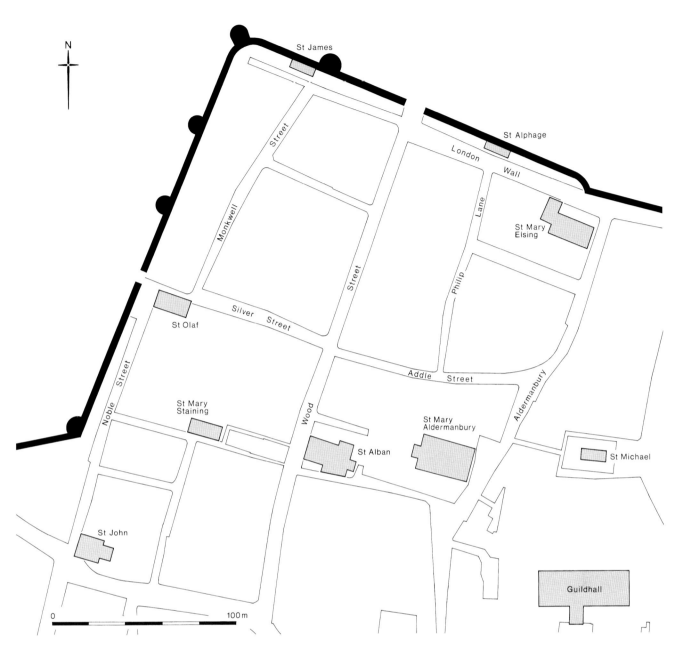

Fig 143 Sites of churches in Cripplegate study area shown in relation to 1940 street pattern.

This information can now be assessed alongside the earliest documentary record of the streets (Fig 143), as recorded by Ekwall (1954): for example, this shows that, since there is a pre-Conquest reference to Cripplegate, then Wood Street, the road that leads to it from Cheapside, might therefore be seen as the primary thoroughfare in our study area. Staining Lane (AD 1181) must have initially served as a back lane separating the yards of properties fronting onto Wood Street to the east and Noble Street to the west, so must have been in place by *c* AD 950. Its own frontages might not have been developed significantly until after the Conquest, as was the case with other back lanes in areas that have been intensively studied (see eg Pudding Lane: Horsman *et al* 1988, 112–16). Oat Lane (AD 1319) and Love Lane would seem to

be secondary lanes cutting across the insulae to give access to the churches of St Mary Staining and St Alban, so should presumably have been in place by AD 1050. Silver Street (AD 1279) and Addle Street (AD 1304) seem to mark the northern edge of eleventh-century development, while the occupation of Monkwell Street (AD 1200) and Phillip Lane (AD 1170) are seen as post-Conquest additions to the streetscape. It should be noted that Phillip Lane leads directly to (from) the church of St Alphage on the wall, which is in all likelihood a mid to late eleventh-century foundation around which parishioners subsequently clustered. It might therefore have been built on relatively open ground initially, rather than in the centre of an already densely occupied parish.

Churches and settlement expansion (Fig 144)

As for the other churches considered in this report, it would seem that St Alban's was set in an area that was first developed intensively between AD 950 and 1000: on its location alone, a foundation date of *c* AD 1000 would not therefore seem unreasonable, and such a date is not contradicted by the site stratigraphy or finds recovered from the associated excavations. The site did not produce any mid Saxon material, even from 'residual' contexts, and Nathalie Cohen's study of the associated stratigraphy, foundation types and subsequent development all suggest that St Alban's could be an eleventh-century foundation. This statement is of more than passing interest for in many previous studies of the medieval City, St Alban's has been argued to be of substantially earlier date (eg Biddle *et al* 1973, 20; map 3), a chapel associated with a Saxon palace. This often repeated tradition can now be laid to rest as a result of the most recent research, but deserves further comment (see below).

Given that this chronology of development and occupation of the streets in the Cripplegate area is accepted, then some general comments might be made concerning the nature of the new population that was occupying the new insulae. One of the churches established in the eleventh-century extension of the Cripplegate grid south of Silver Street/Addle Street was dedicated to St Olaf, the Norwegian king who died in 1030. This was a popular dedication in London, for there are five others if the one at the Southwark bridgehead is included. Other churches with Scandinavian connections include St

Nicholas Acon, or Haakon, in which the suffix presumably refers to its founder; St Magnus, St Clement Danes and St Bride's, which is now thought to be a dedication brought over from Ireland by Vikings from Dublin (Brooke 1975, 139–40). This distribution suggests that Scandinavian immigrants had taken up residence and roots in the harbour area (St Magnus), within the old 'Saxon' town as laid out in AD 900 (St Nicholas Haakon, St Olave Bread Street); in new insulae being developed to the east and north of that core (St Olave Hart Street; St Olaf Broad Street); in the extramural suburb extending along Fleet Street (St Bride's; St Clement Danes) as well as the area north of Cheapside (St Olaf Jewry; St Olaf Monkwell Street). Between the last two churches lies St Lawrence Jewry and the site of the Guildhall Yard excavations (Bateman 1994; Betts *et al* 1995; Porter 1997) where Nicholas Bateman and his team have recovered considerable evidence of eleventh-century occupation, buildings and artefacts that show Scandinavian influence. London, it will be remembered, was besieged and taken by the Danes in 1016, after which King Cnut and his line ruled until 1042.

By combining the evidence of excavation, topography and church dedication a case can thus be made for suggesting that a significant proportion of the population that was settling the expanding town of London into new areas such as that in Cripplegate were Scandinavian immigrants, arriving here in the early eleventh century. Alternative interpretations are of course possible. It could be said, for example, that the choice of St Olaf as a dedication might be seen as reflecting an anti-Danish mood, since Olaf was a

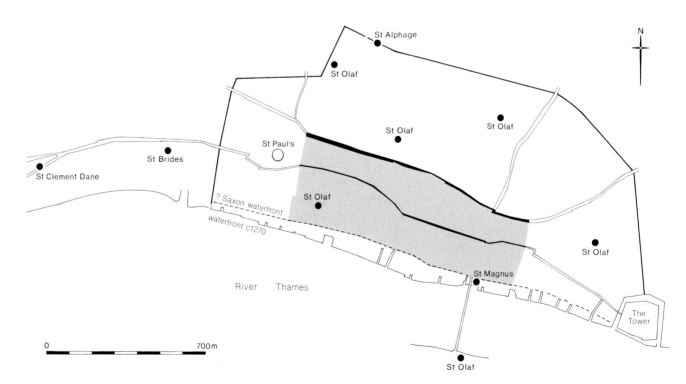

Fig 144 Sites of some of the churches that might be associated with eleventh-century Scandinavian settlement in the City shown in relation to the primary tenth-century settlement core and the minster church of St Paul.

Norwegian king who actually fought against the Danes. In this case, the sudden popularity of the saint during a period of Danish occupation could simply reflect defiant English sentiment in the newly settled areas. The churches dedicated to St Alphage and to St Edmund, a bishop and a king both martyred by the Danes, might also represent this same attitude. The politics of church dedication might also be reflected in the immediate post-Norman conquest period, when churches like St Swithin adopted their English dedications. Whatever the reasoning behind the choice of saint might have been, topographical studies show that most of St Olaf's London churches lie outside the original Alfredian core settlement, and therefore represent settlement expansion in the eleventh century. Beyond that phase of expansion lies a ring of twelfth-century extramural churches, including St Sepulchre, St Gile's Cripplegate and the three St Botolph's at Aldersgate, Bishopsgate and Aldgate (Brooke 1975, 144–7). Together with consideration of other twelfth-century institutions such as Holy Trinity, Aldgate (1108) just inside the walls and St Bartholomew's (1123) just outside, a City wide pattern of progressive expansion from the core area can be surmised. The archaeological study of the street development in the Cripplegate area based on the work of the RMLEC does not contradict that overall picture, but adds detail and precision to it.

This topographical study coupled with consideration of the changing density of settlement discussed in Chapter 3, can also be viewed alongside historical research looking at the City's population (Barron 1995b, 24; 29). Derek Keene has suggested, for example, that London was substantially larger in 1300 than in 1500, discarding the previously held view that the City grew continuously throughout the medieval period (Keene 1985, 20). The archaeological evidence from Cripplegate, fragmentary as it is, supports a picture of rapid expansion and increasingly intensive settlement in the eleventh–twelfth century, followed by major changes in or by the fourteenth century with the amalgamation of properties and the establishment of fewer but larger houses and halls. The detail of those changes would clearly benefit from in depth documentary research (beyond the scope of this volume) as was conducted on a similar sized sample area in neighbouring Cheapside, just to the south-east of Cripplegate (Keene 1985). The pattern of occupied plots and land values in that central location both show a pronounced but broadly negative trend from 1300 to 1550: a similar picture in Cripplegate seems likely. Another interesting development highlighted in the Cheapside study is the change in occupations represented: leather workers (ie tanners, tawyers, fellmongers and leather sellers) were prominent up to 1300 in the area just north of Cheapside itself. Presumably this is a reflection of the area's connection with the cattle market and the drove road of Addle Street. By 1400, mercers, silkwomen and drapers outnumber the older crafts (Keene 1985, 18). Again, analogous changes probably occurred in the Cripplegate area. Detailed documentary

study coupled with the results of the more recent MoLAS excavations at Shelley House in Noble Street, for example (NST94; Howe and Lakin forthcoming), should throw light on the matter. Something can be said of the economy and industry represented by the artefactual evidence recovered from the RMLEC sites in Cripplegate beyond the recovery of the important assemblage of late Saxon loomweights from St Alban's (WFG22). This concerns the ceramic crucible fragments discovered in the City ditch fills, and reported on by Jacqueline Pearce (Chapter 2). They provide evidence for the processing of precious metals in the period 1050–1150, and thus illuminate the derivation of the name Silver Street as the street of the silversmiths. Such activities are not subsequently represented archaeologically until the sixteenth century, perhaps suggesting that the area's economic base changed as much as its population density.

The tradition of a Saxon palace at Cripplegate

Given that Saxon London was such a notable centre of population and prosperity, it is not unreasonable to expect that the contemporary kings had a base there. Documentary records from AD 680 onwards confirm that there was indeed a King's Hall in the town, although its precise location is never made explicit. Aldermanbury, the Alderman's Burh or stronghold, has often been seen as the site of the palace of the Saxon King up to the time of Edward the Confessor, who moved out to Westminster to the site now occupied by the Abbey and the great hall. There is also a reference to King Ethelbert having a palace near Aldermanbury in the seventh century, and a tradition that the church of St Alban's Wood Street was built for King Offa (757–96) and served as the chapel for the City palace (eg Biddle 1973, 20; Brooke 1975, 18; Schofield and Dyson 1980, 42–4; Wheeler 1935, 103–4). This view was and is widely held and is repeated in many common reference works including Pevsner's volume on London's buildings (1973, 34, 142) and *The London Encyclopedia* (Weinreb and Hibbert 1983, 688), although the source is a thirteenth-century reference of dubious validity, as will be discussed below. The 'tradition' that there was a Saxon palace in the Cripplegate area is in fact a conglomeration of several different references that have been considered at length by Tony Dyson, to whom particular acknowledgement must be made for the summary that follows:

(a) 680: there is a reference to a hall (or *selde*) of the Kentish kings in London, but it is not known whether the building was in Lundenwic or within the confines of the old Roman town walls

(b) 1000: Ethelred's IV Law Code mentions that Aldersgate and Cripplegate were in the hands of the guards, perhaps suggesting that they were under royal protection, ie next to a palace site

(c) 1017: Florence of Worcester's Chronicle records that when King Cnut was in London at Christmas in 1017, there was a murder in the palace, and a body was thrown over the City wall into the ditch, implying that the palace was inland and not next to the Thames

(d) 1060s: Edward the Confessor moved his palace site from somewhere within the City walls to Westminster. Subsequently he made extensive grants of lands in the St Martin le Grande, Cripplegate and Aldersgate area to various persons. This implies that Edward's palace site in the City had been in that general area of Cripplegate

(e) Mid thirteenth century: Matthew Paris, the chronicler of St Alban's Abbey, Herts, recorded that the palace of its founder, one Offa, king of Mercia (759–96), once adjoined St Alban's church in London. That comment seems to refer to one of the many entries relating to Abbey owned property, which a dubious official called Adam the Cellarer modified (or simply invented) in the mid twelfth century, while 'improving' the Abbey's property titles. The original account is therefore, at best tendentious: 'in any event, the unsupported word of Mathew Paris is poor evidence for traditions of a much earlier period' (Brooke 1975, 111)

(f) 1531–3: St Paul's accounts make reference to buildings in Aldermanbury 'on the site of the ancient dwelling...where St Ethelbert King & founder of St Paul's had sometime his palace'. This comment is made because the church thought it had been granted the land from the King: this is not the case, for it was actually derived from a bequest of Sir John Beauchamp, who died in 1360

Taking all this documentary material together, it seems that there might well have been an eleventh-century royal hall in the north-west corner of the City. This does not, however, prove that a mid Saxon palace had previously occupied the site. Nevertheless, the RMLEC's discovery of the Cripplegate Roman fort added fuel to that particular fire, providing, it seemed, a ready made royal precinct within the City walls. For Martin Biddle, writing enthusiastically a quarter of a century ago, 'the possibility that this (Saxon palace) enclosure could have been formed by the still surviving defences of the Roman fort... opens a new and so far unexplored inquiry' (Biddle 1973, 20). Certainly Professor Grimes was prepared to give support to the early palace tradition by declaring that the earliest phase of St Alban's church was Saxon: 'All the indications are therefore that the first church of St Albans was indeed Saxon and at least of 8th-9th century date: its proportions resemble those of the slightly larger Saxon church of All Hallows Barking...Presumably then this was the chapel of King Offa' (Grimes 1968, 206–7).

That lead has been followed by many subsequent writers: even the discovery in 1985 of the mid Saxon settlement of Lundenwic to the west of the City has not dampened the ardour of the Cripplegate palace supporters. Rather than claiming that the mid Saxon palace should now be sought in the Aldwych area, they suggested that settlement was a polyfocal one, in which

the commercial area lay to the west in Lundenwic itself, with the *villa regalis* to the east within the old Roman walls of the fort, distinct from the civilian settlement. Our reassessment of the RMLEC data provides grim reading for proponents of that thesis:

(a) It has already been shown that the south and east walls of the fort were demolished in the third century and the ditch infilled: thus no ready made precinct survived to be reoccupied by Saxon kings

(b) The alignments of both St Alban's and St Mary Aldermanbury do not respect the line of the fort walls or the Roman buildings underlying the churches, showing that the fort walls were not a topographical constraint at the time the churches were built

(c) No pottery earlier than the late tenth-eleventh century came from either the St Alban's or St Mary Aldermanbury church site

(d) All Hallows Barking, the parallel quoted to support the mid Saxon date for St Alban's in the 1968 report, has subsequently been redated to the eleventh century: (Vince 1990, Schofield 1994)

(e) Study of street pattern development in the area as a whole shows that occupation expanded from south to north in the tenth–eleventh century onwards, with no earlier focus within the fort area. This statement is supported not only by the RMLEC finds study, but also by the results of later excavations conducted by the Museum of London teams on sites to the south at Wood Street and at Shelley House to the west (MoLAS 1998, 28)

In sum, there is no positive evidence to support the suggestion that there was a mid Saxon focus of any sort near St Alban's church, while there is now mounting negative evidence that the early palace was not on that site. Even if the tradition of a St Alban's palace is thus no longer sustainable, such an advance should be seen as a positive benefit to our knowledge of Saxon London and the research directions that should be taken: the site of that royal focus still needs to be identified.

An area that clearly was the focus for a high status Saxon settlement is that within the bounds of the disused Roman amphitheatre (Bateman 2000), between what is now Guildhall and the church of St Lawrence Jewry (Betts *et al* 1995; fig 2; Porter 1997). Here a sequence of timber buildings was recorded in 1993, but they seem to date to the period 1040 to 1140, and thus apparently too late for Edward the Confessor's palace.

Perhaps a better case could be made for the location of that palace on the site of the precinct of St Martin le Grande (see eg Vince 1990, 57). This is just south of Aldersgate, west of Cheapside and, significantly, due north of St Paul's and of the original site of the Folkmoot, an ideal position for the King's Hall, separate from but close to the Church, the Cheapside market, the urban settlement and the moot itself. The site also lies south-east of Aldermanbury, 'the defended enclosure of the Alderman':

this presumably refers to Aethlred the Ealdorman of Mercians, to whom King Alfred entrusted the government of the newly established town, as recorded in the Chronicle of Florence of Worcester in 886. Excavations near St Martin le Grande on the Newgate Street site in 1976 recorded beam slots thought to represent the remains of a late Saxon building some 9m long × 4m wide (DUA 1976, 400). This substantial structure was clearly not an outhouse, but neither was it built with its gable on the principal street frontage, as late medieval urban properties usually were: instead it was aligned east–west and set well to the north of Newgate Street. If its dating is confirmed, then it is not impossible that it was part of the complex associated with the King's Hall, although too modest in its proportions to represent the 'palace' itself.

Dating the wards (Fig 145)

The topographical studies of the Cripplegate area can also be extended from the skeleton of the street pattern to the administrative structure of the ward system that was imposed upon that settlement. It has been suggested that the tenth-century settlement occupied a discrete area within the old Roman walls to the south of Cheapside, and that occupation subsequently spread out over what had been fields. If that model can be accepted, then it provides a powerful tool to investigate other aspects of the town's development, such as the chronology and dating of its parish and ward structure. In this section, an attempt is made to relate what is known about the growth of settlement in the intramural area to the complex layout of London's ward boundaries, to see if that layout can be dated by association with the underlying streetscape, for which a chronology has now been offered.

Since 1550 the City has been divided into 26 administrative districts termed wards, each one represented by an alderman who initially seems to have exercised proprietary rights, but by 1249 was an elected official (Williams 1963, 34). The precise origin of the ward system is open to debate but is clearly associated with the need to ensure that London was able to defend itself adequately, by drawing on the services of men from each ward, just as was the case in the administrative land divisions termed 'hundreds'. William Page suggested that at least some of the wards developed from sokes, which he saw as areas of land under private jurisdiction, such as the soke of Ethelredshithe, which became Queenhithe Ward (Page 1923, 173). Professor Brooke concluded that 'the wards grew up in the 11th century, though their remote origin may be older' (Brooke 1975, 170), a view largely shared by Dr Vince (1990, 91–2). As for the manning of the defences, the document known as the Burghal Hidage (Hill 1969) suggests that four men were needed to defend every pole (c 5m), then some 20,000 men would have been required to cover the line of the land and riverfront defences of the City. How those arrangements would have been put into practice would depend on the ward structure, and it would not seem unreasonable to

suggest that its origins might well lie in the planned resettlement of the intramural City in c AD 900. After all, the prime reason for relocating the citizens from Lundenwic was probably to take advantage of the superior defences provided by Londinium: to make best use of the walled circuit presumably implies that some sort of ward structure was already in place in the early tenth century. Some topographical evidence to support this suggestion will be presented below.

A list of properties that St Paul's owned or leased survives from c 1127, arranged not by parish, but by ward. This early and most valuable documentary reference shows that there must have been at least 20 wards extant at that date, although they are referred to by the name of the alderman rather than by the present day names (Brooke 1975, 166): Farringdon ward, for example, still takes its name from the Fardon family (Williams 1963, 32). Nevertheless, it has been suggested that of all the wards that cover or abut the Cripplegate study area, Aldersgate, Cripplegate, Farringdon and Cheap might all have been operative at that date (Page 1923, 176). Three additional wards (including Bassishaw, just to the east of our study area) had been formed by 1228 (Page 1923, 176–8). The first territorial (rather than proprietary) listing of London's wards was that of 1285 (Williams 1963, 33). Up until 1393 there were 24 wards, but the following year there were 25 when Farringdon, which lay half inside and half outside the City wall, was divided into two (Farringdon Within and Farringdon Without: Fig 145, no 13).

It is suggested here that the ward system, or its direct ancestor in all but name, must have been instigated in c AD 900 as the new intramural settlement was laid out. The subsequent changes in the number of wards and in the shape of their boundaries summarised above are seen as reflecting the change in the area of settlement and ensuing population density. Thus it can be argued that there were initially some ten or so wards covering the core settlement, from Bread Street and Queenhithe in the west to Billingsgate in the east, each relatively small in area (Fig 145, nos 1–10). The broad shape and extent of most of this core group has largely been retained since c AD 900. There is, however, one obvious interloper in this neat tenth-century pattern, and that is Bridge ward (Fig 145, no 9), which seems to carve or extend its boundaries out of earlier wards on all sides, even almost cutting Langbourn ward in two (Fig 145, no 7). This reflects the simple fact that the Alfredian town boasted no fixed link with the Surrey shore, but was content to be served by ferries. The archaeological evidence for the first Saxon bridge is sometime after AD 970, possibly around AD 1000, according to the dendrochronological evidence from the Fennings Wharf site in Southwark, where the remains of the southern bridgehead were found (Watson and Dyson 1997; Watson et al 2001), and from the St Magnus House sites on the north bank (Steedman et al 1992), where a substantial piled feature initially interpreted as a jetty could, in fact, represent the northern bridgehead.

The construction of the bridge in *c* AD 1000 heralded major changes in the organisation of the London harbour, since the bridge acted as a barrier or at least an impediment to vessels coming up river from the estuary. Some of those changes are enumerated in Ethelred's IV Law Code, which might date to this precise period and provides the first specific documentary reference to the new bridge. The new bridge also heralded a change in the ward boundaries, since men would be required to work on its maintenance and defence, for example. Thus the elongated Bridge Ward can be argued to date to *c* AD 1000. Since it is clearly a later addition to the pattern upon which it is imposed, it implies that the other wards in the settlement core must have been established at an earlier date: they could thus have been laid out in or slightly later than AD 900.

Abutting the core wards were four or five much larger, but not as densely populated wards, extending out to the town wall and often beyond them, eg Farringdon in the west (Fig 145 no 13), Portsoken and Aldgate in the east (Fig 145, nos 22, 23). The form of this group has been subjected to many boundary changes over time, presumably in an effort to ensure an equitable division of population and responsibility. Present day electoral boundaries are similarly subject to change to keep pace with changing population densities. It seems clear that Farringdon ward, for example, has been reduced in area by the later addition of Aldersgate and Cripplegate Wards (Fig 145, nos 15, 16). This suggests that the latter two are creations postdating the initial developments of AD 900, a date when the area north of Cheapside was not intensively settled. A context for the establishment of those two additional wards must therefore be the increase in population of the insulae either side of Wood Street, a development that archaeology has shown to date to the period 950–1050. Once again, a picture is produced in which 'secondary' wards that are unlikely to have been created before the late tenth century are arguably imposed on the primary structure, which should therefore be of early tenth-century date.

It is worth observing that Ethelred's IV Law Code also refers to both Aldersgate and Cripplegate, both of which, we are informed, are to be in the charge of the guards, presumably a new arrangement that differed from those elsewhere on the wall. This could suggest

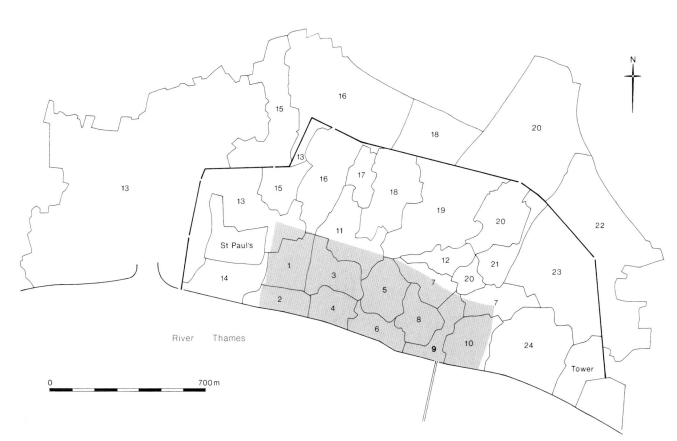

Fig 145 Schematic representation of late medieval wards of London is shown in relation to City wall and tenth-century settlement core. It seems that core area was initially divided into a group of relatively small wards, while much larger wards covered area between core and wall, where settlement was less intensive. Bridge Ward (no 9) is clearly a later imposition on initial pattern. The late medieval ward structure of the City of London is shown in relation to the tenth-century settlement area and waterfront line: 1 Bread Street; 2 Queenhithe; 3 Cordwainer; 4 Vintry; 5 Walbrook; 6 Dowgate; 7 Langbourn; 8 Candlewick; 9 Bridge; 10 Billingsgate; 11 Cheap; 12 Cornhill; 13 Farringdon (Within & Without); 14 Castle Baynard; 15 Aldersgate; 16 Cripplegate; 17 Bassishaw; 18 Coleman Street; 19 Broad Street; 20 Bishopsgate; 21 Lime Street; 22 Portsoken; 23 Aldgate; 24 Tower.

that both gates in the north-west corner of the City had recently been reopened, rebuilt or modified in a major way, perhaps as a consequence of the increasing population seeking new, more convenient access routes.

Thus our retrogressive analysis of the ward structure has suggested that an early tenth-century pattern of large and small wards, closely reflecting the Alfredian core settlement area and outlying fields, was subject to major changes. Some of those changes can be dated, as in the case of the building of the bridge in c AD 1000, or the gradual settlement encroachment over the formerly unoccupied Cripplegate area. Since these archaeologically detectable changes took place after AD 950–1000, then a case can be made for assuming that the initial disposition of the ward structure must date to the early tenth century.

6 *Si Monumentum Requiris, circumspice*

Cripplegate's medieval monuments

In addition to acting as honorary director of the RMLEC, WF Grimes was also the archaeological consultant for the Corporation of London, advising them on matters relating to their ancient monuments and how they might be displayed. He attended many meetings with Corporation officials and the Ministry of Works at which preservation issues and the display of the City wall were discussed: the correspondence file mentions one such in November 1965, for example, which would have considered the implications of the Barbican Wallside development, following the recent discovery of Bastion 11a. This role is also mentioned in a letter from the Corporation in November 1972, which alludes to the 'discussions which have taken place between yourself and various officers of the corporation, on many occasions', on such matters. He was being asked for his 'observations on the treatment of the wall and associated works in order that these could be incorporated in the proposals under consideration' (WFG22a Cor). Grimes was still acting in this role at least as late as 1980, some seven years after he had retired, as the correspondence files show (eg WFG2, Cor 29/10/79; 27/5/80).

The displays of the City wall and of the remains of the first church of St Alphage were one such matter, which was resolved and published with pride by the Corporation (Forty 1955) as has been discussed above (see Fig 10). Although the south facing elevation of the City wall had been treated as a visible monument since the nineteenth century (as the weathered commemorative plaque states), the north face had not been exposed to public gaze for some centuries. The Blitz provided the opportunity for the Corporation to reveal and consolidate it, working under the guidance of Professor Grimes for the academic input. Similar exercises were made with the Bastions 12 to 14 (Figs 146 and 147), while special arrangements were called for when Bastion 11a was unexpectedly discovered in 1965. Here the truncated stubby foundations were deliberately extended to form a complete plan of the base of the tower, so as to make the monument more meaningful to the public. This was a relatively novel departure for Professor Grimes, who but rarely agreed to embellishing surviving masonry monuments, beyond the work required for their consolidation and safety.

The problems posed by the nearby tower of St Mary Elsing also exercised the minds of the Corporation and their consultant, but the solution adopted was not commemorated with a publication as had been the case with the St Alphage wall (Figs 148 and 149). This was presumably because the result was a rather unhappy compromise in which the partly demolished remains of a medieval church tower were 'preserved' in situ while the Barbican redevelopment plans continued unsympathetically around them. Unlike some of the other medieval elements retained in the post-war designs, the preservation of St Mary Elsing was quite clearly an afterthought, its survival depending on accident and argument. Part of the tower that survived the Dissolution of the Monasteries, the Great Fire of London and the Blitz is still standing, albeit incarcerated inaccessibly in a walled compound next to a six lane highway. Somewhat surprisingly for such a 'miraculous survival' (Huelin 1996, 34), it can claim to be the most neglected and least known medieval monument in the City.

In truth in could be argued that the otherwise laudable drive to conserve and consolidate sections of the City's medieval and Roman heritage in the Cripplegate area as elsewhere was a task only half completed in the immediate post-war era. The monuments were certainly there for all to see, but the associated explanations and interpretations were all too often at best uninspired or at worst, non existent. This oversight was much improved with the development of the City Wall Walk plaques and handbook, which were officially launched as late as 1986 (Chapman *et al* 1985). Some of these information boards are now showing their age, and the time is coming for new initiatives to enhance our understanding and appreciation of the City's ancient monuments, the last fixed points in a townscape in which many of the multistory office blocks that Professor Grimes saw rising from the bomb rubble in the 1950s and 1960s have themselves been rebuilt.

The large scale rescue excavation programmes conducted by the Museum of London, which began in the early 1970s, long after the RMLEC had withdrawn from the City, have also exposed sections of the town wall and other medieval monuments. The marked change of ethos that accompanied this work has meant that few sections have been preserved for future generations to observe. Much of the late thirteenth-century medieval extension of the defences in the Fleet valley was excavated in the early 1990s, but none of that section is now visible, for example. Exceptions to this sad rule are the fifteenth-century postern at Tower Hill, a fragment of the Blackfriars range in Carter Lane, and a chapel from Holy Trinity Aldgate. All in all a modest collection of medieval monuments when set beside what was achieved by the impoverished RMLEC.

Archaeology after the Blitz: excavation or evaluation?

This volume has examined the conditions and concepts that constrained the RMLEC's excavation programme, and has re-evaluated its work in the light of more recent analysis, both on the artefacts and on

Fig 146 Ancient monument in a blitzed townscape: Bastion 12 in 1947 looking east. (The Sphere)

the field records. Although excavation methodologies and recording techniques have now changed, we have tried to show that there is much that is new and can be learned from such a reappraisal of 50-year-old records, especially when considered alongside modern research. This, at least, is the general thrust of the previous chapter. The vision and the opportunity were certainly there in 1947 but not, alas, the resources to realise the full potential of the situation. Very few long sequences of stratigraphically related features and associated finds were recorded: the 17-year RMLEC programme produced many sections, but all too few phased plans when compared with what might be expected from a more recent urban site.

As a sampling exercise the RMLEC's results have proved most instructive. This is in itself an important lesson, for it suggests that major long term open area excavations are simply one way of acquiring useful archaeological data: intensive sampling programmes also have their place, programmes in which, by contrast, many (relatively) small observations are made over a wide area. This was the pattern adopted out of necessity by the RMLEC, and it has much in common with the present state of archaeological investigations within the City walls. From 1973 to 1998, the Museum of London teams were used to mounting major open area excavations as a matter of course, utilising

resources on a scale that the RMLEC could not have begun to consider in that age of austerity (eg Rowsome 2000). Since the imposition of Planning Policy Guidance Note 16 in 1990, more time has increasingly been spent on smaller scale evaluation work, in which a single trench might be used to determine the archaeological potential of a site in advance of the granting of permission to redevelop it. Thus London's field archaeologists now collect site evaluation data from such small excavations in a way and would be strangely familiar to Professor Grimes. Consequently, if they wish to discuss what the long term value is of recording data in such a fashion (eg Philpotts 1997), they would do well to consider the results achieved by the RMLEC.

From all this it follows that the old field records need to be as carefully curated and conserved as any field monument if they are to have lasting value: they can only be reinterpreted and new lessons drawn from them if they survive and if they remain accessible. It was argued that the RMLEC records of the St Bride's excavations of 1952–4 had improved with age, in the sense that more recent work had provided a richer context into which to review them in 1994 than was available to Grimes 40 years earlier (Milne 1997, 114). The same is surely true of the Cripplegate records, for we now have detailed work conducted on sites in the

Fig 148 The starkly consolidated remains of the fourteenth-century tower from the Elsing Spital, later St Alphage church, as laid out beside the new London Wall highway in 1963. (Guildhall Library)

Fig 147 Ancient monument in a modern City: Bastion 12 in 1990 projecting into new 'City ditch', looking eastwards over the Barbican. (GLA GRR15L)

newly discovered amphitheatre to the east (Bateman 1994), on medieval developments to the south and west, and a far better understanding of the growth of Saxon London than was possible in 1968. In other words, the old excavation results need to be continually reassessed in the light of new work if their full value is to be extracted. The case for positively investing in London's archaeological archives rather than disbanding or disowning them could not be clearer.

To conclude, the reappraisal of the results of the RMLEC's visionary programme of archaeological excavations on the bomb sites of London have produced data that are still valid. The study of that material has, for example, facilitated the compilation of a cohesive pattern of medieval development within the study area. The reinterpretations of the old data not only challenge our ideas on the medieval City, but also provide new models and fresh insights into the development of the town as a whole. That those records could support and sustain such reworkings should stand as a major tribute to the RMLEC, who had battled against all odds to collect that evidence. It should not be forgotten that the most immediately tangible consequence of Professor Grimes' work after the Blitz in the Cripplegate area was that many of the

*Fig 149 The remains of the Elsing Spital in 1996, viewed from the south-east. (*Ken Walton, *London Archaeological Research Facility)*

medieval features discussed in this report are still visible today: Bastions 11a, 12, 13 and 14, sections of the town wall, an approximation of the associated ditch, the remains of the hall of the Barber Surgeons, the churches St Alphage, St Mary Aldermanbury and the towers of St Alban's and of the hospital of St Mary Elsing. All have been deliberately preserved within the City's ever changing post-war townscape, in spite of the very considerable pressure to redevelop this part of the war ravaged town around the line of the infamous Route 11 (the highway now known as London Wall). Some of these monuments are actually visible from within the Museum of London itself: indeed, their proximity to that institution was one of the reasons why it was built on the Cripplegate site (Sheppard 1991, 163–5). The survival of these precious remains is surely a monument not just to medieval London, but particularly to the work of three long serving members of the Roman and Mediaeval London Excavation Council: Francis Forty (from the Corporation of London), B St John O'Neil, (for the Ministry of Works), and of course to the honorary director of excavations, Professor WF Grimes himself.

Bibliography

Attwater, D, 1965 *A Dictionary of Saints*

Baddeley, J, 1922 *Cripplegate: one of the 26 wards of the City of London* (privately printed)

Ball, M, 1977 *The Worshipful Company of Brewers*, London

Barron, C, 1974 *The Medieval Guildhall of London*, London

—, 1995a Centres of conspicuous consumption: the aristocratic town house in London 1200–1550, *London J*, **20.1**, 1–16

—, 1995b London in the later Middle Ages 1300–1550, *London J*, **20.2**, 22–33

Bateman, N, 1994 The London Amphitheatre, *Current Archaeol*, **137**, 164–71

—, 2000 *Gladiators at the Guildhall*, London

Bayley, J, 1992 Metalworking Ceramics, *Medieval Ceramics*, **16**, 3–10

—, forthcoming, *Post-medieval ceramics and crucibles from the City ditch at Cripplegate*

Beck, R, 1970 *The Halls of the Barbers*, London

Bell, W, Cottrill, F, and Spon, G, 1936 *London Wall through Eighteen Centuries*, London

Beresford, M, and Hurst, J, 1971 *Deserted Medieval Villages*, London

Bertram, J, 1987 Gleanings from City churchyards, *Mon Brass Soc Trans*, **14.2**, 143–50

Betts, I, 1994 Appendix: medieval floor tiles in London churches, in Schofield 1994, 133–40

Betts, I, Bateman, N, and Porter, G, 1995 Two Late Anglo-Saxon Tiles and the early history of St Lawrence Jewry, London, *Medieval Archaeol* **39**, 165–70

Biddle, M, 1966 Excavations at Winchester 1965: fourth interim report, *Antiq J*, **46**

—, 1967 Excavations at Winchester 1966: fifth interim report, *Antiq J*, **47**

—, 1968 Excavations at Winchester 1967: sixth interim report, *Antiq J*, **48**, 250–84

—, 1969 Excavations at Winchester 1968: seventh interim report, *Antiq J*, **49**

—, 1970 Excavations at Winchester, 1969: eighth interim report, *Antiq J*, **50**, 277–326

Biddle, M, Hudson, D and Heighway, C, 1973 *The Future of London's Past*, Worcester

Birch, W (ed), 1887 *Historical Charters and Constitutional Documents of the City of London*, London

Blackmore, L, 1986 Early and Middle Saxon Buildings in the Greater London Area, *London Archaeol*, **5.8**, 207–16

Bloe, J, 1948 Report on the visits made to the site of All Hallows, Lombard Street, *Trans London Middlesex Archaeol Soc*, **9.2**, 180–87

Boddington, A, and Rhodes, M, 1979 Excavations at 48–50 Cannon Street, City of London 1975, *Trans London Middlesex Archaeol Soc*, **30**, 1–38

British Museum 1907 *Guide to the Medieval Room*, London

Brooke, C, 1989 *The Saxo-Norman Kings*, Glasgow

Brooke, C, and Keir, G, 1975 *London 800–1216: The Shaping of a City*, London

Butler, J, 2001 1600 years of the City defences at Aldersgate, *London Archaeol*, **9.9**, 235–44

Butler, L, 1986 Church dedications and the cults of Anglo-Saxon Saints in England, in *The Anglo-Saxon Church* (eds L Butler and R Morris), CBA Res Rep, **60**, 44–50

Camps-Linney, J, 1997 St Mary Elsing Spital: from hospital priory to parish church, unpubl BA dissertation, Inst Archaeol, Univ London

Carew-Hazlitt, W, 1872 *The Livery Companies of the City of London: their origin, character development and social importance*, London

Carter, P, 1913 *A History of St Mary the Virgin, Aldermanbury*, London

—, 1925 *History of the Church and Parish of St Alphage London Wall*, London

Chapman, H, Hall, J, and Marsh, G, 1985 *The London Wall Walk*, London

Chew, H, and Kellaway, W, 1973 *London Assize of Nuisance 1301–1431*, London Rec Soc, **10**

Chew, H and Weinbaum, M, 1970 *London Eyre of 1244*, London Rec Soc, **6**

Chitwood, P, and Hill, J, 1987 Excavations at St Alban's House, Wood Street, *Archaeol Today*, **8.11**, 13–16

Clarke, B, 1966 *The Parish Churches of London*, London

Clarke, H, 1898 *The City Churches*

Clifton-Taylor, A, 1972 *The Pattern of English Building*, London

Cobb, G, 1989 *London City Churches*, London

Cohen, N, 1994 Church Investigations in the City of London 1878–1968, unpubl BA dissertation, Inst Archaeol, Univ London

—, 1995 The Birth of Church Archaeology in London, *London Archaeol*, **7.12**, 315–20

—, 1997 The hall of the Barber-surgeons, *London Archaeol*, **8.6**, 163–7

Cotter, J, 1992 The mystery of the Hessian Wares, in *Everyday and Exotic Pottery from Europe 650-1900* (eds D Gaimster and M Redknap), 256–72, Oxford

Cowie, R, and Whytehead, R, 1989 Lundenwic: the archaeological evidence for mid-Saxon London, *Antiquity*, **63**, 706–18

Daniell, A, 1907 *London City Churches*, London

de Boe, G, and Verhaeghe, F (eds), 1997 *Urbanism in medieval Europe: papers of the medieval Europe Brugge 1997 Conference*, **1**

de Gray Birch, W, 1887 *Catalogue of Seals in the Department of Manuscripts*, British Mus

de Shortt, H, 1965 *Old Sarum*, London

DUA 1976 Archaeology in the City: March–April 1976, *London Archaeol*, **2.15**, 400–401

Dunning, G, 1932 Medieval Finds in London, *Antiq J*, **12**, 177

—, 1933 A Medieval Copper Bowl from London, *Antiq J*, **13**, 170

—, 1937 A 14th-century well at the Bank of England, *Antiq J*, **17**, 414–18

—, 1940 London Medieval Pottery, *Medieval Catalogue*, London Mus, 210–19

Dyson, T, 1980 Aldermanbury: a possible case for continuity? in J Schofield and T Dyson (eds) 1980, 42–3

—, 1984 LUD82 Ludgate Hill: historical survey, unpubl archive rep, MoL

—, 1993 London's City Wall: an assessment of documentary sources, unpubl rep, MoLAS

Dyson, T, and Schofield, J, 1984 Saxon London, in *Anglo-Saxon Towns* (ed J Haslam), 285–313, Chichester

Eeles, F, 1910 Discoveries during the demolition of St Michael Bassishaw, *Trans London Middlesex Archaeol Soc*, **2.1**, 164–78

Ekwall, E, 1954 *Street Names of the City of London*, Oxford

Flintham, D, 1998 Archaeological Investigations into the English Civil War Defences of London, *London Archaeol*, **8.9**, 233–5

Forty, F, 1955 *London Wall by St Alphage Churchyard: exposure and preservation of Roman and Medieval London*, Guildhall Miscellany **5**

Garmonsway, G (ed), 1972 *The Anglo Saxon Chronicle*, London

Gilchrist, R, 1995 *Contemplation and Action: the other monasticism*, Leicester

Glendinning Nash, J, 1919 *History of St Alphage, London and Elsing Priory*

Gordon, C, and Dewhirst, W, 1985 *The Ward of Cripplegate in the City of London*, London

Goss, C, 1947 A history of the Parish of St Mary the Virgin Aldermanbury, *Trans London Middlesex Archaeol Soc*, **9**, 113–64

Grainger, I, and Hawkins, D, 1988 Excavations at the Royal Mint site 1986–8, *London Archaeol*, **5.16**, 429–36

Grimes, W, 1968 *The Excavation of Roman and Medieval London*, London

Guildhall Museum 1908 *Catalogue of the Collection of London Antiquities in the Guildhall Museum*, London

Hammerow, H, 1993 *Excavations at Mucking. Volume 2: the Anglo-Saxon Settlement*, HBMC Archaeol Rep, **21**

Hammond, N, 1995 The Sunken Featured Buildings of the Late Saxon City of London, unpubl MA dissertation, Univ of Durham

Hanson, J, 1989 Order and structure in urban design: the plans for rebuilding of London after the Great Fire of 1666, *EKISTICS*, 334/5, 22–41

Harben, H, 1918 *A Dictionary of London*, London

Harding, V, 1992 Burial Choice and Burial Location in late Medieval London, in *Death in towns: Urban responses to the dying and the dead, 100–1600* (ed S Bassett), 119–35, Leicester

Harris, J, and Tait, A, 1979 *Catalogue of the Drawings of Inigo Jones, J Webb and Issac de Caus at Worcester College Oxford*, Oxford

Haslam, J, 1988 Parishes, churches, wards and gates in eastern London, in *Minsters and Parish Churches: the local church in transition* (ed J Blair), 35–43, Oxford

Hauer, C, 1997 The Church of St Mary the Virgin, Aldermanbury, *Ecclesiology Today*, **14**, 9–11

Hauer, C, and Young, W, 1994 *A Comprehensive History of the London Church and Parish of St Mary the Virgin, Aldermanbury*

Hebditch, M, 1978 Towards the Future of London's Past, in *Collectanea Londiniensia* (eds J Bird, H Chapman, and J Clark), LAMAS Spec Pap, **2**, 23–31

Hill, D, 1969 The Burghal Hidage: the establishment of a text, *Medieval Archaeol*, **13**, 84–92

Hill, W, 1955 *Buried London*, London

Hobley, B, 1988 Lundenwic and Lundenburh: two cities rediscovered, in *The Rebirth of Towns in the West AD 700–1050* (eds R Hodges, and B Hobley), CBA Res Rep, **68**, 69–82

Holling, F, 1977 Reflections on Tudor Green, *Post-Medieval Archaeol*, **11**, 61–6

Hope, V, Birch, C, and Torry, G, 1982 *The Freedom: the past and present of the livery, guilds and City of London*,

Horsman, V, Milne, C, and Milne, G, 1988 *Aspects of Saxo-Norman London, 1: building and street development*, LAMAS Spec Pap, **11**

Howe, E, and Lakin, D, forthcoming, *Cripplegate*, MoLAS monogr

HMSO 1942 *Front Line 1940–41 The official Story of the Civil defence of Britain*, London

Huelin, G, 1966 *Vanished Churches of the City of London*, Guildhall Library

Hurst, DG, 1969 Medieval Britain in 1968, 2: the Church of St Mary Aldermanbury, *Medieval Archaeol*, **13**, 251

Hurst, JG, Neal, D, and van Beuningen, H, 1986 *Pottery produced and traded in north-west Europe 1350–1650*, Rotterdam Pap, **6**

Hyde, R, Fisher, J, and Cline, R, 1992 *The A–Z of Restoration London*, London Topogr Soc Publ, **145**

Jeffery, P, 1996 *The City Churches of Sir Christopher Wren*, London

Jenkinson, W, 1917 *London Churches before the Great Fire*, London

Johnson, D, 1980 *The City ablaze*, London

Jope, E, and Pantin, W, 1958 The Clarendon Hotel, Oxford, *Oxoniensia*, **23**, 1–129

Keene, D, 1985 *Cheapside Before the Great Fire*, Economic and Social Research Council

—, 1995 London in the early Middle Ages, *London J*, **20.2**, 9–21

Kendrick, T, and Radford, C, 1943 Recent Discoveries at All Hallows, Barking, *Antiq J*, **23**, 14–18

Kingsford, C, 1917 Historical Notes on Medieval London Houses, *London Topogr Rec*, **11**, 28–81

Lakin, D, 1992 Preliminary Survey of the Visible Sections of the Roman and Later City Wall, unpubl archive rep, MoLAS

Lambert, G, 1890 The Barber's Company, *Trans London Middlesex Archaeol Soc*, **6**, 125–89

Lobel, M, 1989 *The British Atlas of Historic Towns, 3: the City of London from Prehistoric Times to 1520*, Oxford

London Museum 1940 *Medieval Catalogue*, London

Maloney, J, and Harding, C, 1979 Duke's Place and Houndsditch: the medieval defences, *London Archaeol*, **3.13**, 347–54

Marsden, P, 1965 St Nicholas Acon church, Nicholas Lane, *Medieval Archaeol*, **9**, 185–6

—, 1967 Archaeological finds in the City of London 1963–4, *Trans London Middlesex Archaeol Soc*, **21**, 189–221

—, 1968 The church of St Michael Bassishaw, *Trans London Middlesex Archaeol Soc*, **22**, 14–16

Matthews, L, and Green, HM, 1969 Post-medieval pottery from the Inns of Court, *Post-Medieval Archaeol*, **3**, 1–17

McCann, B, 1993 Fleet Valley Project; interim report, unpubl archive rep, MoLAS

McHardy, A (ed), 1977 *The Church in London, 1375–1392*, London Rec Soc **13**

Merrifield, R, 1965 *The Roman City of London*, London

—, 1983 *London, City of the Romans*, London

Mills, P, 1996 The Battle of London 1066, *London Archaeol*, **8.3**, 59–62

Mills, P, and Oliver, J, 1962 *The Survey of Building Sites in the City of London after the Great Fire of 1666*, London Topogr Soc Publ, **5**

Milne, G, 1990 King Alfred's Plan for London?, *London Archaeol*, **6.8**, 206–7

—, 1992a *Timber Building Techniques in London* c *900–1400*, LAMAS Spec Pap, **15**

—, 1992b (ed) *From Roman Basilica to Medieval Market*, London

—, 1997 *St Bride's Church London: archaeological research 1952–60 and 1992–5*, English Heritage Archaeol Rep, **11**

Milne, G and Wardle, A, 1993 Early Roman development at Leadenhall Court and related research, *Trans London Middlesex Archaeol Soc* **44**, 23–170

MoL, 1987 *Museum of London: Department of Urban Archaeology Archive Catalogue*, London

MoLAS, 1997 Assessment Report of Excavations at Shelley House EC2, unpubl rep

—, 1998 *Annual Review for 1997*, London

Morton and Muntz (eds), 1972, *Carmen de Hastingae Proelio of Guy Bishop of Amiens*, Oxford

Munday, A, 1633 *John Stow's Survey of London*, London

Nenk, B, and Pearce, J, 1994 Two Stamford-type ware modelled birds from London, *Medieval Ceramics*, **18**, 77–9

Norman, P, 1903 *Ancient Halls of the City Guilds*, London

Orton, C, 1988 Post-Roman pottery, in *Excavations in Southwark 1973–6* (ed P Hinton), LAMAS/ Surrey Archaeol Soc Joint Publication, **3**, 295–364

Oxley, J, 1978 The Medieval Church Dedications of the City of London, *Trans London Middlesex Archaeol Soc*, **29**, 117–25

Page, W, 1909 Religious Houses, *Victoria County History of London*, **1**, 535–7

—, 1923 *London its origin and early development*, London

Parnell, G, 1993 *The Tower of London*, London

Pearce, J, 1992 *Post-Medieval Pottery in London 1500–1700 vol 1: Border Wares*, London

—, 1994 The pottery from excavations at Boston House 90–94 Old Broad Street (BRO90), unpubl assessment rep, MoLAS

—, 1996 Medieval and later pottery from excavations at Shelley House, 3 Noble Street (NST94), unpubl assessment rep, MoLAS

—, forthcoming (a), *A collection of fine redware cups from the City of London and evidence for the early 16th-century Surrey-Hampshire Border Ware industry*

—, in preparation (b), *The 16th-century pottery sequence and metalworking ceramics from Cripplegate Buildings, City of London*

Pearce, J, Vince, A, and Jenner, M, 1985 *A dated Type-series of London Medieval Pottery 2: London-type Wares*, LAMAS Spec Pap, **6**

Pearce, J, and Vince, A, 1988 *A dated Type-series of London Medieval Pottery 4: Surrey Whitewares*, LAMAS Spec Pap, **10**

Pevsner, N, 1973 *The Buildings of England: London, the Cities of London and Westminster*, London

Philp, B, 1977 The Forum of Roman London: excavations 1968–9, *Britannia*, **8**, 1–64

Philpotts, C, 1997 London evaluations in the 1990s, *London Archaeol*, **8.5**, 137–9

Platt, C, and Coleman Smith, R, 1975 *Excavations in Medieval Southampton 1953–69*, Leicester

Porter, G, 1992 Archaeological Survey of the City Wall: Bastion 12 and adjacent wall at Barbican Waterside CTW91, unpubl archive rep, MoLAS

—, 1997 An early medieval settlement at Guildhall, City of London, in G de Boe and F Verhaeghe 1997, 45–56

Powys Marks, S, *1964* The Map of Mid-16th-century London, London Topogr Soc Publ, **100**

Pritchard, F, 1984 Late Saxon Textiles from the City of London, *Medieval Archaeol* **28**, 46–76

Rahtz, P, 1976 *Excavations at St Mary's Church Deerhurst 1971–3*, CBA Res Rep, **15**

Rahtz, P, Watts, L, Taylor, H, and Butler, L, 1997 *St Mary's Deerhurst*, Woodbridge

Rawcliffe, C, 1984 The Hospitals of Later Medieval London, *Med Hist*, **28**, 1–19

RCHM 1929 *London vol 4: the City*, Royal Commission on the Historical Monuments

Reynolds, H, 1922 *The Churches of the City of London*, London

Reddaway, T, 1940 *The Rebuilding of London after the Great Fire*, London

Robertson, A, 1925 *The Laws of the Kings of England from Edmund to Henry I*, Cambridge

Rodwell, W, 1997 Landmarks in Church Archaeology: a review of the last 30 years, *Church Archaeol*, **1**, 5–16

Rowsome, P, 1984 Excavations at 1–6 Old Bailey (LUD 82), unpubl archive rep, London

—, 1995 Number One Poultry, initial findings *Rescue News*, **65**, 3–6

—, 2000 *Heart of the City*, London

Rutledge, T, 1994 A 12th-century building on the London waterfront, *London Archaeol*, **7.7**, 178–83

Salzman, L, 1952 *Building in England down to 1540*, Oxford

Samuel, M, and Milne, G, 1992 *The Ledene Hall and medieval market*, in G Milne (ed) 1992, 39–46

Sankey, D, 1992 Archaeological Survey of the City Wall: Bastion 14 and adjacent wall at Bastion House, Barbican CTW91, unpubl archive rep, MoLAS

Saunders, H, 1951 *Westminster Hall*, London

Schofield, J, 1984 *The Building of London from the Conquest to the Great Fire*, London

— (ed), 1987a *Museum of London: Department of Urban Archaeology Archive Catalogue*, London

—, 1987b *The London Surveys of Ralph Tresswell*, London Topogr Soc Publ, **135**

—, 1994 (1996) Saxon and Medieval Parish churches in the City of London: a review, *Trans London Middlesex Archaeol Soc*, **45**, 24–133

— 1995 *Medieval London Houses*, London

Schofield, J, Allen, P, and Taylor, C, 1990 Medieval Property Development in the area of Cheapside, *Trans London Middlesex Archaeol Soc*, **41** (1994), 39–237

Schofield, J, and Dyson, T, 1980 *Archaeology of the City of London*, City of London Archaeol Trust

—, 1984 Saxon London, in *Anglo-Saxon Towns* (ed J Haslam), Chichester

Schofield, J, and Maloney, C (eds), 1998 *Archaeology in the City of London 1907–91: a guide to records of excavations by the Museum of London*, MoL Archaeol Gazett, **1**

Schofield, J, and Vince, A, 1994 *Medieval Towns*, Leicester

Sharpe, R R (ed), 1899–1912 *Calendar of Letter-books preserved among the archives of the City of London: A–L*, London

Shepherd, J, 1998a *The Temple of Mithras, London*, English Heritage Archaeol Rep, **12**

—, 1998b *Archaeology in the City of London 1946–72: a guide to records of excavations by Professor WF Grimes held by the Museum of London*, MoL Archaeol Gazett, **3**

—, forthcoming *The Roman Fort at Cripplegate, London*, English Heritage Archaeol Rep

Sheppard, F, 1991 *The Treasury of London's Past*, London

Simmons, T, 1879 *The Lay Folks Mass Book*, Early English Text Society, Ordinary Ser, **71**

Snell, L, 1978 London Chantries and Chantry Chapels, in *Collectanea Londiniensia* (eds J Bird, H Chapman, and J Clark), LAMAS Spec Pap, **2**, 216–22

Steedman, K, 1992 *Aspects of Saxo-Norman London, vol III*, LAMAS Spec Pap, **14**

Sturdy, D, 1975 The Civil War Defences of London, *London Archaeol*, **2.13**

Tabor, M, 1917 *The City Churches*, London

Tatton-Brown, T, 1986 The Topography of Anglo-Saxon London, *Antiquity*, **60**, 21–30

—, 1990 Building Stone in Canterbury *c* 1070–1525, in *Stone: quarrying and building in England AD 43–1525* (ed D Parsons), Roy Archaeol Inst

Taylor, F, 1945 All Hallows Lombard Street, *Trans London Middlesex Archaeol Soc*, **9.2**, 187–9

Terry, J, 1905 On the Cripplegate Bastion of London Wall, *Trans London Middlesex Archaeol Soc*, (NS) **1.4**, 356–9

Thomas, H, 1828 *The Wards of London* (vols 1 and 2)

Thomas, C, Sloane, B, and Philpotts, C, 1997 *Excavations at the Priory and Hospital of St Mary Spital, London*, MoLAS monogr, **1**

Thompson, A, 1937 *History of the Hospital and New College of the annunciation of St Mary in the Newark, Leicester*, Leicester

Trevil, P, and Rowsome, P, 1998 Number 1 Poultry: late Saxon and medieval sequence, *London Archaeol*, **8:11**, 283–91

Unwin, G, 1908 (rev ed 1966) *The Gilds and Companies of London*, London

Vince, A, 1984 The Aldwych: mid-Saxon London discovered? *Current Archaeol*, **93**, 310–12

—, 1985 Saxon and Medieval Pottery in London: a review, *Medieval Archaeol*, **29**, 25–93

—, 1990 *Saxon London: an archaeological investigation*, London

—, 1991a (ed), *Aspects of Saxo-Norman London II: Finds and Environmental Evidence*, LAMAS Spec Pap, **12**

—, 1991b Early Medieval London: refining the chronology, *London Archaeol*, **6.10**, 263–71

Vince, A, and Jenner, A, 1991 *The Saxon and Early Medieval Pottery of London*, in A Vince (ed) 1991a, 19–119

Watson, B, 1992 The excavation of a Norman fortress on Ludgate Hill, *London Archaeol*, **6.14**, 371–7

—, 1996 Excavations and observations at Minster Court and Minster Pavement, Mincing Lane in the City of London, *Trans London Middlesex Archaeol Soc*, **47** (1998), 87–103

Watson, B, and Dyson, T, 1997 *London Bridge is broken down*, in G de Boe and F Verhaeghe 1997, 311–27

Watson, B, Brigham, T, and Dyson, T, 2001 *London Bridge: 2000 years of a River Crossing*, MoLAS monogr, **8**

Watts, L, and Rahtz, P, 1985 *Mary-le-Port, Bristol: Excavations 1962–3*, Bristol

Weaver, L, 1915 The Complete Building Accounts of the City Churches (parochial) designed by Sir Christopher Wren, *Archaeologia*, **66**, 1–60

Weinbaum, M, 1976 *London Eyre of 1276*, London Rec Soc Publ, **12**

Weinreb, B, and Hibbert, C, 1983, *The London Encyclopedia*, London

West, S, 1985 West Stow. The Anglo-Saxon Village, *East Anglian Archaeol Rep*, **24**

Westman, A, 1987 The Church of St Alphege, *Archaeol Today*, **8.11**, 17–22

—, 1994 Recording Bastion 14 of the City Wall, unpubl archive rep, MoLAS

Wheatley, H (ed), 1956 *Stow's Survey of London*, London

Wheeler, R, 1927 *London and the Vikings*, London Mus Catalogue, **1**

—, 1934 The topography of Saxon London, *Antiquity*, **14**, 290–302; 443–7

—, 1935 *London and the Saxons*, London Mus Catalogue, 6

—, 1944 The Rebuilding of London, *Antiquity*, **18**, 151–2

Wickham, D, 1999 All Hallows Staining, Mark Lane and the crypt of Lambe's Chapel, *Context, J City London Archaeol Soc*, **39**, 26–8

Williams, A, 1958 unpubl RMLEC field notes, MoL Grimes London Archive

Williams, G, 1963 *From Commune to Capital*, London

Wilson, D, and Hurst, G, 1969 Medieval Britain in 1968: churches and chapels, *Medieval Archaeol*, **13**, 250–52

Wood, M, 1965 *The Mediaeval House*, London

Wroe-Brown, R, 1998, Barber Surgeons Hull Garden, Monkwell Square London EC2, unpubl evaluation rep, MoLAS

Index

by Veronica Stebbing